WINE

AN INTRODUCTION FOR AMERICANS

M. A. Amerine
and
V. L. Singleton

WINE

AN INTRODUCTION FOR AMERICANS

University of California Press
Berkeley and Los Angeles 1968

University of California Press
Berkeley and Los Angeles

Cambridge University Press
London, England

© 1965 by The Regents of the University of California

Fourth Printing, 1968

Library of Congress Catalog Card No. 65–11785

Printed in the United States of America

PREFACE

Although there are many books on wine, each with particularly informative or pleasurable sections, none seem to be without deficiencies for the general reader. Those which dwell on the romantic aspects tend to entertain but not inform. Those which surround the subject with arbitrary admonitions and mysticism frighten and confuse. Those which discuss the technology of wine usually ignore the origins and uses of wine. Often one type of wine or one country is emphasized and others are ignored. Books on wine in English are often by Englishmen or expatriates, or are translations and reflect attitudes and descriptions which may not be pertinent or correct from an American viewpoint.

This book attempts to give a broad introduction to the whole subject of wine for Americans. It is intended to be factual where facts are available and give considered opinions where they are required. Sufficient detail is offered to explain the underlying principles and the nature of the world of wines. Since nearly 90 per cent of the wine consumed in the United States is of American origin, a great majority of this from California, the production practices, commercial situation, and legal requirements in the United States market are emphasized. Key references and suggestions for further reading are given for those wishing verification, more detail, or different viewpoints.

The authors wish to acknowledge that helpful suggestions and criticisms for various portions of the manuscript have been made by our colleagues. Our thanks are particularly offered to Professors William V. Cruess, Albert J. Winkler, and A. Dinsmoor Webb. We are also indebted to Miss Genevieve Rogers and Mr. Ernest Callenbach for editorial assistance.

The Wine Institute has kindly furnished many of the photographs presented here.

Davis, California

M. A. AMERINE
V. L. SINGLETON

CONTENTS

Contents

INTRODUCTION

There are many reasons and rewards for the study of wine. The grape has been said to be the only fruit that naturally preserves itself and there is historical justification for the statement. At a time when our modern techniques of storing fresh food were undreamed of, and fresh vegetables and fruits were available only during the short local season, wine was indeed the gift of God. With only modest intervention by ancient man, the grape and its associated yeast produced wine. Here was a food with a flavor like the fresh fruit which could be stored and transported under the existing conditions. At least part of the time it survived in drinkable condition from season to season or even occasionally for many seasons.

The fact that wine produced euphoria was not lost on ancient man, and it became not only a regular part of the diet but also a social beverage used for feasting, celebrating, and entertaining guests. The great variability possible in quality and type of wine naturally led to quality rating and selection of wine; the best wine for auspicious occasions or esteemed guests, the poor or ordinary wine for everyday use. So wine early became an item of commerce with appropriate quality judgments, records, and connoisseurship. As a result of all this, wine has deeply penetrated the social fabric and culture of times and countries from which we spring.

Introduction

Wine still occupies a unique position among foods and beverages. In some areas wine is on the table in the poorest homes and is one of the least expensive comestibles. In other regions it may be served only on special occasions. Students of wines and wine lore, by hobby and avocation, abound. Those who make a profession of wine production and sale cannot escape the historical background of their product. Neither can the romanticist, connoisseur, and historian really know wine without a knowledge of the grape-growing and wine-making practices which result in the myriad kinds of wine.

Social ills are also associated with alcoholic beverages, and their understanding and control require study of the nature and effects of such beverages in general and wines in particular whether we seek to avoid such problems and still enjoy wine or wish to control the social consequences of overindulgence.

Opinions and attitudes on wine may be frivolous or passionate, doting or deploring, but are seldom insipid, for example:

> "There is evil in every berry of grape."—The Koran

> "If penicillin can cure those who are ill,
> Spanish sherry can bring the dead back to life."
> —Sir Alexander Fleming

> "Tis pity wine should be so deleterious
> For tea and coffee leave us much more serious."
> —Lord Byron

> "Come, come, good wine is a good familiar creature if it
> be well used; exclaim no more against it."
> —Shakespeare

> "Wine is the drink of the gods, milk the drink of babes,
> tea the drink of women and water the drink of beasts."
> —John Stuart Blackie

"I wonder what the vintners buy one half so precious as
the stuff they sell."—Omar Khayyam

"Wine makes a man more pleased with himself; I do not
say it makes him more pleasing to others."
—Samuel Johnson

A subject about which there is so much history, romance,
and dispute is surely fascinating and cannot be treated in a
coldly technical manner—but this is intended to be a factual
discussion. It is hoped that you will find it useful whether you
are seeking to learn how wine is made, and what types come
from which countries, or just want to enjoy wine more by knowing more about it.

To define wine simply is not easy, for the definition would
vary according to the context and the attitudes of the definer
and his audience. Wine is often defined very differently in the
detailed laws of various countries, and in popular usage wine
means different things to different people. In Chinese the un-
qualified word for wine also means "alcoholic beverage"; so
beer becomes a "wine" and may be translated "appetite wine."
Perhaps this accounts for the fact that we speak of rice wine, a
literal translation from Chinese. Even within the group of beverages which certainly are wine, there are many products with
varied origins and uses. For our purposes, the most generally
satisfying definition seems to be that wine is a beverage resulting from the fermentation by yeasts of the juice of the grape
with appropriate processing and additions. Before devotees of
blackberry wine and such take us to task, it should be pointed
out that for both legal and commercial reasons a product labeled simply wine would be considered misleading if it obviously tasted like blackberries. Qualifying terms are necessary,
such as blackberry wine, apricot wine, and so on.

Wine, that is, fermented grape juice, has had a long and
varied history; and the many variations on this theme may be-

3

wilder the novice. An outline of the major types of wine may clear up his confusion. Wines can be assigned to one or the other of two major groups, with rare exceptions. The first group in point of historical origin includes the "natural wines" which result from a more or less complete fermentation. The fermentable sugar has been consumed and further growth of yeasts is prevented by lack of "food"; spoilage organisms such as the vinegar bacterium do not develop if the wine is kept from contact with the air. Owing to the limit of sugar present in ripe grapes, the alcohol content of such wines is normally about 12 per cent. The major subclass of these wines is the still (without noticeable carbon dioxide) wine group. Further subdivision of this class depends upon color and residual sugar. Although all the fermentable sugar is consumed as completely as possible in many of these wines, and historically they are all "dry" (without noticeable sweetness), various artful and scientific procedures have produced wines of this class today which have moderate or high amounts of residual sugar.

ONE SYSTEM OF
BROADLY CLASSIFYING WINES

A. *"Natural" wines, 9–14 per cent alcohol*

(Their nature and keeping qualities depend heavily on a "complete" yeast fermentation and protection from air.)

  I. *Still wines* (no excess carbon dioxide)
    a. *Dry* (no noticeable sweetness) *table*

B. *Dessert and appetizer wines, 15–21 per cent alcohol*

(Their nature and keeping qualities depend heavily on the addition of wine spirits.)

  I. *Sweet wines*
    a. White (muscatel, white port, angelica)

(continued)

wines, intended for use during meals

1. White
2. Rosé (pink)
3. Red

(Further subclasses based primarily on grape variety or region of origin.)

b. *Slightly sweet table wines* ("Mellow," "vino" types)

1. White
2. Rosé (pink)
3. Red

c. *Sweet table wines*
1. White

d. *Specialty types*

1. Lightly carbonated types, both red and white

II. *Sparkling wines* (excess carbon dioxide)

a. White (champagne, sparkling muscat)
b. Pink (pink champagne)
c. Red (sparkling burgundy)

b. Pink (California tokay)
c. Red (port, black muscat)

II. *Sherries* (white sweet or dry wines with oxidized flavors)

a. Baked types
b. Aged types
c. *Flor* sherry types (secondary aerobic yeast fermentation)

III. *Flavored, specialty wines* (usually white port base)

a. Vermouth (pale dry, French, Italian types)
b. Proprietary products

1. Special natural wines

2. Other "brand name" specialty wines

As a class the still natural wines are table wines, intended to be a part of a meal. The other major subclass of natural wines are the opposite of still; they are the sparkling wines. They have undergone not one but two complete fermentations and the carbon dioxide of the second has been retained as the "sparkle." For reasons that will become clear later (Chap. 9) they should not be called "carbonated," but the effect is superficially similar. The sparkling wines belong in the class of natural wines, since they are derived from table wines and have similar alcohol content. They may be served with meals, but are often served on other occasions as well.

The other major group includes the dessert and appetizer wines. As their name implies, they are usually served before or at the end of a meal but not during the main courses. These wines are of higher alcohol content. The nature and keeping qualities of these wines depend heavily on the addition of spirits distilled from wine. The consumer often presumes that this addition is intended merely to raise the alcohol content for his benefit, but this is not so. The amount of extra alcohol added to these wines is just about the minimum at which one can be certain that the wine will resist spoilage by further growth of yeasts or other organisms. A major subclass of these wines are sweet wines. The addition of wine spirits serves to arrest the yeast fermentation with part of the sugar unfermented and make it stable in this condition. The alcohol level is too high to permit further yeast fermentation. Sherries, a second subclass, may be sweet or dry and are characterized by flavors induced by various types and degrees of oxidation. The third major subclass is that of the flavored wines such as vermouths and trade-named specialty wines.

One might wonder why all the sparkling wines are in the natural class and all the oxidized types and flavored wines are in the group fortified with wine spirits. There would seem to be no reason why carbonated port, or herb-flavored or oxidized table wine, could not be sold. Ignoring the fact that such products might not be palatable (and some have been marketed inadvertently or otherwise), the difference lies in the manner of consumption. A natural wine, still or sparkling, is ordinarily consumed immediately after opening. Servings are usually fairly generous and often several people are dining together Such wines store poorly in partly empty containers and, if not entirely consumed in one meal, the remainder of a bottle is usually a disappointing remnant of its former self within hours, owing to aroma loss and other changes, especially if loss of "sparkle" is also involved. The fortified wines, however, owing partly to their alcohol content and partly to their richness in sugar and other flavors, are usually served in small portions and even several guests may not consume a whole bottle. They do keep fairly well after opening, and may still be very good after some time. But a carbonated port would be too rich for a few guests to consume the whole bottle after dinner, and the remainder of the wine would lose its identity. A vermouth-like wine or a sherry with a natural wine base would probably be too full-flavored for complete consumption of a bottle at a single sitting by a small dinner party. Moreover, its low alcohol content would allow spoilage organisms to grow.

The general classification of still and sparkling natural or table wines and of sweet, oxidized, or flavored dessert or fortified wines, modified to suit yourself as your acquaintance with wine increases, will enable you to categorize wines and, with a minimum of tasting, become credited with a broad, if not deep, knowledge of wine. It is surprising how many people confuse port with table wine, sherry with chablis, and so on. Even persons versed in the pleasant intricacies of one type of wine may be uninformed about others.

To place the basic categories of wines in perspective in relation to the wine consumption of the world, consider the year 1965, when 190 million gallons of wine and 9.9 million gallons of brandy were consumed in the United States. Yearly per capita (all persons regardless of age) consumption in the

United States was about 0.98 of a gallon of wine compared to 1.5 gallons of distilled spirits, 16 gallons of beer, about 28 gallons of coffee, and 8 gallons of tea. Comparable figures for per capita annual wine consumption are approximately 32 gallons in France, 29 gallons in Italy, and 26 in Portugal, and from 10 to 20 gallons for a long list of countries including Argentina, Chile, and Spain. If the total annual consumption of *alcohol* per adult is estimated, however, the United States consumption is more than 30 per cent of that in France and 60 per cent or more of that of other countries having at least ten times our wine usage. That wine does not represent nearly so high a proportion of the total alcohol consumed in beverages in this country as it does in many other countries is clear from these figures.

The wine consumed in the United States in 1965 consisted of about 83 million gallons of dessert wines (including sherry), 9 million gallons of vermouth, 16 million gallons of other flavored wines, 8 million gallons of sparkling wines, and 74 million gallons of table wines. In recent years the trend of consumption in the United States has been upward in all these categories except dessert wines, which have been decreasing. If we estimate an average retail cost of $1 per bottle or $5 per gallon of wine, this consumption represents $950,000,000 spent by the American consumer for wine. Over $107,350,000 of federal excise taxes were collected on wine and over $103,000,000 on brandy in 1965.

Chapter 1

HISTORY OF THE GRAPE AND WINE INDUSTRY

In the eighth chapter of Genesis, Noah's Ark is said to have
come to rest on Mount Ararat, which is in the Caucasus Mountains in Armenia. Later it is noted, in Genesis 9:20–21, "and
Noah began to be a husbandman, and he planted a vineyard;
and he drank of the wine and was drunken." Certain it is that
a grape-growing Neolithic civilization developed first in a region
which is now northern Iran, or possibly between the Black and
Caspian seas. This is an area where the grape grows wild. It
is quite probable that mead (honey wine) and beer are older
alcoholic beverages than wine. Honey was available in the
forests. Grains, from which beer is made, seem to have been
cultivated at an earlier date than grapes. However, the cultivation of the grape is a very ancient industry, as is indicated by
the remnants of grape seeds which have been found in villages
dating from several thousand years B.C.

The wine industry certainly dates from at least 3000 B.C.,
probably in the area indicated above. Since yeasts are every-
where abundant, fermentation would be no problem. Some
early housewife probably left crushed grapes in a jar and
found, a few days later, that an alcoholic product had been
formed. All these early wines must have been of very poor

quality, just as the early beers were of poor quality. The wines were probably drunk during or soon after the primary fermentation before it "turned" to vinegar.

The antiquity of wine is indicated by the words which have been used for it. The Hittites, who were the dominant linguistic group in the Middle East in 1500 B.C., referred to wine as *uiian-* or as *uianas*, which in the Luwian language became *uin-*. The earliest Greek scripts speak of wine as *woinos*, but in the classical Greek the *w* was lost and the word became *oinos*. From this the Latin and Etruscan *vinum* was derived and later words such as *vino, vin, Wein,* and wine. Even the neighboring languages accepted the Hittite word: in Armenian it is *gini*; in Mingrelian *gvin-i*; and in Georgian *-gvino*. Even the Semitic languages used the word: *vayin* in Hebrew; *wayn* in Sabaean; and *wa-yn* in Arabic and Ethiopian.

The best evidence for the early development of a wine industry comes from Egypt in the predynastic period. There is evidence of the production of red and white wines from the Delta area and in other areas to the south. Hieroglyphics reveal there was a small but rather well-developed grape industry, including arbors and pruning, Figure 1. They also had a form of wine press. However, wines were used almost entirely by priests and royalty. Some medicinal use of wines is indicated. Beer was the usual beverage of workers and rulers.

In the "fertile crescent" area where wine was especially common it was taxed, and at a fairly early date both the common people and the rich drank wine. The problem of dilution of wine with water was already noted in the Code of Hammurabi, which dates from ca. 1792–1686 B.C. There is some evidence that at this period the effect of temperature on wine was known, since many of the wines of Asia Minor and the Caucasus were stored in jars which had been sunk in the ground or in containers cut out of stone and plastered to prevent leakage. They had evidently begun to learn the harmful effects of air on the wine, for the tops of the amphorae were usually covered.

FIG. 1. Harvesting grapes and making wine in the Eighteenth Dynasty (about 1500 B.C.) Courtesy Bruckmann Photo.

Even so, the wines of the pre-Hebrew and pre-Greek period must have been very poor indeed, and must have been drunk very soon after their fermentation.

But as the Greek civilization began to develop the wine industry reached a much higher degree of perfection. Homer's Iliad and Odyssey contain excellent descriptions of wines. The Greeks made wine one of their most important articles of trade, and Greek wine containers have been found scattered throughout the Mediterranean, Egypt, and the Middle East. Wine was not only an important item of trade for the Greeks, but it was also a part of Greek religious ceremonies during the Homeric period. Wine was also pictured as having been offered to comfort a weary man, as in the Iliad, when Hector returns to Troy and his mother Hecuba gives him wine. Most Greek doctors continued to use wines medicinally. They may even have been used as apéritifs before meals, but more often wine was taken with meals, frequently diluted with water. Many of the Greek wines were blended with odorous materials, or grated goat's-milk cheese and white barley were added before consumption. This would not indicate high-quality wine.

The practice of adding herbs or other materials suggests the intention of covering up undesirable odors associated with wine spoilage. And there can be no doubt that the wines contained alcohol. The cults of Bacchus and Dionysos indicate that a group devoted to wine and having an orgiastic character had

11

developed in Greece, certainly no later than the seventh century B.C.

Archaeologists have shown that the Celtic leaders had acquired a taste for wine and imported Greek and Roman wines. Cups and flagons for drinking or serving wine indicate that wine reached Celtic Europe from the Mediterranean during the pre-Christian period.

Wine was important to the Hebrews also. The Bible includes many reports, other than that of Noah, about grapes and wine. It is recorded that Moses sent spies into the Promised Land, and that one grape cluster was so heavy that it required two men to carry it back to the waiting Israelites. The good and bad effects of wine, including that on Noah himself, are reported, and there is considerable moralizing on both the good and bad effects of wine, particularly in Proverbs.

In the New Testament, wine is not only the beverage recommended for Timothy's stomach, but it became a part of the religious ceremonial of the Church. Two of the New Testament quotations deserve explanation. The first, that of the Feast of Cana, in John 2:3–10:

> And when they wanted wine, the mother of Jesus saith unto him, They have no wine.
>
> Jesus saith unto her, Woman, what have I to do with thee? mine hour is not yet come.
>
> His mother saith unto the servants, Whatsoever he saith unto you, do *it*.
>
> And there were set there six waterpots of stone, after the manner of the purifying of the Jews, containing two or three firkins apiece.
>
> Jesus saith unto them, Fill the waterpots with water. And they filled them up to the brim.
>
> And he saith unto them, Draw out now, and bear unto the governor of the feast. And they bare *it*.
>
> When the ruler of the feast had tasted the water that was made wine, and knew not whence it was: (but the

servants which drew the water knew;) the governor of the feast called the bridegroom,

And saith unto him, Every man at the beginning doth set forth good wine; and when men have well drunk, then that which is worse: *but* thou hast kept the good wine until now

This indicates that the wine which had been made from water was better than that which had preceded it. And the guests remarked that the host must be a very wealthy man to be able to serve a good wine after bad wine, which was not the usual procedure. Normally, the host served the good wine first and when the guests had become tipsy and less critical he served the bad wine. The implication is clear: there was very little good wine available and the host had to get the guests to drink the good wine first and then pawn off on them whatever other wines could be found.

The other New Testament quotation is that of the parable of not putting new wine into old bottles:

> And no man putteth new wine into old bottles; else the new wine doth burst the bottles, and the wine is spilled, and the bottles will be marred: but new wine must be put into new bottles. (Mark 2:22)

This translation makes little sense unless we realize that instead of "bottles" the translators of the King James Bible should have written "goatskins." The explanation is that new wine, which is subject to fermentation from residual sugar, should not be placed in old goatskins, which are hard and will not stretch. Fermentation and the pressure of the carbon dioxide produced would then break the goatskin and the contents would be lost. New wine should be put into new goatskins. The new skins being pliable, the gas from the fermentation would stretch them and be less likely to cause them to burst. Actually, this has a symbolic significance. According to modern theologians, the parable is an admonition not to try to put the new

13

religion in the forms of the old religion. Nevertheless, it indicates that in Hebrew times there was a recognition of the differences in quality of wine and the differences in characteristics of new and old wine and that this knowledge was so widespread that it could be used to illustrate a theological idea to the common people.

Before the beginning of the Christian Era grapes and wines had considerable significance for Middle Eastern and Mediterranean peoples. Fresh grapes had a high caloric value, being about 20 to 25 per cent sugar, which is higher than that of most of our common fruits, and the caloric value of dried grapes was even higher, for they may contain as much as 80 per cent sugar. Thus grapes constituted one of the few sources of sweet material and one of the few easily stored and transported food sources of high caloric value. Dried grapes were and still are very popular with nomadic peoples of the Middle East. They were used not only alone but in cooking, or were boiled as a source of a sweet syrup. The importance of such high-calorie foods in the diet of primitive peoples has not been adequately studied.

A number of favorable factors made wine important to ancient peoples. It was actually less likely to be contaminated than water, particularly in cities where public sanitation was difficult and water-borne diseases were common. The pleasant effects of wine were early noted, and seem to be at the basis of the use of wine as a beverage. Furthermore, the effects of wine were somewhat quicker and greater than those from beer, a beverage of lower alcohol content. This must have been a very important factor in the pre-Christian period, since life was not pleasant for either the rich or the poor. Winter was difficult, even in the southern regions, and the vicissitudes of life, with wars and slavery, made wine a welcome beverage, enabling people to forget their problems and ease their aches. This is, of course, an effect of alcohol.

Wines as well as beers were drunk soon after fermentation

and were cloudy, consequently they were an important source of vitamins from the suspended yeast cells. Not until much later were methods for easy and early removal of suspended solids developed. Wines were valued for other reasons too. Homer, especially, seems to have been aware of the aesthetic pleasures of drinking old wines, but he is by no means unique. The many poetic connoisseurs in classical Greece had their favorites: Pramnian, Lesbian, Mendaean, Chian, Saprias, and so on. There was even a book in verse on drinking and eating—*The Deipnosophists*. The Greeks, moreover, had a wine-drinking game, *kottabos*.

We do not know whether the ceremonial and mystical use of wine originated from the alcohol it contained or from the fact that the red wines, at least, were associated with blood and therefore with life itself. Certain it is, however, that the use of wine in ceremonials was prominent in all early religions and adapted itself naturally to the Christian religion.

The process of making wine was well established by the first century of the Christian Era. The Greeks made wine an article of commerce and Greek colonies had spread the culture of the vine as far west as Spain and as far east as the shores of the Black Sea. The quality of much of the wines must have been rather poor because of the warm climate and the poor storage containers. Some aged wine of relatively high quality seems to have been available. In spite of the general lack of quality, wine was appreciated as an article of diet and as a part of the culture of peoples of the Mediterranean and the Middle East.

The Romans built upon Greek civilization, adapting from it varieties of grapes and wine-making procedures so that the long period of trial and error in the Middle East and Greece did not have to be repeated in Italy. Greek colonists settled in Italy in the eighth century B.C. They probably found indigenous vines, but doubtless brought some of their own vines and wines. However, the contributions of the Romans to the wine industry are very great.

15

History of the Grape and Wine Industry

The first good classifications of grape varieties we owe to the Romans, especially to Pliny, who classified grapes as to color, time of ripening, diseases, soil preferences, and types of wines which might be produced. The Romans had a good idea of the cultivation of grape varieties. Columella, particularly, favored certain varieties over others. The Romans were rather skilled in pruning the vines and in improving the yield of grapes by fertilization. The pruning knife appears to be their invention; the edict of Numa Pompilius that no wine might be offered to the gods unless it was made from the grapes of pruned vines indicates an appreciation of vine production and wine quality. However, growing grape vines in trees was definitely a retrograde trend which developed during the Roman period—the vine cannot be properly pruned, overcrops, and the fruit seldom ripens properly. The Romans continued to use the amphora of the Greek period, but in the late Roman period the first wooden cooperage was introduced, possibily in Gaul or northern Italy.

This was a very great advance for the wine industry because it permitted wines to be stored out of contact with air for longer periods of time. The art of cooperage was a real achievement, since a barrel is a rather unstable engineering creation. It is necessary to have the wooden staves exactly coopered to fit together. They must be bent so that pressure is exerted equally at both ends of the staves. To get the heads to fit into the barrel and be leakproof is a rather difficult engineering problem which some early cooper solved satisfactorily. In their wine making the Romans were not much better off than the Greeks, for the concept of the bacterial origin of wine spoilage and the methods of control lay nearly 2,000 years in the future. However, they had learned that by putting wine under warm conditions, usually in smoke-filled rooms, the undesirable changes could be slowed down. This heating of wine probably constitutes an early form of pasteurization.

But because the wines were frequently acetic and had a tendency to spoil, a wide variety of treatments were developed in

16

the Roman period. These included the addition of alkaline materials to reduce the acidity and of foreign materials to cover up the acidity. The use of salt water to make the colors more bright and possibly to dilute off-flavors was also common. The Greek custom of adding spices and herbs to wines was also widespread in Rome. Whether the Greeks or Romans first added resin to wines is not known, but Allen (see references, p. 327) does not believe it was in Greece. The use of gypsum seems to have originated in North Africa and spread to Italy (and Spain). It helped to correct deficiencies in the total acidity.

The blowing of glass became more common in the Roman period and some wines were placed in bottles and kept for various periods of time. Wine goblets were common.

Thus the literature of the Roman period in appreciation of wine is much greater and perhaps better than that of the Greek period. Many passages in Horace and Virgil praise the quality of the wines and indicate that something more than alcohol had been achieved. Thus a 160-year-old Opimian Falernian wine was praised. Even wine snobs appear, recommending wines to please the smart set in Rome.

The Romans carried vine culture into western and eastern France and as far north as the Rhine in Germany, to the southern part of England, and eastward along the Danube. Wine was exported from Italy to the Roman colonies, but as the latter became better established, particularly in Spain and southern France, they produced the wines they needed for their own use. The wines of the south of France were roundly deprecated by Pliny and other Roman writers, but whether they were actually poor or whether this was the sour grapes of regional pride is not known. In fact, in the first century the Emperor Probus prohibited the growing of grapes in France and even passed a law that the vineyards in the Rhone Valley and other parts of France must be removed. This was apparently to prevent competition of the wines of Gaul with those exported from Italy,

17

though it may also have been due to a need to increase grain production. Not only did the Romans carry vine culture to the far parts of the empire but they also carried their methods of growing grapes and possibly some of their varieties. And some of their wines must have been great. The famous physician Galen was a connoisseur who prescribed wine in his medical practice.

With the downfall of the Roman Empire agriculture gradually deteriorated, the vineyard industry with it. There are many indications of this: the lack of appreciation of wine in the Dark Ages, the small amount of wine produced, and the chaos that was present in Europe from A.D. 400 to as late as the thirteenth century. Charlemagne may have planted a vineyard or two, and occasional poets praised wines, probably more for their alcohol than their quality.

One important contribution during the Dark Ages is the probable introduction into Europe of grape varieties brought back from the Middle East by the Crusaders. It is now generally believed that the Petite Sirah was brought to the Rhone by one of the Crusaders, and a number of other varieties were probably introduced into France at this time. The best indications are that most of the varieties now in Europe were present there by the twelfth or thirteenth century.

The need of the Church for wine for sacramental purposes was probably the most important factor in the preservation of the wine industry through the Dark Ages. Virtually the only stable organizations, as far as agriculture was concerned, were the monastic establishments which grew to prominence during the tenth to the fifteenth centuries. Not only were the monasteries free of most of the taxes but they were also spared much of the marauding which made agriculture hazardous for private individuals, Figure 2. The important wine districts of Europe were either discovered by or preserved by monastic organizations, particularly in Burgundy and in Germany, where large monastic orders owned extensive vineyards and developed

18

Fig. 2. Gathering grapes and wine making in a fifteenth-century monastery vineyard. Courtesy Bruckmann Photo.

19

wine making to a much higher plane than it had in the period from 400 to 1200. Remnants of monastic wineries can still be found in France, Spain, Germany, Austria, Yugoslavia, and other countries.

Not only did the monasteries preserve the growing of grapes and production of wine but they also, for the first time, made a point of the regional classifications of wine. Taking a justifiable pride in the wine industry they were developing, the monasteries naturally praised the local wines of each region. Since the monasteries had a certain stability, they could keep wines over a period of years, especially now that wooden casks were available. Some monasteries kept good records, which made it possible for them to classify the wines and compare them with wines of other districts. Thus by the end of the Middle Ages the monasteries presented to the Western World a well-developed wine industry to which private enterprise later added. In Germany, at least, they became expert coopers and built large and excellent oak casks for wine storage.

As the Middle Ages became politically more stable, trade developed and wines were shipped to various parts of the Western World. Many documents show that the wine trade was carried on even in the worst periods of the Dark Ages, particularly for the purposes of the Church and the nobility. Trade continued between Bordeaux and England throughout the Dark Ages and some German wines seem to have been exported as far west as Ireland during this period. In Germany the Hanseatic League of city-states was very active in the importation and exportation of wines not only between the member states but to foreign countries. But not until the fourteenth and fifteenth centuries did the international wine trade assume large proportions.

The international trade in wines had an important effect on standardization and classifications of wines. When wines are shipped long distances for foreign trade it is necessary to have some guarantee of the quality. This forced the producers into classifying their wines and selling them at prices appropriate to the quality. Still, wines were probably not as widely distributed among the common people in the Middle Ages as they had been in the Roman period. Nevertheless, as the feudal system gradually dissolved, the improved standard of living of the middle class demanded more and more wines, and the vineyard acreage, particularly in France and Germany, increased rapidly during the fifteenth, sixteenth, and seventeenth centuries. Trade of England and the southern European and Mediterranean countries was especially important. Shakespeare refers to the wines of many countries, but particularly to those of Spain.

By 1850 the wine industry was well established in all parts of Europe south of the Rhine and extending into Austria along the Danube and into the Crimea and Caucasus in Russia. Wines were imported, particularly from France, Spain, Portugal, and Madeira, to England and elsewhere, and from Germany to the countries to the north. Many wines from Germany reached England during this period. The countries which produced no wine, such as Belgium and Holland, developed a flourishing import trade for wine, primarily from France. The trade of port from Portugal to England was particularly important. The fortification of port, dating from the eighteenth century, led to the aging of these wines and their popularity with English connoisseurs. The development of vintage claret for the English market followed soon thereafter. Italy was still, in 1850, primarily a collection of city-states and, although wine making was very common, not much wine was exported from Italy until the end of the nineteenth century, with the exception of vermouth from Turin and of some wine from Tuscany and Sicily. Surprisingly, all the Western countries carried on trade with Cyprus, since there seems to have been more appreciation of sweet wines in this period than of table wines. Constantia, a sweet wine from South Africa, was brought to Europe in the eighteenth and nineteenth centuries.

21

There is probably a very good reason for this appreciation of the higher alcohol sweet wines. They were undoubtedly more stable than the table wines and easier to care for. Furthermore, central heating had not come into use in this period in northern Europe and the sweet wines gave more calories per volume than the table wines. Nevertheless, Rhine wines and Bordeaux wines as well as Champagne and Burgundy had achieved a recognition for quality in England by 1850.

In 1850 more wines were being bottled and more wines were being aged than at any previous time. Yet it has been estimated that at least 25 per cent of the wine spoiled before fermentation was complete, and much of the wine was certainly of very poor quality. But some, owing to the market with the court and rich leisure classes, must have been very fine.

A series of disastrous vine diseases swept through Europe: downy mildew, oïdium (powdery mildew), and black rot were inadvertently introduced into Europe from America in the period immediately after 1850. These diseases made it difficult for the grapes to ripen properly, or indeed to ripen at all.

About 1870 some American rootstocks were imported into English and French botanical gardens and on these rootstocks a root louse, phylloxera, was introduced into Europe. The American species of grapes are resistant to this root louse, but the European grape, *Vitis vinifera,* was not immune and rapidly succumbed. The destruction of vineyards between 1870 and 1900 was unparalleled in agricultural history. Virtually all the vineyards of France were destroyed during this period, most of the vineyards of Spain were ruined before 1910, and the root louse caused widespread damage to vineyards in Austria, southern Germany, Rumania, southern Russia, and other parts of the world, including California. The French quickly recognized that the only feasible remedy was the importation of vigorous and phylloxera-resistant American rootstocks to which European grapes could be grafted. Several viticultural expeditions were sent to this country and thousands of American cuttings were sent to France. Gradually the best of these were selected and widely distributed throughout the world as rootstocks upon which European grapes could be grafted. Unfortunately, in the interim a number of American varieties which were ill suited to the European climate and the European palate were planted not as rootstocks but as direct producers of grapes in order that some form of wine industry could carry on. Greece, which was not subject to phylloxera, exported a very large amount of raisins to Europe to be converted into wine.

The rootstocks now used in California were brought to California from France and not directly from the eastern United States. Phylloxera caused widespread migration of grape growers from France to other parts of the world as well as from Italy to the New World and to South America. The economic crisis in the wine industry made the production of quality wines more difficult, and there were few great vintages in France during the period 1875 to 1893. Phylloxera had one beneficial result. When the vineyards were replanted only a few varieties were used, compared to the very mixed plantings in the pre-phylloxera period.

The most important contribution of the mid-nineteenth century we owe to Louis Pasteur. At Lille, where he was teaching, sugar beet molasses was being fermented for the production of alcohol for distillation. Investigating poor sugar utilization in an alcohol distillery, he found that the conversion of alcohol to acetic acid was the cause of the poor yields of alcohol. Later he turned his attention to the wine industry and demonstrated conclusively that the spoilage of wines was due to aerobic micro-organisms of the *Acetobacter* type, i.e., organisms producing acetic acid. He found that if the wines were kept out of contact with the air *Acetobacter* could not develop. After this great step forward, the acetification of wines has been gradually brought under complete control. He also demonstrated a number of anaerobic diseases of wine and prescribed treatments for controlling them.

23

Louis Pasteur thus represents the application of the scientific revolution to the wine industry. The application of scientific principles to fermentation and the care of wines is still continuing today. The wine industry has made many strides in the application of pure yeast cultures to secure clean fermentations, the use of mild antiseptics, such as sulfur dioxide, to prevent the growth of undesirable organisms, and the clarification of wines by means of various fining agents to produce greater stability and clarity.

But another revolution that took place in the nineteenth century is as important as the scientific revolution: the industrial revolution. Many types of machinery were devised for cultivating vineyards, for handling or crushing grapes, for pumping crushed grapes to fermenting tanks, for filtration or pumping wines from one tank to the other. The application of technology to the grape and wine industry reduced the cost of production markedly and led to a great expansion in the wine industry in the latter part of the nineteenth century.

Thanks to these revolutions and their applications to the wine industry, we are now living in the golden age of wines, for never before has so high a percentage of fine wines been produced. And these are being produced at a lower relative cost than ever before. The production of grapes per acre is greater. We have developed better varieties, grow them with less injury from insects and fungus diseases, and bring them to the winery in better condition. The scientific revolution has made it possible to process these wines more rapidly, with less cost and greater assurance of success. Much of the guesswork has been taken out of the wine industry. Within the next twenty years we shall probably be able to control even more of the factors that determine wine quality, and thus further increase the percentage of fine wines produced. The present excessive prices of some imported wines is certainly not a permanent development.

24

History of the Grape and Wine Industry

Summary.—The antiquity of the wine industry is recognized by all historians. The Greeks and Romans made wine an item of trade and spread the culture of grapes throughout Europe.

During the Middle Ages the monastic orders maintained grape culture and international trade began to develop. International trade was an important factor in creating unique types of quality wines.

Phylloxera created unprecedented economic problems which were only solved by replanting the vineyards on resistant rootstocks. Pasteur personifies the application of scientific principles to the wine industry. The industrial revolution greatly lessened the burden of making wine.

Because of the scientific and industrial revolutions, we are living today in the golden age of wines as far as quality and availability are concerned.

Wherefore by their fruits shall ye know them.—MATTHEW 7:20

Chapter 2

GRAPES FOR WINE

The wine grape is a unique fruit and its particular qualities have made "wine" synonymous with "grape wine." It has several characteristics which adapt it to the making of a fermented beverage with less difficulty and fewer problems than is possible with most other fruits or fermentable materials: notably, an unusually high content of fermentable sugar, relatively high nitrogen content, and the natural association of fermenting yeasts with the grape berry. While, with modern science and technology, limitations of other fruits can be overcome and the natural characteristics of the grape have been enhanced by selection, wine would probably not have become a part of the culture of man so early or so importantly without the Old World grape.

The quality of the wine can be affected by the grape variety and its management in the vineyard, by the fermentation technique, and by the processing and aging of the wine. All must be proper for good wine; lack of attention to any one can spoil it. Without grapes that are adapted for the wine intended, the production of good wine is foredoomed to failure.

Grapes belong to the botanical family Vitaceae (Order Rhamnales, Class Dicotyledoneae, Division Spermatophyta-Angiospermae). The Vitaceae (vines) include no other food plants, but do include several of interest as ornamentals such as Virginia creeper and Boston ivy. There are eleven genera in the family and that of grapes is *Vitis*.

The major commercial grape of California and most of the rest of the world is the species *Vitis vinifera*, also called the European grape. It was native to the area around the Caspian Sea and was one of the first domesticated plants. It has been under cultivation for at least 5,000 years and was important in the agriculture of ancient Phoenicia, Egypt, Greece, and Rome. Selection over this long time has produced a wide range in size and shape of clusters and berries, color, leaf shape, and growth habit, and at least 5,000 named cultivars of *V. vinifera* are known. Many different varieties are grown commercially; each may be valued for its flavor, beauty, time of ripening, pest resistance, adaptation to a locale's soil or climate, high yield, or some other special feature.

The European grape was taken along (as seeds, cuttings or rooted plants) during exploration and colonization. It was brought to Mexico, Argentina, Chile, through Baja California to California, into Australia, and into South Africa. In these areas as well as in Eurasia the European grape was and is the primary grape used for making wine.

The explorers and colonists encountered other grapes growing wild in many parts of the world, especially the North Temperate Zone. Leif Erikson found so many wild grapes growing in the New World that he called his discovery Vineland. Many old place names reflect the profusion of wild grapes native to America, for example, Martha's Vineyard. Of the many American species of *Vitis*, *V. labrusca* is by far the most important for fruit production. This species was called the "fox" grape and grew wild in the Mid-Atlantic States. The native American species have been domesticated only about 300 years, but 1,500–2,000 pure varieties and hybrids have been developed. The Concord may be considered the typical *V. labrusca*, since more acreage is planted to it (about 80 per cent of non-European grape plantings) and more people are familiar with it in the form of the grape juice and jelly of the American supermarket or from backyard culture. Other important varieties deriving at least in part from this species included Delaware, Catawba, Ives, Niagara, and Isabella.

Another American native is *Vitis rotundifolia* of the South Atlantic States. These are known as muscadine grapes, of which Scuppernong is one variety. There are many other species of native grapes. Some, such as V. *rupestris* (the sand grape) or V. *riparia* (the river grape), are useful as rootstocks or breeding material, but none of these are themselves important as fruit producers. The fruit from the American species all have rather distinctive, strong "wild" flavors which usually carry over into crosses with V. *vinifera*. These flavors are liked by Americans who are familiar with them and who also like V. *vinifera* flavors, but they are foreign to the European wine types. The drinker of European wines describes the flavor of wine made with V. *labrusca* grapes, such as Concord, as "foxy." Presumably the term comes from the old name of fox grape, although some people claim to note an "animal-den" odor in some wines from V. *labrusca*. The foxy flavor is produced partly by the presence of methyl anthranilate, a flavor substance which is added to synthetic grape "pop" drinks. A harsh or bitter flavor often develops in wines from these grapes as they age or oxidize. Being of simple, strong flavor, wines made with grapes of American varieties are likely to be of limited interest and monotonous even to those who like these flavors. Although it is often attempted, the matching and justifiable labeling of wines from these varieties with names derived from traditional European wines, i.e., burgundy, chablis, sauterne, etc., is nearly impossible and usually disappointing to both groups—those liking Concord flavor and those liking traditional wine types.

The American species do, however, contribute much to viticulture. Growing wild as they did in areas having very cold winters, humid summers, and many natural enemies, they are more resistant to these conditions than the European varieties The root louse, phylloxera, introduced into Europe from the New World, spread rapidly and became a scourge which nearly wiped out grape growing until it was recognized that scions of the European varieties could be grown as grafts on rootstocks of the resistant American species. Varieties of American species can be grown in areas so humid that European varieties succumb to various pathogens, particularly oïdium (powdery mildew), downy mildew, and fruit-spoiling molds. The American varieties resist winter cold better and usually require a shorter growing season. These facts explain the growing of American varieties in preference to European varieties in subtropical (humid) regions as well as in the coldest areas where grapes can be grown. Crossing and back-crossing among American species and *Vitis vinifera* varieties are being used to develop grapes with fruit like the European and resistance like the American species These are sometimes referred to as "direct producers" since some of them can be grown on their own roots without grafting in the presence of phylloxera.

Many distinctive wine types *are* or require specific grape varieties. Many varieties are inherently of poor quality for some wine types, and some varieties can be converted into good or standard qualities of several wine types. In California it is common practice to label wines which contain mostly a single variety of grapes (51 per cent legal minimum) with the name of that grape variety. This varietal labeling is useful only if the variety has a generally recognized distinctive quality. A wine from a variety of grape without a reputation for some special quality is ordinarily marketed under a class or generic label. In some countries the same result is achieved by using a single variety or a limited number of varieties of grapes for the wines. Thus, although given geographical labels, the character of the wines reflects the specific variety or varieties grown in the region.

29

Grapes for Wine

It is notoriously difficult to describe flavors in a generally meaningful way, but it is possible to divide grapes into a few classes which can be readily recognized with a little experience in tasting their wines. The flavor of the wine, even when freshly made and certainly after aging or further processing, may be different from that of the fruit as picked. However, if the wine from one variety is distinctive and usually recognizable by experienced tasters compared to the same type of wine from other varieties, the difference is attributable to the nature of the grape. Not every lot of wine produced from grapes of varieties with distinctive flavors will be flavored intensely and characteristically enough to be recognized even by the expert taster. The subtlety and variability in flavor qualities between wine from different varieties of grapes and even the same variety as produced by different wineries, in different lots, and in different years contribute much to the enjoyment of wine by those who observe and become acquainted with these differences.

A classification of varietal flavors into four groups will help the novice become acquainted with the broad range of possible flavors: non-*vinifera*-flavored varieties, muscat-flavored varieties, other distinctively flavored varieties, and nondistinctively flavored varieties. The non-*vinifera*-flavored variety group is dominated by the grapes such as Concord which have the flavor described as "foxy," "wild-grape," or perhaps preferably *"labrusca"* flavor. Muscadines and grapes of other species are included here, although their flavors are not the same as the Concord-*labrusca* types. The muscat-flavored group are *vinifera* varieties and a few *vinifera* crosses with other species that have a distinctive perfumy, floral aroma which is often quite intense and is easily recognized, once experienced, both in the grape and in the wine. The group of *vinifera* varietals which are not muscat-flavored and yet are recognizable is a heterogeneous group which includes a wide range of flavors and most of the varieties famous for quality wine production. The

30

nondistinctive varieties include all those that produce wines the flavor of which is generally best described as "vinous." Good standard wines are produced from some members of this group and, owing to high yields or other factors, some of the most widely planted and largest total tonnage varieties fall here, but the flavors are very similar. As an illustration, most of the *vinifera* grapes seen in the fresh-fruit market such as Thompson Seedless make wines which would place them in this class. Such varieties are often used in wine types whose characteristic flavors depend on processing rather than grape variety.

An attempt has been made to list most of the major and some of the minor varieties (in terms of use in wines which are available in the United States) according to these groups in the accompanying tabulation. There is no substitute, of course, for personal experience in recognizing flavors and listings are subject to differences of opinion based upon personal experience and interpretation. We are *not* saying that within the four classes given there are no differences between varieties —far from it! Not all *labrusca* varieties make wines with the same flavor, nor do muscats, or the other two classes. Even if the basic flavor is similar, differing levels of intensity, different nuances, and differing features other than flavor, such as red versus white color, produce a wide range of very noticeably different grapes and wines in each general class.

Groupings according to Recognizable Flavors of the Fruit (as Wine)

A. *Varieties with distinctive non-vinifera flavors:* Derived from American species and crosses; carry more or less strong native-grape flavors into young table, sparkling, or young port-type wines made from them. Mostly not planted in large acreage; often used for fresh fruit, etc., instead of for wines.

31

Grapes for Wine

1. *Vitis labrusca*–type flavors, foxy aromas
   a. Red wine types: Concord, Ives (Ives Seedling), Fredonia, Early Niabell, Niabell, Pierce, Isabella (also used for white wine), Sheridan, Jewell
   b. White wine types (several have red pigment in skin, but are used mostly for white wines): Catawba, Delaware, Diana, Duchess, Iona, Missouri Riesling, Niagara, Noah, Ontario, Ripley, Elvira
2. *Vitis rotundifolia*–type flavors, muscadine grape aroma (*not* muscat)
   a. Red wine types: Mish, James, Eden, Thomas
   b. White wine types: Scuppernong (sometimes loosely used for all muscadine grapes)
3. Derived from several species with flavors described as raw, herbaceous, post oak, mustang, etc.
   a. Red or pink-skinned types predominate; although white wines are made from some, and white-skinned examples exist. Norton, America, Bailey, Beacon, Fern Munson, Herbemont, Lenoir, Clinton, Empire State, Taylor, Beta, Ellen Scott, Salvador, Jacquez, and many direct producers bearing names of developers followed by a number, such as Seibel 1000, Couderc 4401, Baco No. 1, Seyve-Villard 12309, etc.

B. *Muscat-flavored varieties:* Fruity-floral muscat aroma makes these grapes very attractive as fresh fruit and carries into the wines. All but one are pure V. *vinifera.*
   1. Red or pink wine types: Aleatico, Muscat Hamburg
   2. White wine types: Muscat blanc (Muscat Canelli, Muscat de Frontignan), Muscat of Alexandria, Malvasia bianca, Orange Muscat, July Muscat, Golden Muscat (a cross which is more "foxy" than muscat-flavored)

C. *Other distinctively flavored varieties* (*besides muscat or native-grape-flavored*): This group is the most important to high-quality wines of world, but is very heterogeneous as to nature and degree of distinctiveness of grape's aroma and

Fig. 3. Gamay Beaujolais grapes, illustrating the tight clusters of thin-skinned berries common among *Vitis vinifera* varieties for wine. Source: The Wine Institute.

wine's flavor. Suggested descriptive adjectives are intended to be complimentary, and flavors are more delicate than the terms imply. These descriptions may aid in developing your own tasting vocabulary, but are *not* to be taken too literally.

1. Red wine types: Cabernet Sauvignon (green olive, herbaceous), Ruby Cabernet (green olive, weedy, tannic), Cabernet franc (green olive, weedy), Malbec (krautish, soft), Merlot (green olive), Pinot noir (pepperminty), Gamay Beaujolais, Figure 3 (fruity, tart), Gamay de Burgoyne (fruity, tart), Napa Gamay (fruity, tart), Pinot St.-George (Red Pinot, not highly distinctive), Zinfandel (raspberry), Grenache (fruity, estery, may become harsh), Barbera (very fruity, tart), Petite Sirah (possibly Durif, Shiraz, more than one variety carries this name; fruity, tannic), Grignolino (more than one variety sold under this name, also frequently blended; spicy-fruity, tends to pinkish-orange color), Souzão (rich, fruity), Tinto cão (rich, fruity), Tinta Madeira (prunish, cheddar, rich), Nebbiolo (fruity, licorice)

2. White wine types (fruity-floral aromas sometimes difficult to distinguish from muscat, but other flavor factors distinguish them): White Riesling (Johannisberg Riesling, fruity-floral, tart), Müller-Thurgau (slight muscat), Sylvaner (Franken Riesling, fruity, tart, not highly distinctive), Grey Riesling (spicy-fruity, not highly distinctive except when grapes are very ripe), Gewürztraminer (resembles muscat), Emerald Riesling (fruity, sometimes spicy, possibly slight muscat, tart), Chardonnay (Pinot Chardonnay, applish, intensity varies with degree of ripeness of grapes), Flora (fruity, spicy), Helena (fruity), Sauvignon vert (fruity, spicy, possibly slight muscat), Chenin blanc (Pineau blanc de la Loire, White Pinot; fruity, appetizing, not highly distinctive), Folle blanche (fruity, tart), Pinot blanc (weedy, rich), Melon (similar

FɪG. 4. Sauvignon blanc. Source: The Wine Institute.

to Pinot blanc), Sauvignon blanc, Figure 4 (fruity, green olive, faintly herbaceous), Sémillon (figs, faintly cigar-like), Fernão Pires (very fruity-floral)

D. *Nondistinctive varieties:* Very important on acreage-gallonage basis; quality of wines ranges from very ordinary to good or even excellent, but generally no recognizably distinctive flavors derive from grape itself.

    1. Red varieties (low-colored varieties also used in white dessert wines and sherries): Carignane, Mission, Refosco, Alicante Bouschet, Mataro, Pagadebito, Emperor, Flame Tokay, Valdepeñas, Aramon

    2. White varieties: Aligoté, Thompson Seedless (Sultanina), Clairette blanche, French Colombard, Palomino (Golden Chasselas), Burger, Saint-Émilion (Ugni blanc, Trebbiano), Grillo, Chasselas doré, Feher Szagos, Green Hungarian, Red Veltliner

Summary.—The characteristic compositions, flavor, and other qualities of the grape variety are extremely important variables in the making of wine. No one can be personally acquainted with all the world's grape varieties and the wines that could be made from them. New varieties are continually being bred and selected. Each variety must be tested for several wine types, over several seasons, and in different areas before the distinctiveness and value can be estimated. Decades may elapse before the place of a variety in a given viticultural economy is secure and even then may be upset by many factors. The winegrower and the wine consumer can profit from this diversity by learning to exploit it according to their own needs and tastes. A grouping of varieties with respect to their recognizably different flavors has been presented. Together with later discussions of the effects of climatic differences, vinification practices, and adaptation of certain varieties for certain wine types, this table and some tasting experience should help the novice to advance rapidly in understanding and appreciation of wine.

Chapter 3

GROWING WINE GRAPES

Viticulture—the growing of grapes—is a very large agricultural
industry. On a world basis, the grape probably enters the human diet in a larger amount per capita and in more different
forms of commercial importance (raisins, many kinds of wine,
fresh fruit, canned fruit, juice, jellies, etc.) than any other fruit.
California is by far the most important state viticulturally in
the United States. It produces about 90 per cent of all grapes,
100 per cent of the raisins, about 90 per cent of the table
grapes, and about 80 per cent of the wine consumed in this
country. This production involves property and facilities with
a total replacement value estimated at $1,000,000,000, includ-
ing, in 1965, 227 wineries and 486,000 acres of vineyard (about
95 per cent in bearing). The total annual production of grapes
in the United States is about 4 million tons, and about half of
this is crushed by wineries. Although this production is of great
importance from the national viewpoint, in terms of the world's
total commercial output California produces about 3 per cent
of the wine, 40 per cent of the raisins, and 15 per cent of the
fresh table grapes. Since the acreage is less than 2 per cent of
the world's total, California's viticulture is seen to be relatively
efficient. Several other states, notably New York, Ohio, Penn-

sylvania, and Michigan, have appreciable wine-grape production and some grapes are produced in most states, adding an estimated total of 400,000 tons per year to the commercial grape crop of the United States.

The total wine production of the world is estimated to be about 7.0 billion gallons per year. Of this total, European countries produce about 5.7 billion gallons. The remaining 1.4 billion gallons are produced by Algeria (300 million gallons), Argentina (500 million gallons), and several other countries such as the United States (190 million gallons). Generally speaking, the countries with a large production of wine also have high consumption and as a result do not export a high proportion of their wines. The foreign wines seen in the United States do not usually reflect the typical wine of the country of origin. Only a small proportion of the wine with the most renown and highest price may be selected for exportation in many cases. Also, wines which can be sold at low prices on the American market are often exported. Therefore, we cannot speak knowingly of the "wines of country X" without understanding many details of weather, viticultural practices, and wine-making procedures and their relation to the typical wines as well as to the wines exported to America from country X. Writers have tended to emphasize wines worthy of export, not the standard district wines. This encourages snobbism and shallow knowledge of both domestic and foreign products.

The sources and types of wines consumed in the United States in 1965 are shown in the accompanying table. The figures for the rest of the United States were obtained by subtracting the wine entering distribution channels from California from the total consumption of wine produced in the United States. The transfer of California wine directly to wineries in other states for blending or further processing particularly between subsidiaries and affiliates of single organizations is believed to have inflated the apparent proportion of wine contributed by the rest of the country.

PERCENTAGE OF UNITED STATES CONSUMPTION (1965)

Source	Dessert wine	Table wine	Sparkling wine	Vermouth	Other flavored	Total
California	85.5	71.1	41.8	21.8	91.5	76.3
Other States	12.5	16.8	39.5	31.1	8.5	15.1
Foreign	2.0	12.1	18.7	47.1	——	3.6
Per cent of total wine	43.9	39.1	4.0	4.8	8.2	100.0

Viticulture is a complex science. Each viticultural area has its own problems. Considering the great number of varieties of grapes and the several types of wine, it is fortunate for the student of wines that it is not possible to grow every variety of grapes and produce every type of wine efficiently in every area and that certain guiding principles govern the choice. A general knowledge of the growing of grapes and the production of wine is necessary for those who would understand wine.

In the spring as soon as the average daily temperature reaches about 50° F. the dormant vine begins to grow and put out the shoots which will bear this year's crop. The flower-clusters emerge with the new shoots and about 45 days later the inconspicuous flowers bloom. After the berries set, the small, hard, green, acid berries grow rapidly for a time then undergo no great visible change until the beginning of ripening. By the beginning of ripening cell division in the berries has ceased but a second period of growth owing primarily to cell enlargement begins. At this time the concentration of tartaric and malic acids in the cell fluids of the berry is at its maximum, totaling about 3 per cent. The sugar content is very low, less than 4 per cent. From this stage until the fruit is ripe, the concentration of sugar in the fruit will rise to over 20 per cent. This means that the plant is using its tremendous photosynthetic capacity to produce sucrose, which is translocated in low concentration (0.5 per cent or so) from the leaf to the fruit and concentrated there. The grape is very unusual among fruits in

39

that the disaccharide sucrose is hydrolyzed between the leaf and the berry where it is stored in high concentrations of approximately equal proportions of the constituent monosaccharides, glucose and fructose. Most other fruits store carbohydrates as either starch or sucrose and do not produce so high a concentration of soluble, fermentable sugar. During the final cell enlargement stage the volume of the berry increases about fourfold to fivefold. If the *amount* of acid in a berry remained constant during this period, the *concentration* would decrease in proportion to the dilution produced by the accumulation of juice in the enlarged state. Part of the acid is respired and so the concentration of acid decreases even more than can be accounted for by dilution. The proportion of the acid which is respired is affected by the temperature. In hot weather most of the malic and part of the tartaric acid may be lost by respiration in the fruit; in cooler weather more is retained. As an example, if 100 green berries at 1 gram each contain a total of 3 grams of acid (3 per cent), they may weigh 5 grams when ripe and contain 2.5 grams of acid, giving a concentration of 0.5 per cent acid in the ripe berry. Other changes occur, of course, during the later stages of ripening—flavor compounds are produced, chlorophyll is lost, and, in red varieties, the red anthocyanin pigments form.

As an example of this grand sequence in the northern central valley region of California, say the Lodi district, the grapes should "push," begin to sprout from the dormant buds, about April 1. Blooming should occur about May 15, ripening begins about July 15, and the berries should be fully mature about September 15. These estimates are approximate, of course, for a mid-season grape variety and an average year. Individual grape varieties vary in their required growing season from as little as 90 days for a very early variety to about 195 days for a late variety. The vine should continue green and active but with limited growth after fruit maturity. When the weather becomes cool in the fall it turns dormant and drops its leaves, often with a brilliant display of fall colors which makes vineyard areas a tourist attraction at that time of year. After the vines become dormant, the vineyardist prunes them and the process is ready to begin again in the spring.

The manner of pruning can affect the yield and quality of the next crop. The fruit for next year's crop develops from buds upon the canes which grew this year. Thus the number of fruitful buds left when the vines are pruned helps control the size of the following crop. If too many are left, the vine probably cannot mature all the fruit; the result is that the fruit matures slowly and its quality may be impaired. If too few fruitful buds are left, the quality is generally good, but the yield is impaired. Economics and human nature conspire to produce more errors on the "too many" side. Much skill and considerable luck are required to prune every year to obtain the maximum yield consistent with optimum quality, since grape variety, vine health, the weather, berries set per cluster, and the wine to be made all contribute in determining the optimum crop in any one season for a certain vineyard. The heaviest-producing varieties of grapes, particularly if over-cropped, may produce 16 tons of fruit per acre, but California production averages 8 tons per acre for raisin varieties, 7 tons per acre for table-grape varieties, and 5.3 tons per acre for wine varieties. Production in New York and in Europe is usually only 2 to 5 tons per acre, depending upon variety.

The varieties of grape which can be recommended for planting in a given vineyard are limited by the local climate and the marketing situation. If the growing season (between frost-free conditions) averages 120 days, it is obvious that varieties requiring 180 days to mature should not be planted. For less obvious reasons, among them the fact that early varieties tend to be shy producers and to produce lower quality wine under these conditions, it is not usually a good idea to plant early-maturing wine-grape varieties in an area with a long, hot growing season. In latitudes toward the poles, grape growing is

41

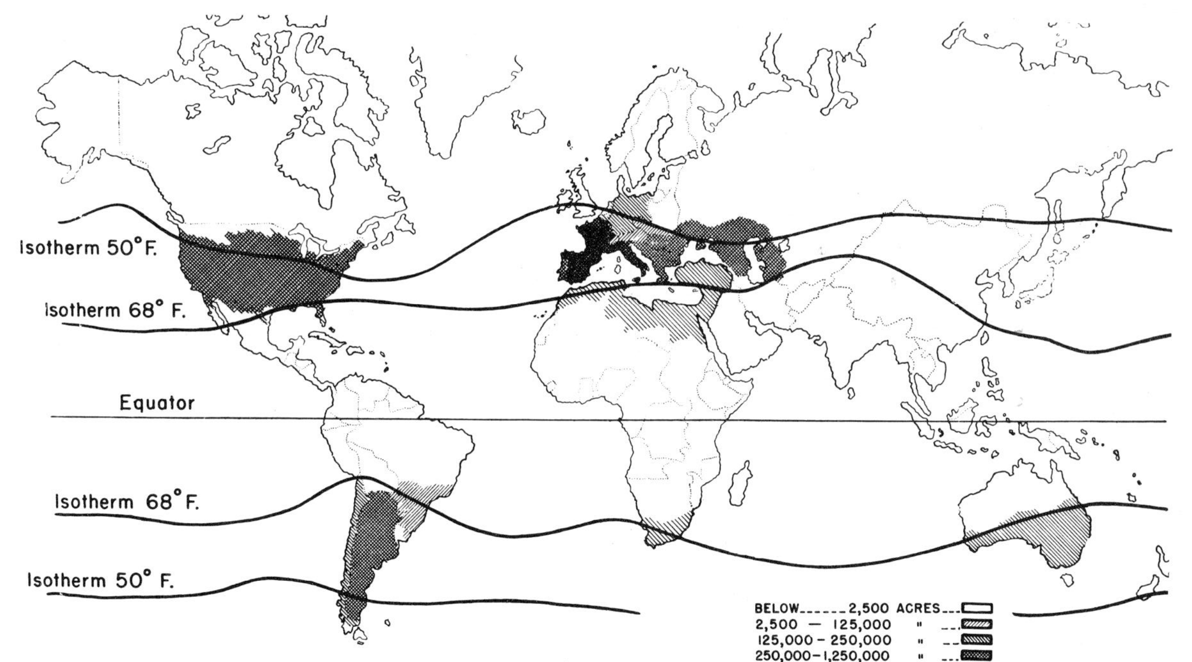

Fig. 5. Distribution of grape plantings in the world.

limited by a short growing season and severe cold. A short period of 0° F. is likely to kill European vines. Nearer the equator, grapes suffer from the lack of a winter dormant period and perhaps from high humidity. Hence the planting of grapes for commercial-scale wine production must be limited to an ill-defined belt in the Northern Hemisphere including California and the Mediterranean area, and in the Southern Hemisphere including South Africa, Australia, Chile, and Argentina. However, grapes are not grown in all places where they could be, and local geography and weather may limit profitable grape growing to a much greater degree than is implied by the extent of this "double belt" around the earth.

Grape vines are adaptable to most well-drained soils, even relatively infertile ones. They have very extensive root systems and can withstand more drought than some other fruits. If irrigation is possible, grapes are not limited by lack of rainfall. In fact, since the grape vines dislike cold, waterlogged soil and are susceptible to pathogens such as mildew in wet or too humid conditions, the absence of summer rains is often a favorable characteristic for a wine-growing area. If summer rains do occur (as in many European areas), their timing, the amount of rain, and the time before the free water drains away and drying conditions return are critical. Since moisture is moisture to the vine root, the opinion that irrigation is detrimental to wine quality compared to rainfall is erroneous. Rains during blooming may cause a poor set of berries resulting in a light crop. Rains, particularly if followed by several humid days late in the ripening period, may delay ripening and produce lowered quality or perhaps complete loss by encouraging berry cracking, bunch rot, and so on. Fog and high humidity without rain may have similar effects, producing mildew on the leaves and causing berry damage. Localities with frequent hailstorms are undesirable for grapes. When the shoots are small and brittle, hail can damage a vineyard severely. Later, hail decreases the yield and quality of the year's vintage and may weaken the vine.

43

The effects of wind can be severe on grapes; areas of strong or poorly timed windstorms are unsuitable for grapes. Tender shoots may break off and the crop will be reduced by high winds. Leaves may be ripped from the vine, decreasing its ability to produce sugar and mature the fruit. If strong winds occur later in the season, the fruit may be damaged by whipping and may be exposed to decay and sun damage.

Sunburn and heat damage have various effects depending upon the timing. At temperatures of about 105° F. or more the grape berries are likely to be damaged, particularly those exposed to the direct sun. If this occurs early in the season, the damaged berries will be shrunken and hard. The yield will be decreased, but the remaining berries will develop normally and the quality of the wine will not be impaired. Later in the season the damaged berries will dry up and become raisined and caramelized in flavor. This may not cause much reduction in yield, but off-flavors will lower the quality of the wine. Relatively uniform temperatures are important, especially in the spring and fall. Temperatures just below freezing after the shoots have begun to develop or before the vine has turned dormant will seriously damage or kill the vine and affect the amount of the crop in the spring or its quality, if it is still on the vine in the fall.

All these factors influence the success of grape growing and the quality of the wine in a given area. However, not only the climate of a viticultural area is important, but also the "microclimate" of each vineyard. By establishing vineyards on gentle slopes with maximum exposure to the sun or in valleys protected from wind, the vineyardist can minimize possible climatic problems. By centuries of observation of success and failure in the older viticultural countries and more recently by scientific study, especially in the newer viticultural areas, the successful vineyard and grape-wine complex is developed. The types of wine produced, the varieties of grapes which should be grown, the proper management of vineyards and wineries are characteristic of a given area. There is always room for the innovator,

44

FIG. 6. A Sémillon head-pruned vine showing the location of the clusters. (The rocky soil might be poor for other crops, but it is typical of many areas famous for grapes.) Source: The Wine Institute.

45

and the "best" management practice today may be superseded by better information tomorrow, but the producer who flouts the fundamental viticultural, enological, or economic "laws" in his operations is doomed to failure.

One of the most successful methods of clarifying the relationships between different areas both for grape growing and wine making has been the "heat-summation" method of classifying vineyard regions. The grape does not grow or mature its fruit when the average daily temperature is below about 50° F. The growing season for grapes is the total number of days during the summer (based upon a ten-year average) when the average daily temperature is above 50° F. The rate of metabolism and growth of plants is generally faster under warmer conditions. The heat-summation scale used for grapes is obtained by totaling the number of degrees above 50° F. for the days of the growing season. Thus, if the average daily temperature is 70° F. today, this contributes $70 - 50 = 20$ "heat" units, air-temperature growth units, or "degree-days" to the grape-growing season. Ten days at 51° F. would be equivalent in these units to one day at 60° F. average temperature. The average daily temperature is ordinarily estimated by averaging the minimum and maximum temperature for each 24-hour period.

Based upon these units, the coldest regions where grapes are grown commercially have heat summations of the order of 1,700 degree-days and the hottest regions reach about 5,200 degree-days. The grape-growing areas have been conveniently classified in five "regions" of heat summation, Figure 7. The coldest, Region I, has 2,500 or fewer degree-days and would be represented by areas near the towns of Napa, Santa Cruz, and Santa Rosa in California, much of Switzerland and the districts of the Rhine, Moselle, and Champagne in Europe. Region II, still fairly cool, has a heat summation of 2,501–3,000 degree-days and would characterize the middle of the Napa Valley, the Sonoma Valley, and the Santa Clara Valley of California and the region near the city of Bordeaux, France. Region

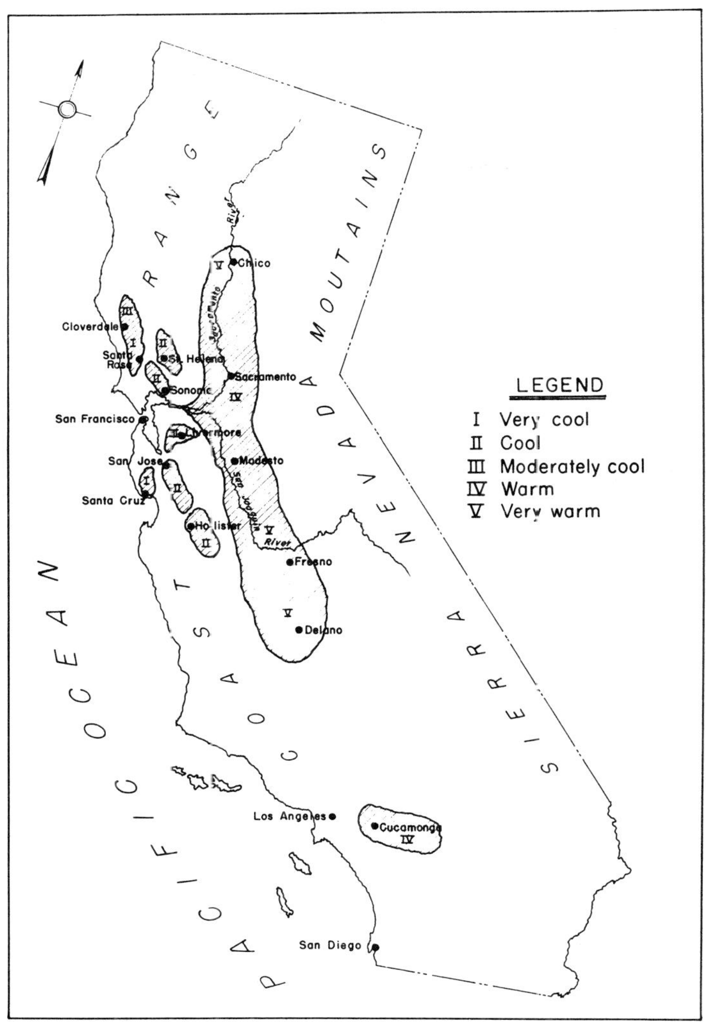

FIG. 7. Wine districts of California.

III, 3,001–3,500 degree-days, is typical of the northern Napa Valley and Livermore in California and Tuscany in Italy. Region IV, 3,501–4,000 degree-days, characterizes areas near the California towns of Ukiah, Davis, Lodi, and Cucamonga, and much of Sicily, Greece, and central Spain. Region V is the hottest, 4,001 degree-days or more, and characterizes the majority of the Sacramento and San Joaquin valleys of California, as well as the vineyard areas of Morocco, Algeria, and southern Spain.

The general characteristics of these regions and more specifically the average heat summation in a specific vineyard tell us much about the type of grapes and wines that should be produced in the vineyard and why this is so. In a Region I vineyard the growing season is short, temperature is low, and only early-ripening varieties will mature. Obtaining sufficient sugar in the grapes may be a problem and the acidity of the juice tends to be high. As a result, table wines are the preferable type to produce, since they are dry or nearly so, tart, and of relatively low alcohol content. In a vineyard in Region V the grapes can mature later and will tend to have high sugar content but low acidity, with the result that good dessert wines can be produced.

The same grape variety grown in one region, say III, will have, as compared to a warmer region, say V, more total acid when ripe in III than in V because a higher proportion of the acid is respired under warmer conditions. The fruit will reach a higher sugar content on the same date or reach a given sugar content earlier in V (warmer) than in III (cooler). A variety of grape with red pigmented fruit will ordinarily have more red pigment in the cooler region than in the warmer at the same degree of ripeness. The fruit from the cooler region will ordinarily taste fruitier and more tart; the fruit (of the same variety) from the warmer region will be sweeter but more flat.

The interrelationships described here help make it clear that, as grape-growing regions the cooler coastal valleys of California have much in common with such cool regions as Germany and

Burgundy and Bordeaux in France. The hotter parts of the San Joaquin Valley have much in common, viticulturally, with southern France, Spain and Algeria. The range of conditions in California is unusually wide and makes possible the production in California of good quality wines of all the basic types.

The heat-summation figures given are based upon a ten-year average and do not reveal another important feature. For consistent success and a stable wine-growing industry, wide deviations from the average climate are undesirable. The climate of intracontinental areas is more variable than that of areas modified and made more uniform by nearness to the oceans or other sizable bodies of water. The growing of wine grapes beside the Finger Lakes in New York and the influence of the Mediterranean Sea upon the countries surrounding it are examples of this. Many of the vineyards in the important viticultural areas of the world which are noted for their grapes and wines depend partly on the more equable climate which results from the influence of an adjacent body of water. California is particularly fortunate in the relative uniformity of its climate. This is one reason why the climatic-region (I–V) concept has been developed and made particularly useful in this state.

The statement is often heard that every year is a vintage year in California. In the sense that the grapes are able to ripen to an adequate sugar level in California and are not threatened unduly by late rains this is generally true. In many regions of the world, in as many as three or four years out of five sugar must be added to the grapes and lowering of the acidity must be encouraged in order to produce a properly balanced wine. The vintage years traditionally extolled for these areas are the years in which the grapes were able to ripen optimally. Although California, the source of most of America's wine, is relatively fortunate in this respect, vagaries of storm and season still cause variation in the product from year to year and from vineyard to vineyard. The fact that wine, in contrast to most food products, does vary and is still often handled in small batch lots, and

49

similar products from several years' production may be available simultaneously, enables the student of wine to seek out and enjoy these variations. High-quality milk is envisioned as having a single identical flavor regardless of source. Standardization of wine to the same degree is, fortunately, unlikely. Wine surely would lose most of its interest for the sophisticated adult if it did not display so many variations, both obvious and subtle, in its qualities and attributes from the vineyard to the dining table and fireside.

Summary.—Commercial viticulture is limited to certain areas of the world with 1,700 or more heat-summation units during the summer season, without excessive rain or humidity in summer, and having a continuous winter dormant period with no excessive or prolonged cold temperatures nor unseasonable warm spells. Vineyard sites and cultural practices are selected in order to produce the best grapes of the chosen variety for the type of wine to be made. The environment of the vine has important effects upon its metabolism and influences the composition of the fruit and, in turn, the quality of the wine. Consistently successful commercial growing of high-quality wine grapes depends upon a correct matching to wine type of variety, viticultural operations, climate, and not a little good fortune.

Chapter 4

MICROORGANISMS AND WINE

Two plants are necessary to make wine: the fruit from the grapevine and yeasts for fermentation. The grape, a seed-bearing member of the plant kingdom, or spermatophyte, has been discussed. The other essential plant for wine, the yeast, is a member of the thallophytes. This division includes the algae, lichens, and fungi or mycetes. In the broad group of fungi will be found the yeasts, bacteria, and molds, all of interest to students of wine. The genus called *Saccharomyces* (sugar fungus) includes the yeasts of most significance in all forms of commercial production of alcohol from sugar. The species *Saccharomyces cerevisiae* (the name referring to cereal and the goddess Ceres) is the yeast commonly used in panary (bakery) and vinous fermentations. Selections of S. *cerevisiae* and another species, S. *carlsbergensis*, are generally used for distillery and brewery fermentations also. The yeast which is most important in wine fermentations is S. *cerevisiae* var. *ellipsoideus*, so called from its slightly elongated oval shape compared to the more nearly spherical form of other varieties. (In older books this wine yeast may be listed just as S. *ellipsoideus*.) This variety of yeast is well adapted to fermenting grapes to wine and is often found on the skin of the ripe wine grape in sufficient numbers to make possible the fermentation of the crushed grape without further inoculation. The visible white coating of the grape berry, the bloom, is a waxy material produced by the

51

fruit and *not* yeast cells, although a considerable yeast population may fall on it and stick to it.

Yeasts are widely distributed in nature and most other fruits as well as the grape carry some associated yeasts. The numbers and species of the natural microflora on the surface of a healthy fruit are influenced by many factors. While the ripe grapes in wine-producing areas often carry sufficient cells of the wine yeast *S. cerevisiae* var. *ellipsoideus* on their skins to ferment the grape to wine when crushed, it is more usual today to add an inoculum of a strain of this "tame" or "domesticated" yeast selected for its desirable attributes. Several problems are avoided by this procedure. The relatively high cell numbers and the known growth characteristics of the strain added produce more prompt and predictable fermentations. If microorganisms are present in the crushed grapes which would otherwise begin to multiply, they are "swamped" by the large number of wine-yeast cells added, and the resultant rapid vinous fermentation prevents appreciable modification of the wine by these other organisms.

Among the microorganisms that may be present on grapes for wine are the "wild" yeasts, which often belong to other genera such as *Kloeckera*, *Torulopsis*, *Pichia*, and *Hansenula*. These are also referred to as the apiculate yeasts because the cells of some of them have pointed ends (apices) somewhat like the shape of a lemon. Cells of these yeasts as a group are often much more numerous on grapes than are wine-yeast cells. During the early stages of fermentation, particularly if no inoculum has been added, these wild yeasts multiply. The relative growth of the wine yeast is favored by the addition of sulfur dioxide, because most of the other yeasts are more susceptible to its inhibitory effects than is the wine yeast. The wild yeasts are usually inhibited by about 4 to 6 per cent or more alcohol; as soon as this level is exceeded, the wine yeast becomes predominant and most of the wild yeasts cease appreciable growth or fermentation.

52

Microorganisms and Wine

There has been much speculation with little firm conclusion as to the importance of the type or strain of yeast to the flavor and quality of the wine. A particular strain of *Saccharomyces cerevisiae* var. *ellipsoideus* is usually chosen for such attributes as rapid fermentation, high alcohol yield per gram of sugar consumed, high alcohol tolerance, ease of removal of the yeast cells from the finished wine, and ability to ferment at low temperatures rather than for specific flavor effects. Differences between fermentations with single pure strains within this variety in respect to flavor contribution appear to be relatively minor. This may not be true when other species and genera become involved in the fermentation. Although the wild yeasts produce alcohol, they can also produce a higher proportion of other products which contribute to flavor. *Hansenula*, for example, is noted for a relatively high production of odorous esters. Even though the growth of most of them is stopped at 4 to 6 per cent alcohol, the wild yeasts are believed to contribute special flavors from their activity in the early stages of fermentation. Moreover, some species of *Torulopsis* will ferment to 10 per cent alcohol.

Other species within the genus *Saccharomyces* are important in special wine types; *S. beticus* or *S. oviformis* contribute a special flavor to *flor* sherry and certain sweet table wines such as the yellow wines of Jura. Wines made in different areas from the same grape variety with apparently similar fruit composition and processing often do taste noticeably different. It may be that differences in the make-up of the microflora naturally present in the two areas are important in producing the differences in the wines. The natural flora on grapes in vineyard regions where wine has been made for many years usually differs from that found on grapes in an isolated new planting, and often few wine yeasts are found on grapes from new plantings. As a new vineyard produces fruit, some falls on the ground, and insects and other vectors bring in yeasts which multiply in the fallen fruit and perhaps on the surface of healthy fruit.

53

Yeasts can survive from season to season in the soil; as the cycle is repeated over the years a complex flora of microorganisms is built up which may be fairly stable in one vineyard area but differ from that in other areas. In parts of Europe it is believed that special qualities and distinctiveness are introduced into wines by the complex microflora present on the grapes, and inoculation with pure cultures of wine yeasts is not widely practiced.

Many studies have indeed shown that a great variety of yeasts, including *Saccharomyces* species other than the typical wine yeasts, do occur on grapes and can participate in fermentation of the grapes to produce fine wines. It is also true, however, that wines of the highest quality are produced (and more consistently so) in countries where the most modern and scientific technology is used, including routine inoculations with pure cultures of selected strains of wine yeast.

Yeasts, like most living organisms, require as nutrients a metabolizable source of carbon and of nitrogen, minerals, and certain trace substances or vitamins. The usual carbon source is a fermentable carbohydrate. Grape juice contains approximately equal proportions of the 6-carbon sugars (hexoses) glucose and fructose, both of which are readily fermented and support growth of the majority of yeasts. Maltose, the sugar formed from starch breakdown, but not starch itself can be fermented by the yeasts used in commercial fermentations. Sucrose, table sugar, can be fermented by yeasts, since they produce invertase, the enzyme which converts sucrose to invert sugar—an equal mixture of glucose and fructose. Sucrose is sometimes added to grapes and often is added to berry fermentations, but it does not occur in important amounts in ripe grapes. Starch conversion to sugar and then fermentation of the maltose is not involved in wine preparation since grapes do not contain starch, but it is, of course, an important step in beer and spirit production from cereals and starchy materials. Other sugars such as galactose, mannose, and melibiose may or may not be fermented readily at first or even after the yeasts become accustomed to them, but this is primarily of interest as a means of distinguishing strains and species of yeasts from each other, since these sugars are not found widely in fruits. Certain other carbohydrates, particularly pentose sugars such as arabinose, ribose, and xylose, do occur in fruit juices in small amounts and are not fermentable by wine yeasts. As a result, a residue of nonfermentable sugars of the order of a gram per liter remains in the wine even when it is fermented completely "dry," that is, all the fermentable sugar consumed.

As a nitrogen source for producing its own proteins the yeast cell can make use of the amino acids (protein building blocks) in the grape juice. Wine yeasts and yeasts in general, however, do not ordinarily require the presence of amino acids or other complex nitrogen sources. Yeasts can grow, ferment, and multiply quite well simply by using ammonia or ammonium salts. They also can use the nitrogen of many simple organic compounds such as carbamide, but they cannot use nitrates as many higher plants can. Ordinarily grapes contain sufficient amino acids and other forms of available nitrogen that satisfactorily support yeast metabolism during wine fermentation. Grapes are almost unique among fruits in this regard. For satisfactory fermentation of honey, apple juice, and so on, some extra nitrogen source must be added; raisins are often used.

The minerals required by yeasts are known to include most of those required by living organisms. However, the natural substrates such as grape juice ordinarily contain more than enough of each to meet the needs of fermenting yeasts. In fact, the amount required by yeasts of most of the mineral elements is so small that it is difficult to produce a medium sufficiently low to demonstrate the requirement. Phosphorus in the form of phosphate ions and, less often, smaller amounts of others such as potassium or magnesium may be needed for fermenting diluted or partially purified mixtures such as sugar syrup.

The vitamin requirements of yeasts are of interest as diagnostic agents to determine identity or nonidentity of two cultures of yeast cells. Many yeasts have an absolute requirement for biotin; the biotin must be present in the medium or the yeast will not grow. Requirements may also be partial: growth will occur without the substance but will be slower than if it is added. The requirements may also be adaptive: after becoming accustomed to the absence of a substance, yeasts will grow well without it but will not do so at first. Although such requirements are less common and less frequently absolute than the requirement for biotin, a yeast strain may require one or more of the other water-soluble or B family of growth substances such as thiamine, pantothenic acid, pyridoxine, nicotinic acid, para-aminobenzoic acid, or inositol. Riboflavin is readily produced by most yeasts and is produced commercially in high yields from cultures of a yeast, though not a *Saccharomyces* species. All these vitamins and growth factors are commonly found in grape juice in sufficient amounts to permit rapid fermentation by wine yeasts.

Crushed grapes or grape juice ready to be fermented (commonly called "must" in the wine industry) is, then, ordinarily adequate nutritionally for yeasts to develop in it and convert it into wine. Under special circumstances such as refermenting wine, restarting a stopped fermentation, or fermenting fruits and materials other than grapes, yeast "foods" must be added. Various proprietary mixtures are sold to ensure rapid completion of fermentation if the amount of an essential nutrient (other than sugar) is inadequate. These yeast foods usually include ammonium phosphate and perhaps other minerals. As a source of the other trace substances an extract or lysis product from yeast cells which is rich in vitamins, growth factors, and amino acids, may be used.

The production of alcohol during the usual anaerobic (protected from air or oxygen) fermentation of must to wine parallels yeast growth. By growth, when speaking of microorganisms, is meant cell multiplication. Yeasts multiply somewhat differently than do most bacteria and other one-celled microorganisms. Bacterial cells commonly multiply by splitting into two equal new cells; this is called binary fission. Since the new cells are both equally young and at each new "generation" all the cells are again "young," there is no such thing as an old *cell* present but only an older culture. Yeasts, on the other hand, reproduce by forming a daughter bud on the mother cell, Figure 8. This bud grows until it eventually (with most yeasts) splits away and begins to bud itself. The mother cell retains a bud scar; only a few dozen buds can be produced before a given mother cell is "old" and dies. The break-up (autolysis) of the old cells can contribute nutrients to the remaining active cells.

The growth curve of yeast cells during fermentation follows the typical S-shaped form. There is a lag period during which the total number of yeast cells (whether added or naturally present) remains constant and the number of living cells may even decrease as some die from the shock of the new environment. As budding begins and new cells form there is a rapid transition to the second phase—the period of logarithmic growth. During this period the number of cells increases more and more rapidly as each cell becomes 2, the 2 become 4, the 4 give 8, and so on. This period continues until some factor becomes limiting (too little sugar, too much alcohol, etc.) at which time the multiplication slows and eventually stops, marking the third and final phase of the process. If some of the cells are removed to a new container of fresh must, the process begins again.

The growth and fermentation process for a single organism, the wine yeast, is complicated by the presence of other organisms. Grape juice from ripe grapes is rather acidic, having a pH between about 3 and 4 (pH units from 7 downward indicate a more and more acidic solution). Many microorganisms (particularly animal pathogens) will not multiply in or even survive such acidic conditions. During the fermentation, the anaerobic conditions and probably the high carbon dioxide content prevent the growth of a further large group of organisms, molds for example. As fermentation proceeds, the increasing content of alcohol limits even more the organisms which can survive. As a result of all these and other similar factors, relatively few microorganisms can be present and survive, much less multiply, in wine. This is perhaps not important today with modern sanitation and scientific technology, but in the days of polluted water and general ignorance of good sanitation this fact no doubt explained the healthfulness of wine compared to many other foods. No human pathogens or dangerous food toxin producers occur in wine nor, indeed, would they be likely to survive if deliberately added. Certainly this is a source of comfort to both producers and consumers.

The fact that most of the wild yeasts do not develop beyond about 4 to 6 per cent alcohol means that variations in the time it takes different lots of wine to reach about 4 per cent alcohol would permit variations in the contributions of wild yeasts to the final quality and flavor of wine. This is true also of the activity of other organisms present in wine during fermentation. A cleaner-flavored, better product results more consistently when the major fermentation (i.e., that of the wine yeasts) is prompt in starting and properly carried to completion. Again the value of inoculation with a selected yeast is apparent.

Among the limited number of kinds of microorganisms other than yeasts which may grow in wine are the bacteria which produce acetic acid. Several species of *Acetobacter*, such as A. *aceti* and A. *suboxydans*, are used to produce vinegar by conversion of ethanol to acetic acid. They are aerobic (requiring oxygen) and are inhibited by sulfur dioxide so that they are not usually a problem during fermentation. However, they occur in most wineries and a few of their cells may be found in or can get into most wines by contact with previously used casks. Owing to their general presence, nearly any wine produced by natural fermentation (without added alcohol) will

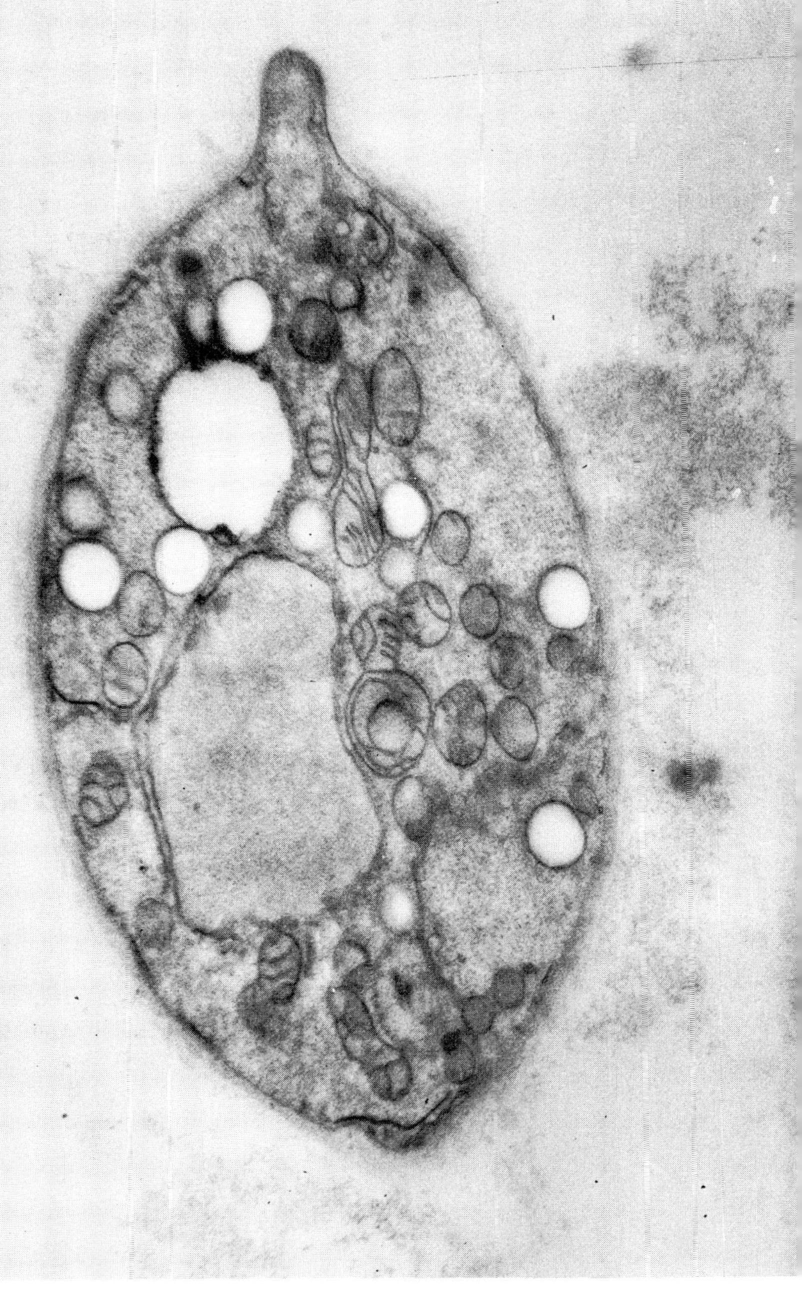

Fig. 8. A yeast cell just beginning to form a bud, as shown
by electron microscopy at about 20,000-fold magnification
Source: Dr. S. F. Conti, Dartmouth Medical School.

become acetic *if exposed to the air*. As the bacteria multiply, more and more of the alcohol is oxidized to acetic acid and part of the acetic acid is combined with more of the ethanol to produce ethyl acetate. Ethyl acetate may also be produced directly. Although a small amount of acetic acid and ethyl acetate occur in wine as natural constituents from the grape and from the yeast fermentation, any appreciable amount indicates activity of acetic-souring bacteria. Most countries have legal limits upon the maximum amount of acetic acid which can be present in products to be sold as wine.

When the growth of *Acetobacter* is encouraged, wine vinegar will result. Encouragement usually takes the form of inoculating the wine with *Acetobacter* cells and allowing free air contact with the surface of the wine so that these aerobic organisms can grow.

Conversely, the winemaker can prevent his wine from becoming vinegar by keeping his equipment and containers clean to minimize the possibility of addition of appreciable numbers of acetic-acid-producing bacteria to his lots of wine. Since some *Acetobacter* cells can be found in most wines, he prevents their multiplication also by keeping the wine containers full to the top to prevent air contact (and thus the growth of these air-requiring bacteria) and by judicious use of sulfur dioxide or other inhibitory additives.

The other major group of bacteria important in wine are the lactic acid bacteria. Organisms of this general class are active in the souring of milk, cheese making, sauerkraut production, and other useful fermentations. Some of them may be spoilage organisms in wine or they may have beneficial action depending upon their effect and manner of occurrence. Several genera of these organisms may occur in wine: notably *Micrococcus* or *Streptococcus* (forms nonpathogenic to human beings), *Lactobacillus*, *Pediococcus*, and *Leuconostoc*. These genera include many species, each with very definite and often complex arrays of nutritional requirements and metabolic products. These bacteria are widely distributed in nature and thus can and usually do occur in grape musts and in wineries. They are anaerobes, are tolerant to the acidity of wines, and some are able to multiply even in solutions with ethanol concentrations too high for yeasts. Hence they can occur in wine and multiply during the yeast fermentation, although they are usually susceptible to sulfur dioxide. They can metabolize sugars to produce lactic acid and other products; however, they are relatively slow-growing organisms (compared to yeasts during active fermentation) and usually are not much of a problem at this stage. After the alcoholic fermentation is finished they still may develop in wine by consuming nutrients not consumed (or not consumable) by the yeasts.

The most important result of the multiplication of lactic acid bacteria in wine is the so-called malo-lactic fermentation. Malic acid, $HOOC—CH_2—CHOH—COOH$ (the name referring to its isolation from apples), is converted by these organisms to lactic acid, $CH_3—CHOH—COOH$, the acid of sour milk, and carbon dioxide is given off. As a result of this action the acidity of the wine is decreased and the pH raised because the two carboxylic acid functions of malic acid are reduced to the single carboxylic acid function of lactic acid. The proportion of the wine's total acidity resulting from malic acid is reduced to half its former amount. Ordinarily, when the malo-lactic fermentation occurs, malic acid is completely converted to lactic acid. The proportion of the total acidity of a wine which is contributed by malic acid is variable by season and by grape variety, but is particularly high when the total acidity is high, sometimes amounting to as much as half. The total acidity may be too high for the most palatable wine, and therefore lowering of the acidity by a malo-lactic fermentation is desirable. This is frequently true in countries with relatively cool weather during the grape-growing and harvesting season. In warm regions (such as California) the malo-lactic fermentation might not be desirable, since it might lower the already low acidity too much and produce "flat"-tasting wine.

Considering the malo-lactic conversion alone is, however, an oversimplification, for the growth of lactic acid bacteria produces other effects than converting malic to lactic acid. A recent study of premium-priced California wines showed that a higher proportion of them (nearly all the red table wines) had undergone the malo-lactic conversion than was true of popular-priced wines. The subtle complexities introduced into the wine's flavor may be advantageous even if acidity-lowering per se is not particularly desirable. The species or strain of lactic acid bacterium which is present is evidently important. The special flavor effects are sometimes noticeably favorable, but in other cases the growth of lactic acid bacteria produces undesirable off-flavors such as "mousiness."

The timing of the malo-lactic fermentation is important. If the malo-lactic fermentation occurs after the wine is bottled, the increase in cells may produce noticeable and undesirable turbidity. The same is true, of course, of any other cellular growth, yeasts included. The wine is then said to have been biologically unstable with respect to clarity. Other effects may also result from the activity of lactic acid bacteria. If the malo-lactic fermentation occurs in the bottle, or if the carbon dioxide produced is not allowed to escape, the wine will be "gassy." With the exception of a few kinds of wine which make a virtue of this effect, gassiness in table wines is considered a negative quality factor. Another type of defect may result from a few members of the malo-lactic group of organisms—"ropy" wine. The organism produces a gelatinous thickening agent much like the dextran used as a transfusion blood-substitute.

Molds do not grow in wine and are not a problem in a winery except for occasional localized "mildew" problems on the outside of casks, on corks, or in improperly cleaned empty containers. This situation is not serious and is easily controlled by proper and frequent housecleaning. Molds can be a problem on grapes, however, particularly inside shipping containers of fresh table grapes.

One of the most commonly troublesome molds on table grapes is an ash-gray mold, *Botrytis cinerea*. This and certain other molds may attack unripened grapes on the vines under high humidity conditions, and berries with cracked skins may be attacked by secondary infections of molds, yeasts, and bacteria. The results are lower yield and reduced suitability of the grapes for wine. But *B. cinerea* can have special effects which have aided in the development of some of the most luscious and expensive wines from grapes upon which this mold has grown. If the humidity is high for a period, spores of *B. cinerea* can germinate and the mold will grow on and through the skin of the healthy grape. If this is followed by a period of low humidity, much of the moisture of the berry is lost through the loosened skin. The berry becomes shriveled like a raisin, but without the caramelized taste of the raisin. The juice obtained from these grapes has a higher sugar content owing to the water loss. Not only is a special delicate flavor introduced by the growth of the mold, but also the grape's natural flavor seems to be more concentrated. As a final dividend, the mold preferentially metabolizes a portion of the acid of the grape so that the juice has about the same acidity as the original juice. Thus a small amount of a very rich, sweet wine can be made from the remaining concentrated juice from grapes infected by the "noble mold." The happy combination and sequence of events leading to this result rarely occur in nature except in certain small regions of the grape-growing world. More will be said about this later, in connection with the Sauternes of France, the *Trockenbeerenauslese* wines of Germany, and the Tokay of Hungary. In California the proper conditions very rarely occur in the vineyards. Study of the right conditions for inoculation, the control of humidity, and development of the correct equipment and technique has led to the production in California of luscious wines from picked grapes inoculated with spores of *Botrytis cinerea.*

Summary.—The major microorganisms of importance to students of wine have been briefly described. The yeasts are the agents for the alcoholic fermentation necessary to convert grape juice to wine. Limited activity of "wild" yeasts may sometimes be important for development of particular flavors, but excessive growth of wild yeasts can be harmful. Since the growth of mixed cultures is unpredictable, the use of inocula of selected true wine yeasts is the only procedure which can be recommended. Organisms other than yeasts are sources of negative or sometimes positive effects on grape or wine quality. Some are used in producing other fermented food products. None constitutes a health hazard. With proper wine-making techniques and the necessary precautions, the microbiological problems of wine production can be controlled and wine quality maintained. Winemakers capitalize upon the special effects of some of these organisms to produce improved and more elegant wines.

Chapter 5

ALCOHOLIC FERMENTATION

In this chapter we shall consider how the yeast acts during the conversion of grape juice to wine and how some of the major constituents of wine arise during fermentation. The very word "yeast" is believed to have reached English from Anglo-Saxon *gist* via Greek *zestos* (boiled), and Sanskrit *yasyati* (it seethes). To ferment is to seethe, or "boil" without a great deal of heat. The term "fermentation" today is used loosely to include all processes in which chemical changes are brought about in organic substances by the action of microorganisms (or less commonly by other cells or free enzymes). Important commercial examples include the production of antibiotics by submerged aerobic mold and actinomycete fermentations. With some exceptions, such as vinegar production, the "natural" food fermentations observed by housewives and farmers of long ago were usually capable of changing foods in sealed or deep containers, that is, were anaerobic. This includes sauerkraut, pickle, and olive fermentations by lactic acid bacteria as well as the alcoholic fermentation by yeasts. This "boiling" without heat was a great mystery to the ancients and was one of the first subjects studied by science. The knowledge resulting from the study of wine fermentations and the so-called diseases of wine was a major contributor to the development and early progress of the modern sciences of microbiology and biochemistry.

Only a little over a hundred years ago it was discovered that alcoholic fermentation could occur naturally only in the presence of small living "ferments," the yeasts. Pasteur, from his studies in the 1860's, defined fermentation as life without air (anaerobic life) in contrast to the respiration of animals and higher plants which require air (are aerobic). In 1897 Edward Buchner reported that yeasts could be broken up and the cell-free juice would still produce alcohol from sugar. Thus the idea arose that there were "organized" ferments (cells of micro-organisms) which could be broken down to "unorganized" ferments. These we know now as the enzymes, proteinaceous molecules which catalyze each of the metabolic reactions of the cell. Originally it was assumed that one enzyme of the yeast produced alcohol from sugar, but further study revealed that separate enzymes carry on steps in the process. The process of sugar catabolism to ethyl alcohol by yeasts and to lactic acid by the muscles of animals was eventually found to be essentially the same process except for the very last steps. This pathway of carbohydrate utilization by living organisms is usually called the Embden-Meyerhof pathway after two of the many scientists who have contributed to our complete understanding of this biochemical process today.

The process of fermentation of one molecule of a simple sugar to alcohol was shown to result in two molecules of ethyl alcohol (more simply called ethanol) and two molecules of carbon dioxide. This was formulated by Gay-Lussac in 1810 into the equation which bears his name. This equation on the over-all process can be written in a slightly modernized version as:

$$1 \text{ glucose } (C_6H_{12}O_6) \rightarrow 2 \text{ ethanol } (CH_3CH_2OH) + 2CO_2 + \text{ about 56 kilocalories of energy}$$

Thus 180 grams of glucose (the molecular weight in grams computed from the atomic weights of carbon 12, hydrogen 1, and oxygen 16) should produce a total of 92 grams of ethanol and 88 grams of carbon dioxide when completely fermented.

Alcoholic Fermentation

This represents the maximum theoretical ethanol yield, which is 51.1 per cent of the weight of the sugar (hexose) fermented. Although actual yields in wine making approach this level, they are slightly lower owing to the diversion of some of the sugar's atoms to other products, incorporation of sugar derivatives into the yeast cells, losses by volatilization, and so on.

The Embden-Meyerhof pathway of conversion of sugars to ethanol does not require oxygen, and in fact the mixture of air into the fermenting solution decreases the yield of ethanol. Under truly aerobic conditions no alcohol is produced even though yeast growth is excellent, and if ethanol is already present the yeast cells can eventually metabolize it completely to carbon dioxide and water in the presence of air. The normal condition for alcoholic fermentation, then, is the absence of air or oxygen. This is relatively simple to accomplish, since the oxygen dissolved in the solution to be fermented is rapidly consumed by the yeast cells during initial (aerobic) multiplication. Access of further oxygen during fermentation in the typical deep liquid layer is not usually a serious problem, particularly since carbon dioxide is produced in large volume and as it escapes it sweeps away the air.

The 56 kilocalories of energy indicated as a product of fermentation of one gram molecular weight of glucose in the Gay-Lussac equation above represents the total energy change during the reaction. If glucose is "burned" either actually or by complete metabolic combustion to carbon dioxide and water, the total heat energy released is 673 kilocalories. The yeast cell ferments sugar *not* to get alcohol and carbon dioxide; it has no use for them and thus they accumulate or escape. It does need energy and this is the "profit" the yeast gains from fermenting the sugar. The energy is needed to do the chemical work of synthesizing the substances of more yeast cells; without it no reproduction of the yeast can occur. It is obvious that, if 673 kilocalories are produced when yeast converts 180 grams of glucose to carbon dioxide and water by complete oxidation and

67

only 56 kilocalories are produced by alcoholic fermentation, more than twelve times the amount of energy is potentially available for producing new yeast cells aerobically than anaerobically. To put it another way, yeasts must metabolize more than twelve times as much sugar to produce the same amount of cellular growth when growing anaerobically as they would if oxygen was available to them. This is fortunate for us because it means that during alcoholic fermentation the yeasts must "process" a great deal of sugar to alcohol with relatively little cell multiplication and therefore relatively little consumption of the sugar and other nutrients to build cells. If our object is to produce a large number of yeast cells, whether for use in inoculation of wine fermentation or as pressed yeast cakes for the baker, the pumping of oxygen (air) through the solution containing the yeast will produce up to twelvefold more cells per unit of sugar consumed and lower or eliminate the production of ethanol. The fact that the addition of oxygen to fermenting yeasts inhibits the conversion of glucose to ethanol, and gives more cells per unit of glucose consumed was observed by Pasteur and is termed the Pasteur effect.

The total amount of energy released during conversion of glucose to ethanol by yeasts (about 56 kilocalories/mole) is not available to the yeast for metabolic work. About 40 per cent of this amount, or 22 kilocalories, is captured in a usable form by the yeast. The rest is lost to the yeast and appears as heat. Thus the temperature of the fermenting solution is increased significantly. The usable energy is captured and transferred to other uses by the yeast cell in the form of a complex chemical, adenosine triphosphate, usually abbreviated ATP. A phosphate ion from the fermenting solution is combined by enzymes of the yeast with adenosine diphosphate, ADP, to give ATP. This illustrates one important reason why yeasts require the presence of phosphate for growth. The formation of ATP requires energy and the energy is obtained by the yeast from specific steps in the conversion of sugar to ethanol. Once

68

"built into" ATP, this energy can be temporarily stored, transferred, and used by the yeast for a multitude of metabolic reactions requiring energy. In fact, ATP is the primary energy-exchanging substance for all activities of living organsms including the muscular work you are doing right now as you breathe.

Converting sugar to alcohol requires at least a dozen enzymes each of which catalyzes one step in the process sequence of the Embden-Meyerhof pathway. The enzymes acting first are those necessary to get the particular sugar being fermented phosphorylated and isomerized into the form of fructose-1,6-diphosphate. This hexose phosphate is necessary for starting the remainder of the breakdown reactions, and two molecules of ATP are consumed in its formation from the fermentable simple sugars. The next reaction splits the 6-carbon unit, fructose-1,6-diphosphate, into two 3-carbon triose phosphates. These are dihydroxyacetone phosphate and glyceraldehyde-3-phosphate, which can be converted one into the other by the action of an isomerase (enzyme). A series of reaction steps, each with its own enzyme, then occurs and eventually two molecules of pyruvic acid result. During these reactions hydrogen is transferred to a coenzyme carrier and two new molecules of ATP are formed for each 3-carbon unit, or a total of four, giving a net gain of two ATP, per sugar molecule fermented. Each new gram molecule of ATP represents about 11 kilocalories of useful energy gained by the yeast and therefore accounts for the 22 kilocalories of energy yeasts gain in converting one mole of glucose to two moles of ethanol.

The pyruvic acid (CH_3—CO—COOH) is converted to acetaldehyde (CH_3CHO) by loss of one molecule of carbon dioxide (or two per original hexose sugar). This escaping carbon dioxide is one of the major products of fermentation. The acetaldehyde is ordinarily reduced by the addition to it of the hydrogen transferred to the coenzyme carrier at the earlier step mentioned. This final reaction, $CH_3CHO + H_2$

$\rightarrow CH_3CH_2OH$, is catalyzed by the enzyme alcohol dehydrogenase. It is reversible and acetaldehyde can be produced from ethanol. All the reactions in this sequence are reversible if the proper conditions, enzymes, and energy are supplied, except that of the decarboxylation (carbon dioxide loss) of pyruvic acid. The reversal of the sequence would produce sugars from smaller molecules, and has several features in common with the way in which the grapevine makes its sugar.

This reaction system may seem a bit complicated, but it has been substantiated by chemists, and is one of the fundamentals of modern biochemistry. It clearly explains the origin of the major products of alcoholic fermentation. It also explains the presence of at least small amounts of many of the intermediate compounds in the sequence such as acetaldehyde and pyruvic acid. Acetaldehyde reacts with sulfur dioxide, or rather the bisulfite ion in solution, to form an addition product which cannot be reduced to ethanol by the coenzyme hydrogen carrier system. The hydrogen is diverted under this condition to reduce the triose dihydroxyacetone to glycerol. Some glycerol (also called glycerine, $CH_2OH-CHOH-CH_2OH$) is produced to the extent of about 0.5 to 1.5 per cent in every wine fermentation, but considerably more may be produced under certain conditions, including the presence of high amounts of bisulfite. Glycerol production for explosives (nitroglycerine) by fermentation was an important development in the First World War. Glycerol is a slightly sweet substance and *may* contribute to the viscosity and apparent "body" of some wines.

Glycerol is a constituent of fats and as such some of it is incorporated into the yeast cell. Pyruvic acid is partly converted to alanine, one of the amino acids of yeast proteins. Reactions such as these divert some of the atoms from the original sugar molecule into yeast-cell constituents and decrease the yield of ethanol. Other reactions, such as the enzymatic reduction of a small amount of pyruvic acid to lactic acid or the conversion of some acetaldehyde to acetic acid, not only divert some of the carbon source to products other than alcohol, but also explain the presence of small amounts of these compounds which may contribute to a wine's flavor.

Yeasts are able to grow aerobically and can convert ethanol to acetaldehyde then, via a series of reactions known as the Krebs cycle, after its discoverer, to carbon dioxide and water. Various degrees of temporary, partial, or incomplete aerobic metabolism can occur or be produced in wine fermentation. In the production of *flor* sherry, for example, the level of acetaldehyde and certain other flavor-producing substances is much increased by aerobic growth of yeast in or on the surface of previously fermented wine. In any typical wine fermentation some oxygen gains access to the wine even though relatively anaerobic conditions must exist to produce wine. As a result, again, more or less of the carbon source is diverted from ethanol production to other products. Among these products are citric acid, succinic acid, fumaric acid, malic acid, and α-ketoglutaric acid. Not all compounds that are found in wine got there from aerobic action of yeasts, however, for the Krebs cycle occurs in grapes, too, and produces the greater part of the total acids found in wine.

These many possible and actual diversions of the carbon of sugar during wine fermentation explain the fact that, whereas 51.1 per cent of the weight of glucose theoretically should appear as ethanol, only about 48 per cent actually does so. Since the yeast does produce 90–95 per cent of the theoretical amount of ethanol, it might be assumed that the small amounts of other products are unimportant. This is far from the truth, because many of the constituents minor in amount in wine are major in importance to flavor and aroma. Many of the important esters and other odorous constituents are present in very small amounts and in complex mixtures which are difficult to analyze; yet they determine the quality and distinctiveness of wines and most other food products. In wines many of these important trace compounds arise from the grapes them-

71

selves, but many are produced or are modified as the yeasts play their role in the process of wine making.

Higher alcohols, sometimes called fusel oils, occur in fermented beverages. By higher alcohols is meant those like ethanol, but with more than two carbon atoms. Particularly the 5-carbon or amyl alcohols, 4-carbon butanols, and 3-carbon propyl alcohols or propanols may occur in wine in various isomers and proportions. These compounds arise in large part during alcoholic fermentation, and their relative concentration in wines and spirits is a factor in the flavor and quality of the product, although they ordinarily total rather less than a tenth of 1 per cent of the wine. It was believed, based upon the work of Ehrlich, that these compounds arose by the action of yeast enzymes upon the amino acids in wine musts. An example is the conversion of leucine into isoamyl alcohol:

$$(CH_3)_2\!-\!CH\!-\!CH_2\!-\!CH(NH_2)\!-\!COOH + H_2O$$
$$\rightarrow (CH_3)_2\!-\!CH\!-\!CH_2\!-\!CH_2OH + NH_3 + CO_2$$

This is an oversimplification because, among other things, more higher alcohols are produced under some conditions than can be accounted for by complete conversion of all the respective amino acids present in the medium. Rather, it is now known, the carbon skeletons which the yeast produces to make its amino acids can also be diverted to produce these alcohols. This is another example of the complex and intimate interplay between the various chemical reactions which characterize the metabolism of living cells and alcoholic fermentation in particular.

As we have seen, the grape berry contains sugars, acids, pigments, tannins, and odorous compounds; and some of these ingredients, particularly sugars and amino acid derivatives, are used and transformed by yeasts during fermentation. Fermentation, particularly the alcohol produced, affects the solvent powers of the fluid and influences the composition of the wine. The pigments, many of the odorous compounds, and part

72

of the tannin compounds are localized within the cells of the skin of the grape berry. Another large portion of the total tannin of the berry is found in the seeds. Some of these compounds are not released at all and some do not go completely into the solution merely as a result of the crushing of the grapes. Time for diffusion from the cells and the extractive effect of alcohol are both provided during fermentation, if the solid parts of the berry remain in the must during this period. The turbulence in the fermentation vessel and perhaps the enzymic actions of the yeast also affect the transfer of less soluble grape-cell components to the solution. Thus, although the grape produces the tannin, anthocyanin pigment, and aroma compounds, and the yeast may not produce any synthesis or chemical change of these compounds, their content in the wine can be strongly influenced by events during the fermentation process.

Summary.—The juice from the freshly crushed grape berry contains sugars, acids, and other cell-sap-soluble components of the easily disrupted cells. Juice-insoluble substances and the contents of cells not easily broken, which may be important to the composition and quality of the wine, are dissolved in the wine by the alcohol and by other effects produced by fermentation. The metabolic activities of the fermenting wine yeast produce a theoretical conversion of 51 per cent of the weight of sugar fermented to ethanol and the rest to carbon dioxide. Actual yields are slightly lower because the yeast produces a series of compounds other than alcohol. Some of the sugar is used to synthesize new yeast cells. The energy necessary for this synthesis and waste heat energy are produced by the yeast during the sequence of fermentation reactions terminating in ethanol, a by-product of the activity of anaerobic yeast. The ethanol, acetaldehyde, higher alcohols (fusel oils), and other products of alcoholic fermentation are important attributes of wine. The variable proportions of them contribute to type, flavor, and quality differences among wines. Some yeast cells break up (autolyze) and contribute their soluble constituents to the solution. Therefore, the composition of the wine may be affected by the grape, by the direct and indirect reactions of alcoholic fermentation on grape must, by yeast-cell breakdown products, by activity of other microorganisms, and by reactions during processing.

The biochemistry of fermentation not only beautifully illuminates and clarifies the ancient art of making wine, but also explains and makes possible a calculated control of many of the "mysteries" which baffled the artisan winemaker. Aesthetics, however, is still a part of (and should not be displaced from) wine production and wine appreciation, but mystique should not remain if knowledge can be substituted.

Chapter 6

CLASSIFICATION OF WINES

Wines can be classified on the basis of geographical origin, color, the amount of carbon dioxide they contain, the sugar content, and many other chemical characteristics.

Actual commercial sales of wines are generally made according to country and district of origin. Climatic conditions, varieties used, wine-making procedures, and custom usually do make the wines of different viticultural regions different from each other. However, the geographical origin of wines requires a special classification for each country and for the many microclimates of each country. For ordinary wines, which differ little from one country to another, the distinction is unnecessary on the basis of either quality or composition.

The classification we shall use is based primarily upon easily recognizable characteristics, such as whether herbs or flavoring materials have been added, the amount of carbon dioxide pressure, the percentage of sugar, and the presence or absence of distinguishable varietal aromas. This classification is intended primarily for students and consumers who are interested in distinguishing one wine from another by tasting.

The question whether a varietal aroma is "distinguishable" is not so easily established. Different varieties contribute more or less distinctive flavors to wines. The distinctiveness varies with the maturity of the grapes (which, in turn, depends on climatic conditions) and on the wine-making and aging procedures. Individuals vary in their ability to recognize varietal aromas. The novice can barely distinguish muscats from nonmuscats. However, the expert can distinguish a fairly large number of varietal aromas. He may not be able to identify the varietal aroma, but he will be able to distinguish it from other varieties. Even within a single varietal aroma there may be a good deal of variation. For example, the varietal origin of most of the wines of Burgundy is Pinot noir. Nevertheless, many experts on the wines of Burgundy are able to distinguish the wines made in one part of the region from those made in another part of the region and even of one vintage from another. The same is true of the wines of Bordeaux, although there the varietal composition is likely to be more complex. This also leads to differences between wines of different chateaux. Long experience with the wines of a region is necessary for one to be able to distinguish such subtle nuances of character. An expert on the wines of one region may be unable to identify the wines of another region with which he is unfamiliar.

In the following classification we have listed as "distinguishable" only the varieties and types of wines which are normally distinctive. A number of varieties listed as having indistinguishable varietal odors may, under certain conditions, be distinguishable. A good example is Nebbiolo, which is listed (if grown in California) as being without a distinguishable varietal aroma, whereas the wines of Barolo often have a distinguishable varietal aroma. Since Barolo wines are made from Nebbiolo, this would appear to be a contradiction, but the Nebbiolo when grown in the Barolo district seems to have more varietal aroma than it does when it is grown in California. The examples given in this list are mainly of American wines, but include a representative number of European wine types. Note that the classification is dichotomous; so, if the wine does not fall into one group, it must be found in the other.

WINES WITH ADDED HERBS OR FLAVORING CONSTITUENTS

Wines with anthocyanin pigments.—The exact flavoring materials which are added to red wines to produce bitter-tasting wines are not always known. One of the most popular wines of this type, Byrrh, contains some cinchona and has a distinctly bitter taste. While most *retsina* is white, occasionally you find a red one containing the typical resin or turpentine odor. A few of the proprietary, flavored California wines have been at least pink in color. The Dubonnet and Byrrh types of wines are consumed in France as apéritifs with or without ice and with or without soda. In this country Dubonnet is used primarily for making cocktails with gin. Several Italian types of wines might also be placed in this category, but none is likely to be popular in this country except as a dilettante drink.

Wines without anthocyanin pigments.—The most characteristic of these are the herb-flavored wines of the dry or French type of vermouth and the sweet or Italian type vermouth. The dry vermouths have a slight amber color when produced and sold in France or Italy. Those exported to or made in this country are mostly very light in color. This is obviously so that more vermouth can be blended with gin for martini cocktails (vermouth being less costly than gin). These vermouths are not actually dry, as most of them contain from 2 to 4 per cent of sugar. The sweet type of vermouth is very sweet, usually with 14 to 16 per cent sugar and 16 to 20 per cent alcohol. Sweet vermouth has an amber color, sometimes with a reddish hue. Both types have distinct and complex odors from the herbs and spices from which they are made. Some dry vermouths on the American market have a low herb character. In all of them the herb mixture should be adjusted so that the odor of no single herb or spice predominates.

Besides the true herb-flavored wines we have nowadays a

wide variety of wines to which other kinds of flavoring constituents have been added. These, known as "special natural flavored" wines in this country, carry proprietary labels, such as Thunderbird and Silver Satin. Many of them are very light in color and appear to have been intended as substitutes for the gin or vodka type of highballs. A few have been produced with an amber color and have even been bottled in whiskey type bottles. These may have been intended as substitutes for the whiskey highball. They usually have about 16 to 20 per cent alcohol and contain 8 to 14 per cent sugar. They have been quite popular in this country and there seems to be a market for them. It is probable that new and different types of flavoring materials may be used in producing these types of wines. Several imported types appear to be imitations of the original American prototypes. Some of these wines are pink and a few are red. They obviously belong in the previous category. The increase in consumption of such wines has undoubtedly lessened the demand for standard dessert wines such as port and muscatel.

Very few medicinal types of wines are produced nowadays. Occasionally one finds a home-made gentian or rhubarb wine, and a small but widespread home industry is engaged in the making of flavored wines for home use. There was, during and just after the war, a fad for a flavored wine which was said to have medicinal property, but this eventually ran foul of the internal revenue laws and disappeared from the market. Some of the favored and widely advertised prescriptions, especially those for female diseases, may owe their attraction and alleged beneficial properties to the alcohol they contain.

WINES WITHOUT ADDED HERBS OR
FLAVORING MATERIALS

Most of the wines produced in the world contain no added flavoring material. Their flavor comes from the variety of grape from which they were produced, from the fermentation process, or from treatments during aging or from the aging itself.

78

Classification of Wines

Wines with excess carbon dioxide.—Excess carbon dioxide in wines may arise from (1) the fermentation of sugar which has been added to the finished wine and which leads to the production of two to six atmospheres of pressure, (2) the fermentation of constituents normally present in the wine, such as residual sugar or malic acid, or (3) the addition of carbon dioxide directly to the wine. In the latter two the pressure is usually much less. Wines containing excess carbon dioxide from the fermentation of added sugar may be further classified as those containing anthocyanin pigments and those which do not contain anthocyanin pigments.

Sparkling wines containing anthocyanin pigments are commonly sold either as pink sparkling wines or as red sparkling wines such as California sparkling burgundy or champagne rouge, depending on the amount of pigment. A small amount of sparkling Burgundy is imported from France. Because of their tannin content in juxtaposition with the carbon dioxide, these wines usually have a slightly bitter taste. Therefore, they are normally sweetened and hence are abhorred, justifiably or not, by many wine connoisseurs.

Sparkling wines that do not contain anthocyanin pigments may be subdivided into those which have a muscat flavor and those which do not. The most important types of muscat-flavored sparkling wines are produced near Asti in northern Italy, known as *muscato spumante*. A small amount of sparkling muscat is made in California.

The sparkling wines that do not contain a muscat flavor include those labeled simply as California or New York champagne, *Sekt, spumante, espumante, shampanskoe,* Champagne, and *mousseux.* The latter refer, respectively, to sparkling wines from Germany, Italy, Spain or Portugal, Russia, and France. In this country if the wine has been fermented in bulk in large tanks it is labeled California or New York or American champagne, bulk process. These nonred types of sparkling wines may be further labeled *brut, sec* (dry or extra dry), *demi-sec,* or *doux.* These usually refer to wines containing less than 1.5

per cent of sugar for the *brut* types and from 2.5 to 4.5 per cent of sugar for the *sec*, 5 for *demi-sec*, and 10 for *doux*. However, some *brut* types, unfortunately, contain more than 1.5 per cent sugar.

The sparkling wines that derive their gassiness from constituents normally present in still wines are of two types. Both contain very little pressure, usually about one atmosphere. More common are the wines which are gassy from the fermentation of residual sugar. These include occasional wines from Germany, France, and Italy, and the *muscato amabile* of California. The last is a particularly interesting type in that it is made from very sweet muscat musts which are allowed to ferment at a very low temperature. It is then bottled with a certain amount of gassiness. In France a number of the Vouvray types are gassy from the fermentation of the residual sugar.

Technically more interesting are the wines which are gassy from the malo-lactic fermentation. The most important types of these are the red and the white *vinho verde* types from the Minho district of northern Portugal (see also p. 236). A number of wines in the Piedmont district of Italy are also gassy from the fermentation of malic acid.

Addition of carbon dioxide is an old practice, and formerly a number of these carbonated wines were found on the market. Those containing anthocyanin pigments were sold as California carbonated burgundy and those not containing anthocyanin pigments were sold as California carbonated wines of the moselle or even of the sauterne type. A number of Swiss wines are evidently bottled with enough added carbon dioxide to give them a slight gassiness. In California some wines contain about a quarter of an atmosphere of pressure, sufficient to give a slightly prickly sensation to the tongue. These may not be called carbonated wines either on the bottle or in their advertising, since that would cause their tax to be increased, but the title of one of them, Ripple, seems to suggest subtly that carbon dioxide may be present.

Wines without obvious excess carbon dioxide.—This includes the most important fraction of wines produced in the world. They can be classified as still (i.e., not gassy) wines. There are three very broad groups on the basis of alcohol content: below 14 per cent alcohol, those between about 14 and 17 per cent alcohol, and those containing over 17 but below about 21 per cent alcohol. The first is commonly known as table wines and the others as dessert.

Alcohol 8 to 14 per cent: The California regulations call for wines to be between 10½ and 14 per cent alcohol if they are red and between 10 and 14 per cent if they are white. The federal regulations require a minimum of 9 per cent by volume of alcohol. The usual European minimum is 8 or 9 per cent. For districts with an *appellation d'origine* in France, the minimum percentage of alcohol is specified by regulations. For example, a wine labeled simply Bordeaux rouge can have a lower minimum of alcohol than one labeled Médoc. The regulations in other countries are very diverse.

Two broad general groups of wines may be differentiated: those with anthocyanin pigments and those without such pigments. The wines containing anthocyanin pigments can be subdivided, in turn, into those which are pink and those which have a full red color.

The pink wines are usually dry, and are labeled as California rosé types or as California Gamay rosé or California Grenache rosé or Grignolino. Some come from a specific district in France or Italy, such as Anjou, Burgundy, or Tavel. Some proprietary blended rosé wines, both American and imported, have appeared on the market. There has been a tendency to make the California rosés with about 1 to 2 per cent sugar. A number of the more popular brands are decidedly on the sweet side. Some eastern United States proprietary-named rosés are very sweet.

The wines with a red color are generally dry, although a few have a small amount of sugar. The dry red wines can be classified as to whether they have or do not have a distinguishable varietal aroma.

81

Among these with a distinguishable varietal aroma the Barbera usually has a high acidity although, because of the use of the malo-lactic fermentation, this may not always be true. Those with a moderate acidity include Barolo, produced from the Nebbiolo grape; Beaujolais, a product of the Gamay variety; the various Bordeaux wines such as Médoc, Saint-Emilion, and château wines from that district, all of which contain some Cabernet aroma; the wines of Burgundy, produced from Pinot noir; the California or Chilean Cabernets; Châteauneuf-du-Pape, produced from Grenache and several other varieties; Chianti, a product of Sangioveto and Colorino; Fresia, named after the variety; Gamay (at least some Gamays in California have a varietal aroma); Hermitage, which owes its distinguishable character to Petite Sirah; California, Chilean, and other Pinot noirs; Rioja, a mixture of Grenache and Tempranilla; Zinfandel; and many others.

Wines without a distinguishable varietal aroma include California burgundy, California claret, California dry red table wine, California red chianti, Carignane, Charbono, Durif, Malvoisie, Mourastel, Pinot St.-George (Red Pinot by error), and many of the *vins ordinaires* and local wines of France, Portugal, Spain, Italy, and other countries. Some of the varietal types under the best conditions may have a distinctive flavor. Although many attempts have been made to introduce characteristic differences between these nonvarietal types, none has been successful, for example, greater color and alcohol in California burgundy compared to California claret. However, the California burgundy of one producer may resemble the California claret of another and vice versa. In France the classification of *vin ordinaire* is often made on the basis of alcohol content— usually 9, 10, and 11 per cent.

Stable sweet red wines of only 8 to 14 per cent alcohol are easily produced with the modern methods of stabilization and pasteurization, and a number of them are found on the market. They include wines of the California vino da tavola type which contain about 1.5 per cent sugar and could be classified as

California red table wines, but they also include a number of kosher-type wines such as Mogen David and Manischewitz which would be classified as sweet red table wines but which have a distinct Concord aroma.

Wines without anthocyanin pigments can be classified into those which have a distinguishable varietal aroma and those which do not. Among those which have a distinguishable varietal aroma, some are sweet and others contain no noticeable sugar. The sweet wines include the German *Auslese* types, the Hungarian Tokay, the California light muscat and light sweet muscat, the Loire wines in years when *Botrytis* develops well, French Sauternes, Sweet Catawba, California Sauvignon blanc and California Sweet Sauvignon blanc, California Sémillon and California Sweet Sémillon, and some of our California Chenin blancs. There may also be some eastern wines with proprietary labels which are sweet and have a methyl anthranilate (Concord) type of odor.

The dry wines with distinguishable varietal aromas include Catawba, Chablis, Chardonnay (sometimes labeled Pinot Chardonnay), Chenin blanc (sometimes labeled White Pinot by error), Delaware, Folle blanche (not always with a varietal aroma), Gewürztraminer, Graves, some Loire wines, particularly from Vouvray, Moselle, California Pinot blanc, California White Riesling (Johannisberg Riesling by error), Rhine, California Dry Sauvignon blanc, California Sauvignon vert, California Dry Sémillon, Sylvaner, and Traminer.

Many California, French, Italian, and other wines do not have a distinguishable varietal character. Thus California chablis, dry sauterne, rhine, white chianti, and similar types are usually blends of several wines—usually wines of ordinary varieties of grapes. Even wines labeled Riesling, Grey Riesling, Veltliner, Rotgipfler, Gutedel (or Chasselas doré) can seldom be distinguished. Many Italian, Austrian, Swiss, Spanish, and Greek white table wines are of this type. As with the reds, many attempts to persuade producers to make some distinction between the types have been without success, i.e., California

83

chablis from California rhine. Some of the wines so labeled of one company are virtually identical. Another company's products may be quite different from these and the types may be carefully distinguished from each other.

Alcohol 14 to 17 per cent: This is a sort of no man's land for wines. There is a good reason for this. Fermentation of sugar often ceases at about 14 per cent alcohol, but bacterial activity continues through 17 or 18 per cent. Consequently, wines which contain residual sugar are usually fortified up to something over 18 per cent of alcohol so that they will not be subject to bacterial spoilage. However, in certain states in the United States the maximum percentage of alcohol is only 16 and for these states wines must be produced which have an alcohol content in this particular range.

The regulations of the Catholic Church are that alcohol can be added to wines only toward the end of the tumultuous fermentation and, in addition, specify that the alcohol should not normally exceed about 18 per cent. Therefore, a number of wines are produced with an alcohol content in this range for ecclesiastical use. A few dry Spanish wines of the *fino* and *manzanilla* types are regularly sold in Spain and occasionally exported with an alcohol content of about 15 to 16 per cent.

These wines can be divided into two groups: those which contain anthocyanin pigments and those which do not. Among those which contain anthocyanin pigments are miscellaneous red sweet wines which are shipped to certain states because of legal restrictions. Sometimes these are called California port; others have proprietary names. A number of these are for kosher or ecclesiastical use and employ either proprietary names or names that would not indicate that they are dessert wines.

The wines that do not contain anthocyanin pigments include a variety of ecclesiastical types which may be labeled California angelica or California muscatel or have various kinds of proprietary labels. The Spanish *fino* and *manzanilla* wines are usually labeled under these names, but would, of course, also carry the name of the producer. A number of the *montilla* wines in Spain have an alcohol content in this intermediate range. Russia produces a number of very sweet wines which have an alcohol content of not more than 16 per cent. These are sometimes labeled muscatel or Pinot gris and contain up to 20 or 23 per cent sugar.

Alcohol 17 to 21 per cent: This is the main group of dessert wines and it can be divided into two groups: those which contain anthocyanin pigments and those which do not. The wines which contain anthocyanin pigments can be divided into those with a muscat aroma and those without a muscat aroma. In this country very little muscat-flavored wine, red or pink, is now produced. The Aleatico is apparently not on the market at the present time, but a number of sweet table wines from Tuscany and Sardinia in Italy do have pink color and muscat aroma. Apparently only one or two companies are producing a red or black muscatel. Some of the South African Constantia wines apparently are of this type, since they are made from a red muscat variety.

We have a number of types of red dessert wines which do not have a muscat aroma. The wine with the very tawny-red or pink color and baked odor is called California tokay. It obviously has some of the characteristics of a sherry, very little characteristics of port, and some of the sugary characteristics of angelica. It is not normally aged very long in California, and enjoys only a limited market, usually among consumers desiring a low-priced wine.

The more important group of red fortified wines without a muscat aroma are those which have the name port. Those which have a slight brownish red or amber tint are usually sold as tawny port, whether from Portugal, California, Australia, or South Africa. The red color is more pronounced than in California tokay. The tawny color should be clearly due to aging and not to baking, since wines made by baking usually have a caramel or burnt odor. The remainder of the ports

85

available in this country are called simply port or ruby port. Vintage ports include the wines that are bottled after only two years or which may be bottled somewhat later, but before they become brown in color. The classical type of vintage port is that produced in Portugal but bottled and most appreciated in Great Britain. Vintage-type wines of both types are made also in California, Australia, and South Africa.

For the wines not containing anthocyanin pigments we can distinguish those which have a muscat aroma from those which do not. A great many white wines with a muscat aroma are produced in various parts of the world: for example, the muscatel of Frontignan and of Lunel from the south of France; the Muscato Canelli from near Asti in the Piedmont district of Italy. Some of these Italian muscats are slightly less than 17 per cent alcohol rather than above. There are also the very sweet muscat wines from the Island of Samos in Asia Minor, the Setúbal wine from near Lisbon in Portugal, and the varieties of muscatel from Russia, South Africa, Australia, and California. While many of these have developed an amber color through aging, some are amber because they were made from fully ripe grapes or were heated. These latter have a raisin or caramel flavor which is undesirable.

A number of white dessert wines have a special odor because of treatment or aging, others have no special odor caused by treatment or aging. The first group includes a diverse collection of wines having a raisin odor, Málaga; a baked odor, California dry, medium, or sweet sherry, and Madeira of Sercial, Boal and Malmsey types; wines with a reduced-must or burnt odor, of the Marsala type; and wines with a *rancio* odor from long aging of sweet wines, such as the Banyuls from the south of France and the wines from the Priorato region near Tarragona in northern Spain.

In another group of wines the special odor arises from the film-yeast process. These film-yeast wines can be divided into dry and nearly dry types. Among the dry types are Californian,

86

Australian, South African, and Russian sherry, many of the *montilla* wines from near Cordoba in Spain, the wines from Château Chalon in France, and some of the Spanish *manzanillas* which have been prepared for export. Among the sweet *flor* types are the *amontillados*, Californian or South African medium or sweet *flor* sherry. Some of the sweet types of Spanish sherries and *montillas* contain little film-yeast wine and probably would belong in the next category.

The last grouping includes wines which do not have a special odor because of treatment or aging. The most important of these is the amber-colored wine called California angelica. The *olorosos* which do not have any *flor*-type odor could also be placed in this category. Some of the cream sherries from Spain might belong here, too. Wines which are somewhat lighter in color, owing to the use of very light-colored juice and possibly, for some wines, the use of charcoal, are sold as California white port. White port from Portugal is more nearly in the category of the California angelica.

Summary.—Wines can be classified on the basis of whether or not they contain added flavoring materials, such as herbs or spices. The nonflavored wines can be separated into sparkling and nonsparkling wines, depending on whether or not they contain a visible excess of carbon dioxide at room temperature. Most of the wines of the world are of the nonsparkling type. These can best be distinguished on the basis of percentage of alcohol: 8 to 14, 14 to 17, and 17 to 21. The intermediate group is of importance primarily for wines produced for certain states or for sacramental purpose. Wines in the 8 to 14 per cent group can be separated as to color, sugar content, and whether or not they have a distinguishable varietal aroma. Wines in the 17 to 21 per cent group can be classified on the basis of color, varietal aroma, sugar content, and production or processing techniques.

Chapter 7

OPERATIONS IN WINE MAKING

Most of the descriptions of wine-making processes given here are based upon commercial practice. This may appear unfortunate to persons interested in home wine making. For this reason a few words on making wine at home are in order. The United States has very detailed and stringent laws regulating the production of alcoholic beverages; the Alcohol and Tobacco Tax Division (often referred to as the A.T.T.D.) of the federal Internal Revenue Service must be consulted regarding the federal and state laws before one engages in such production. The federal laws permit, upon obtaining specific permission, the tax-free production of up to 200 gallons of still wine per year by the head of a family for the exclusive use of his family. This ruling reflects the special place that wine holds as a dietary beverage; such permission is not granted for distilled beverages or beer. In fact, even possessing an unregistered still is illegal; home registrations are rarely approved, and then only for uses other than producing alcoholic beverages (distilled water, etc.).

Assuming that you are the head of a household and have obtained governmental permission to make wine at home, can you be successful? The answer depends upon your idea of success. Many who dabble in home vegetable gardening soon learn that it is difficult to show a profit. Even if land and labor are assumed to be free, satisfactory gardens are rare without expenditure for fertilizer, sprays, and tools. If accounting is honest, you may find that better and cheaper carrots can be obtained from the grocery store than from your garden. The "money-savers" and the "let's try it oncers" are usually better advised not to start gardening (or wine making). If you care to learn how and follow the rules it is possible to produce carrots of prize-winning quality or, for that matter, orchids, at home. Wine making is similar. If you want the pride and thrill of being able to say "I made it myself," or if you have an abiding interest in making a special product not otherwise obtainable (such as wine from your own rare variety of grapes), you can learn to make good wine in small lots (about 5 gallons recommended minimum) in your own basement or garage. However, success depends on attention to all the enological facts which govern the production of good wines commercially. Therefore a description of commercial practices and the reasons behind them will suffice for the home winemaker if he does not cut too many corners. He may be willing to accept a small amount of sediment in his wine and can do without filtration and tartrate removal, but if he does not keep his storage containers full and sealed the wine will become vinegar even more quickly than it does in large commercial operations. A pamphlet with specific descriptions of home wine-making procedures is listed on page 328 (Amerine-Marsh). Most other books for the would-be home winemaker take the form of recipes which are deceptively simple, but rarely culminate in a worth-while product.

COMMERCIAL WINE ANALYSIS

To make the best wine possible with the raw materials available and do so every time the process must be *controlled* from grape to glass. Control implies knowing the necessary facts and acting upon them to modify the process in the desired direction. The facts relate to the microbiological, chemical composition, and sensory quality of the wine at all the important stages. To obtain these facts every winery must use laboratory examinations and analytical procedures. A few of the larger wineries have elaborate quality control and developmental research laboratories staffed with enologists, bacteriologists, chemists, statisticians, engineers, and other specialists. All wineries have at least modest facilities for obtaining the essential minimum of data.

It may be sufficient for the winery to determine sugar, total acid, volatile acid, alcohol, and extract in the musts and wines. Analyses for sulfur dioxide, tannin, pigment, aldehydes, esters, iron, copper, calcium, potassium, and malic acid are occasionally very helpful. Some provision for sensory examination (careful, unbiased comparison and judgment of appearance and flavor) and for microscopic and microbiological control are frequently needed. Consulting organizations may be utilized by smaller wineries for the more complex or less commonly required laboratory studies. Even in Europe, particularly in France and Germany, the small winemakers can and do call on government and private laboratories for assistance.

Total acid content is usually determined by neutralizing a sample of the wine with a solution of alkali. Calculation of the total acid (as tartaric acid) from the amount of alkali required is then possible. The total acid value is a measure of the tartness of the wine or must, and is useful in determining the time to pick the grapes, in preparing blends, and in estimating a wine's stability. Volatile acidity is determined similarly upon a distillate from a wine sample and indicates the soundness or defectiveness of the wine from its acetic acid (vinegar) content.

Alcohol, sugar, and extract can be determined in several ways depending upon the accuracy and specific data needed. Modifications of a single simple method can be used to estimate all three to a degree of accuracy sufficient for most winery purposes. Extract refers to the nonvolatile, nonsugar, soluble solids present in a wine. It is determined on the residual solution after distilling the alcohol from a completely fermented wine sample. The distillate is trapped and condensed and used to determine the alcohol content of the samples. Sugar is not usually determined directly, but is estimated as dissolved solids, since the major portion of the soluble solid in must and sweet wine is sugar, and correction can be made for the extract, non-sugar solids. The total dissolved solids in an aqueous solution (must) or the alcohol in a distillate can be determined by measuring the density of the solution. Density, weight per unit volume, is affected by temperature—the volume of a given weight of solution increases as the temperature rises. Therefore the density determined at the solution's temperature is corrected to a standard temperature and compared to the appropriate table of known density values for sugar or ethanol solutions in water at the standard temperature. To avoid using density tables it is possible to determine the density by means of hydrometers calibrated directly in units of sugar or alcohol concentration.

Hydrometry is based upon Archimedes' discovery that a floating object will sink in a liquid just to the point that the weight of the volume of liquid displaced by the submerged portion equals the weight of the object itself. The hydrometer (sometimes called a "stem" or "spindle" in the winery vernacular) is a sealed hollow glass tube with a bulbous end weighted at the bottom so that it floats vertically, Figure 9. The top portion is made narrow so that a considerable length represents a relatively small increase in displaced volume. This drawn-out portion is calibrated and marked to indicate the density, or a density-related value, of the liquid at the point on this scale intersected by the surface of the liquid when the hydrometer is floating freely. In order that the whole range of values possible in the winery can be read to the desired degree of accuracy (usually ±0.05 per cent), a set of hydrometers, each covering only a part of the range, is needed.

When ethanol is added to water, the density decreases and

91

Fig. 9. Hydrometers illustrating measurement of dissolved solids in juice and ethanol in distillates with a thermometer for use in correcting the values to a standard temperature.

the hydrometer sinks deeper and deeper. Hydrometers for use in determining alcohol in wine distillates are usually calibrated to read ethanol volume per hundred units of solution volume (percentage by volume) at 60° F. It is usual to distill the alcohol from a certain volume of wine and dilute the distillate back to that same volume in order that the alcohol content of the wine may be read directly from the distillate (corrected if necessary to 60° F.). The residual aqueous solution in the distillation flask can be diluted to the original wine volume also and the dissolved solids (extract) determined with a different set of hydrometers.

Dissolving solids like sugar and organic acids in water raises the density and causes hydrometers to float higher and higher. Hydrometers used for the measurement of dissolved solids in wineries are usually calibrated to read zero in pure water at

20° C. (68° F.) and weight units of sucrose (table sugar) per 100 weight units (percentage by weight) for higher density solutions at that temperature. The tables of density values upon which these calibrations are based were first calculated by Balling and later recalculated and improved by Brix. Since the dissolved solid being measured in the winery is not primarily sucrose, it is common to refer to a reading corresponding to the density of 20.0 grams of sucrose per 100 grams of solution at 20° C. as 20.0° Brix or simply Brix 20.0 (pronounced "bricks"). Degrees Balling may also be used in wineries (usually pronounced to rhyme with "ballast"), but Brix is the preferred term in the other branches of the food industry. The numerical values are now the same in any case.

Brix values for the extract of a completely fermented dry wine generally are below 2 for thin white wines and over 3 for the richer red wines. The extract can be determined and subtracted from the Brix of the original must corrected for temperature. The result is a measure of the sugar in the must (or similarly in a partly fermented wine). For most winery operations the temperature-corrected Brix values are ordinarily used directly for determining the time to pick grapes, the alcohol yield to be expected from grapes received at the winery, and for following the course of a fermentation. For these purposes it is important to recognize the approximations involved. Since sugar solutions are denser and alcohol solutions less dense than water, the Brix readings will drop faster during fermentation than does the actual consumption of sugar. At a hydrometer reading of 0° Brix, unfermented sugar is present; when the sugar of a sweet grape must is completely fermented, the alcohol level produces a minus Brix hydrometer reading directly in the wine. Serious errors in Brix values may result if care is not taken to prevent the effects of high levels of suspended insoluble solids, foam in the solution, and unclean hydrometers.

Values for dissolved solids equivalent to the Brix hydrometer readings may be obtained on grape juice by using a refractometer, which measures sugar and other dissolved substances by their effect on the refractive index of the aqueous solution. Pocket-sized models calibrated in Brix equivalents covering the range of about 0–40 per cent sugar are very convenient for use in the vineyard to observe the ripening of the grapes and select the time for harvesting. Only a few drops of juice are needed for a reading, and readings can be taken from several vines in a few minutes. A hydrometer requires a cupful or more of juice and is more fragile and inconvenient for field use.

A convenient formula for estimating the alcohol content to expect in a dry wine is: degrees Brix of the crushed grape (original unfermented must) times 0.55 equals alcohol in percentage by volume after fermentation. This estimate corrects for the conversion of some sugar to other products, takes into account the extract, and expresses the alcohol in the usual wine units. Therefore, grapes testing 20° Brix can be expected to give wine of about 11 per cent alcohol by volume or numerically slightly more alcohol than half the "sugar" (dissolved solids) in the proper units.

PREPARING THE GRAPES

The making of wine actually starts with the harvesting of the grapes. Not only must they be picked at the proper stage of development for the particular wine to be made, but they must arrive at the winery in good condition. They should arrive at the winery with clusters intact and berries without damaged skins or freed juice. The time between picking and the start of actual processing in the winery should be short. If the grapes are handled roughly and held for even a short time, organisms begin to develop. Some of these organisms are likely to be undesirable under these uncontrolled, aerobic conditions. The subsequent wine fermentation may not be as "clean," and the yield of alcohol and the quality of the wine may be lowered. Loss of free juice may reduce the yield of wine. The modern

American practice is to wash the grape containers after each trip from the vineyard to the winery. If the grapes are broken or juice dries on the containers the cleaning process is more difficult. A final important reason for care and dispatch in handling grapes is that enzymes of the fruit, particularly those that cause browning (as on a peeled apple), begin to act when the berry is broken. This may contribute undesirable brown color and possibly other defects to the wine.

The processing of grapes into wine begins as soon as the grapes arrive at the winery. Although there are several stages in the process, there is no stopping place until the wine has passed at least the fermentation and initial clarification steps. The first operation at the winery is ordinarily the removal of the stems and the next is the crushing of the grape berries. Ordinarily both operations are accomplished together in a crusher-stemmer. Various models are used, but the Garolla type is common. It consists of a horizontal cylinder or tube a foot or more in diameter and several feet long, covered with slots or holes large enough to pass the berries but not the stems from the cluster (Figure 10). Along the center of this tube is an axle carrying a series of paddles which rotate at fairly high speed, 500 r.p.m. or more. The tube rotates at a moderate speed (about 25 r.p.m.). The grape clusters are conveyed into one end of the tube and as they travel along it the paddles whip the berries through the holes and the stems remain inside to be carried out the other end. The berries are wiped or knocked through the holes in the rotating cylinder with some force and are thereby crushed either by the paddles in going through the holes, or in hitting the walls of another stationary cylinder surrounding the first which catches and drains the crushed grape mass called "must" into a basin or sump from which it is pumped to the next operation.

The ease of removing the stems and crushing the berries depends upon the variety of grapes. Large clusters with long, tough stems cause problems by winding around parts of the

95

machinery. Withered or raisined berries may hang on the stems or resist crushing. Berries of thick-skinned or pulpy varieties may crush poorly. Table-grape varieties have been selected for stronger skins and large clusters with strong stem attachment to withstand shipment as fresh fruit. As a result they are often relatively difficult to destem and crush for winery use. The object of crushing is to break open 100 per cent of the berries to free the juice for removal or for contact and fermentation by the yeast. The intact berry may pass through a fermentation unchanged and not yield its juice when pressed, thus reducing the yield of wine. Grinding or overly forceful breaking of the berries is usually undesirable. An excess of suspended solids may be introduced and the wine will be difficult to clarify later. Also seeds may be broken up and too much tannin, astringency, and bitterness as well as seed oils contributed from them to the wine.

The dry stems amount to only about 40 to 150 pounds per ton of grapes depending upon the variety, and average about 80 pounds. They contain very little fermentable carbohydrate; unless an unusual amount of juice or tightly held raisins are carried off with them, no appreciable loss is sustained by their removal. The removal of stems from grapes for wines is common practice in California. The stems contain a fairly high concentration of tannin, and this tannin and other substances from the stems add astringency, bitterness, and resinous or peppery flavors to the wine if they are not removed. Stems are also relatively high in ash (mineral) and acid, which may contribute undesirably. Musts without stems pump and handle more easily. Rarely (in California) stems may be left in the must to contribute some tannins to wines otherwise too low in this group of substances for proper flavor and keeping qualities. Sometimes stems are left in or are added back to aid in pressing juice from troublesome lots of freshly crushed grapes that are pulpy and tend to squirt through the press openings instead of yielding their juice.

Fic. 10. Internal view of a crusher-stemmer. Source: The
Wine Institute.

97

SULFURING

Sulfuring is an important operation; wine yeasts tolerate moderate concentrations of sulfur dioxide while most undesirable organisms in musts and wine are inhibited by it. Sulfur dioxide is the pungent gas which is given off as sulfur is burned in air. Formerly sulfur-containing candles and cloth wicks were burned in casks to produce the sterilizing gas. Now, however, metal cylinders of the liquefied gas are more commonly used because they give a more precise and controllable treatment. The sulfur dioxide may be metered directly into the solution (must or wine) or it may be dissolved as a concentrated solution (6 per cent or more) in water (sulfurous acid is the hydrated form of sulfur dioxide) for addition. The bisulfite ion and sulfurous acid may be generated in musts and wine also by the addition of sodium or potassium metabisulfite ($Na_2S_2O_5$ or $K_2S_2O_5$), sodium sulfite (Na_2SO_3), or sodium bisulfite ($NaHSO_3$). These white crystalline solids are no longer used commercially as often as sulfur dioxide gas or solution, but are perhaps more convenient to obtain and to store for use in small operations such as in home wine making.

Sulfur dioxide has three major functions in wine making: to control undesirable microorganisms, to inhibit the browning enzymes, and to serve as an antioxidant. The action of the browning enzymes of grapes is directly inhibited by sulfurous acid, which denatures these enzymes. Sulfur dioxide also helps prevent browning and other oxidative reactions by keeping the system under reducing conditions and reacting with the oxygen present. By this action it becomes an antioxidant and resists or even temporarily reverses the effects of air. Other effects of sulfur dioxide include combination with acetaldehyde, thus causing the formation of more glycerol by fermentation; but the amounts used in normal wine making are too small to change the glycerol content appreciably. Sulfur dioxide may aid in clarification, especially of juice before fermentation. It helps kill the cells of the grapeskin and thereby aids the release of the red pigment for red wines, but it also reacts with the red pigments to bleach some of the color, at least temporarily. No other substance is known which has the combination of desirable attributes of sulfur dioxide, but several different substances are coming into use or are being tested to reduce the total amount of sulfur dioxide needed. Substitutes for sulfur dioxide are desired because its burnt-sulfur, pungent odor becomes noticeable and a negative quality factor at rather low levels. The use of sulfur dioxide should, therefore, be held to the absolute minimum. With close attention to good winery practices it should not be necessary to use objectionable levels of sulfur dioxide.

Owing to the need to inhibit the browning enzymes and the "wild" microorganisms as soon as the grapes are crushed, the sulfur dioxide is often metered in at the crusher-stemmer as the must is pumped to the next operation. Thus the action of the sulfur dioxide begins immediately and the necessary uniform mixing of the sulfur dioxide with the must is accomplished more easily. Since the bound forms of sulfur dioxide such as the aldehyde bisulfite addition compound formed during fermentation are not active as are the free forms, it is often necessary to make further small additions of sulfur dioxide at later stages of wine making.

PRESSING

After the grapes are destemmed and crushed and sulfur dioxide is added, the must is ready for further processing. If white grapes are being vinified (converted to wine) the usual next step is separation of the fluid must or juice from the solids (skins, seeds, and part of the pulp), called pomace or specifically sweet pomace in this case. If red wines are being produced, the separation of fluid (wine) from solid (fermented or dry pomace) occurs during fermentation, but the same type of equipment is used. The must may be held in a large tank for a time and pectin-splitting enzymes may be added to allow some breakdown of the tissues to occur. The free juice may then be drained off through a slotted false bottom in the tank. This juice or wine similarly obtained is termed "free-run" as opposed to "press-run." With care it is often possible to obtain 60–70 per cent of the fluid as free-run. Even if this particular method is not followed, it is usual to collect a free-run fraction which drains off from the press under no pressure or very light pressure and then to collect one or more subsequent portions as the pressing becomes more complete. The wine resulting from the later more drastic pressings may be used in blending, sold as a lower-quality grade, or used for distilling, since it may contain a high level of tannins or other potentially undesirable extractives and may resist clarification.

Vitis labrusca varieties are called "slip-skin" grapes and are difficult to press; other pulpy varieties also are troublesome. Muscat varieties, some table-grape varieties, and a few others such as Palomino are noted for the difficulty with which the juice is recovered from the pulp. Not only is good juice recovery difficult from such grapes but the pulp and skins tend to squirt explosively from the openings in the press as pressure is applied. To resist this effect, pressure is applied very slowly and the press may be lined with cloth or stems. After fermentation the remaining grape pulp is usually disrupted to the point that pressing the pomace is less troublesome. Thus, pressing of pomace from red wine fermentations is usually no problem. The total direct yield of juice (or wine) from grapes is from 140 to 190 gallons per ton and averages 175 gallons commercially. White wines (pressed as juice) usually yield 15 to 20 gallons per ton of grapes less than red wines (pressed after fermentation). The dry weight of the pomace amounts to 40 to 160 pounds per ton of grapes, averaging 100 pounds.

Several types and many models of press are in use in wineries. The major types of presses are rack and cloth presses, basket presses and modifications thereof, and continuous presses. In the rack and cloth procedure, a slotted shallow box, usually wooden, is lined with a coarse-weave cloth. The crushed grape must, perhaps mixed with cellulose fibers or other press aid, is distributed a few inches thick on the cloth, the cloth is folded over the top, and the whole "cheese," or several stacked on each other, is squeezed in a screw or hydraulic pressure frame until the juice desired has run out and been collected in a catch basin at the bottom. This procedure is laborious and slow, but it can handle Concord and other slippery varieties of grapes that are very difficult to press.

Basket presses—the familiar slotted wooden basket with screw or hydraulically operated central piston and press-plate used for cider and other juices as well as wines—are used particularly in small table-wine wineries, Figure 11. They are rather slow and laborious, and are being replaced by modern semiautomatic presses. By pressing less forcefully on a thinner layer of grape pomace the newer models produce a better combination of good recovery with high quality. One press of this kind (the Willmes press) receives the must into a slotted horizontal cylinder (slots too small to pass seeds and skins) with closed ends. The cylinder is rotated to distribute the must around the periphery, and a rubber bag along the axis of the cylinder is inflated with air pressure, forcing the pomace against the sides. The juice (or wine) is caught in a pan at the bottom. The pressure may be released and reapplied to improve the yield. The dry pomace is then expelled, and the cycle is repeated.

Continuous presses on the market today are usually of the screw-press type, although continuous belt presses are under development. The screw press operates by accepting must or partly pressed pomace at one end and compresses it by passing it along a screw rotating in a slotted cylinder. The screw threads and cylinder are pitched at an angle such that progressively higher pressure is applied and the fluid is expressed from the solid mass through the slots. The pomace expelled from the end of the screw may be actually hot from the pressure and friction produced. Although extremely high recovery can be obtained, the quality of the product is apt to be low (high in astringency and bitterness, difficult to clarify, perhaps heated or browned); hence this type of press is usually reserved for recovering wine for distilling.

FERMENTATION

The fermentation of the juice for white wines or the whole crushed grape mass for red wines is the next operation. The fermentation is accomplished in any suitable container large enough so that it is only half to three-quarters full when the must has been added. This precaution is necessary owing to the considerable volume of carbon dioxide produced during rapid fermentation and the resultant expansion in volume and surface foam. The sulfured must is pumped into this tank and the inoculum of wine yeast added (usually about 1 per cent by volume of a rapidly fermenting culture of a selected wine yeast). The whole mass is then mixed well.

Fermentation starts slowly, but after twelve hours or so should be quite active. Heat is released. If the fermentations are in small lots in a cool place, the heat loss from the container may be sufficient to prevent excessive temperature rise in the fermentor. In large commercial lots, however, the temperature must be controlled. As a rule of thumb, the heat produced by fermentation, if it is not removed, will raise the temperature of the fermenting mass about 2.3° F. for each drop of 1° Brix. If the must contains 20 pounds of dissolved solids (primarily sugar) per 100 pounds (20° Brix) and is allowed to ferment to 0° Brix, that is, not quite dry, the temperature could rise about 46° F. The rise of 46° F. starting from normal summer temperatures is sufficient to be highly discouraging if not lethal to yeasts. Therefore it is possible in large fermentors with low rates of heat dissipation for the yeasts to "pasteurize" themselves with their own heat production and halt

102

Fig. 11. Hydraulic press and press cake after pressing. Source
Presse- und Informationsamt der Bundesregierung, Bonn.

the fermentation. This or any fermentation which stops with fermentable sugar remaining is said to be "stuck." It is often difficult and always a nuisance to restart a stuck fermentation; cooling, aeration, and often addition of more yeast and extra yeast "food" such as yeast extract and ammonium phosphate are required. It may be preferable to gradually blend the stuck wine into another actively fermenting must. The final product is usually poorer quality than it might have been. It is much better to avoid the problem than to try to correct it after it has arisen. This is particularly important in wine making, because during the relatively short vintage season (2–3 months) all the wine for the year is made. During this very busy period, efficient haste without waste is crucial, and the investment in extra fermentation tanks to hold "mistakes" while you correct them is not likely to return a profit.

In large wineries, in a warm climate such as that of California, high-capacity cooling systems are required. A common type of temperature-controlling system consists of a large central mechanical refrigeration unit connected to one side of a heat exchanger (an apparatus giving a large conductive surface for exchange of heat between two fluids without any contact or mixing of the fluids) with facilities to pump the fermenting must to be cooled through the other side and back to the fermentor. An alternative, especially for smaller operations, might be one or more portable refrigeration units with cooling coils to be lowered into the fermentors. If the fermentors are small, cooling of the fermenting room, or a cooling coil operated with running water, may be adequate.

Cooling not only removes the extra heat produced by fermentation, but also, by lowering the fermentation rate, decreases the rate of heat production. Other means such as maintaining a high pressure (4 atmospheres or so) in the fermentors can be used to slow the fermentation and allow the heat to escape. The pressure-controlled fermentation method is popular in some countries, notably Germany, but has not been found advantageous in California.

The fermentation is allowed to proceed to the desired point. This may be until it terminates naturally with all the sugar fermented; or the fermentation of the remaining sugar may be arrested by such means as the addition of wine spirits. These details and the related problems of when to remove the grape-skins from red wine fermentations are discussed later with the specific wine types.

AGING AND CLARIFICATION

After the pomace has been separated from the wine and the fermentation has been completed or stopped, the next step is the first racking. The wine is allowed to stand until a ma or portion of the yeast cells and other fine suspended materials has collected at the bottom of the container as sediment or lees. It is then racked: the relatively clear wine is carefully pumped or siphoned off without disturbing the lees. It is important to remove the first or yeast lees and complete the first racking as soon as possible, for, if the yeast cells are allowed to remain in a thick layer at the bottom, they will begin to autolyze and possibly introduce off-flavors into the wine. Early racking also tends to prevent further growth of yeasts and other micro-organisms by removing much of the potential nutrients with the lees. Conversely, leaving the wine for a time on the yeast lees may encourage liberation of some nutrients for the malo-lactic organisms and encourage that fermentation if it is desired.

During the transition period between the tumultuous fermentation and the first racking there is likely to be a slow release of carbon dioxide as the last portion of fermentable sugar is converted and the carbon dioxide escapes from the wine. The wine cannot be sealed tight without causing pressure increase—and yet the carbon dioxide evolution is too slow to prevent air from entering the wine cask. This dilemma is solved by the use of a fermentation bung—an arrangement of valves or water-sealed tubes which allows escape of gas but keeps air from mixing freely with the headspace gas, Figure 12. Gen-

Fig 12. A simple fermentation bung which allows the escape of carbon dioxide. (The water seal prevents access of air to the wine in the barrel.)

erally, after the first racking, most of the carbon dioxide has escaped and the wine cask or tank can be bunged tight. Contact between the wine and the air must be kept to a minimum to prevent excessive oxidation, browning, and the growth of the aerobic vinegar bacteria. This can be accomplished by keeping the container as full as possible and closed except during essential operations.

Wooden containers such as white oak barrels (usually 50 gallons) and casks (100–1,000 gallons) and oak and redwood tanks (several thousand gallons) are believed to serve a special role in aging wine by allowing a very slow diffusion of oxygen through the wood, which, if sufficiently slow and limited, produces some of the desirable changes of aging. The oak of the barrel stave also contributes some flavor and extractives and the wine becomes more complex and mellow. A small but steady diffusion of water and ethanol vapor out of the cask also occurs. Depending upon the relative humidity, the wine may become more concentrated in alcohol (dry conditions) or weaker in alcohol (moist conditions) because of different relative rates of loss of ethanol and water through the wood. As water and alcohol escape, the nonvolatile constituents become slightly more concentrated and the decrease in volume appears as ullage—more headspace. This allows more air to enter the cask. To prevent harmful effects of this air the ullage is made up every week or so by adding more of the same wine from another container. This is called "topping" in many California wineries. Ullage occurs even in impervious containers as the young wine cools to cellar temperature, or there may be overflow if a full container is allowed to warm.

Because of the necessity of keeping all containers full and yet allow for a continual slow loss, the winery must have a variety of sizes of cooperage (winery containers collectively). As the "fill" wine for the ullage of a large cask is used up, the cask is "broken down"; that is, the wine is transferred to one or more smaller containers, more "fill" is set aside (perhaps in

107

a small barrel or glass jars), and the process starts all over. This has always been a problem for wineries which age wine in wooden containers. It is difficult to have stainless steel, glass-lined, or coated concrete tanks just the right size for each lot of wine, Figure 13. This problem is solved today in some wineries by using nitrogen or carbon dioxide atmospheres in the head-space of partly full tanks to flush out and keep out the air. Owing to penetration of oxygen by diffusion this is successful only with tanks having impervious walls.

One quality criterion for wine is clarity. The American consumer is conditioned to suspect any product with sediment and discriminates against it. Brilliantly clear wine is not achieved at the first racking by any means. Several additional rackings, along with filtrations, fining* treatments, and stabilization treatments are required to produce wine that is and will stay clear until purchased by the consumer—stable wine. The clarification of wine is partly accomplished by aging the wine, but it is also partly opposed by aging. With time the proteins, other colloidal substances, and microbial cells tend to precipitate out and the wine becomes clarified. However, also with time, metal ions may be picked up from containers and equipment, oxidation may be producing turbidity, and some microbes may multiply. Even though a wine has been made brilliantly clear, small amounts of sediment often continue to form.

There is much justification for the statement often found upon the labels of bottles of red wine that it is *natural* for fine wines to form a deposit when aged in the bottle. This does not mean that murky wine is better, nor does it justify slipshod clarification practices by the winery, but the consumer is ill informed who objects to all types of slight imperfections in brilliance and stability of clarity. He will never know the "bottle bouquet" and extra quality produced by proper bottle

---

* The verb "to fine" and its derivatives are pronounced with a long *i*, and mean generally to refine, make fine, or purify. With regard to wine the term refers to the use of certain agents to produce a brilliant clarity.

Fig. 13. Oak ovals, stainless steel tanks, and redwood tanks in a California table wine winery. Source: The Wine Institute.

age, of red wines especially, nor will he learn to buy and keep wines in his own wine closet for extra aging.

Various types of turbidity can be present in wine—microbial cells, amorphous precipitates of materials such as proteins and some forms of pigments and tannins, and crystalline precipitates, particularly potassium acid tartrate. Microbiological stability is achieved by removing, killing, or preventing development of the microbes by use of sulfur dioxide and other permitted agents such as sorbic acid or diethylpyrocarbonate, by

109

pasteurization, and by such fine filtration that the cells are removed and the product emerges effectively sterile. The combination of treatments chosen depends upon the type of product and degree of stability desired. It is possible to produce microbiologically stable dry wines and fortified wines with only a modest amount of sulfur dioxide and ordinary fining and filtration procedures. With low alcohol wines having residual sugar, such as naturally sweet table wines and some of the other more recently popularized types ("mellow" reds and slightly sweet rosés), additional treatment is often required.

Fining agents produce a flocculent precipitate which removes (by coprecipitation and adsorption) dispersed elements and colloids which would not readily settle out by themselves. Three major types of fining agent are proteins, adsorbents, and metal-removing substances. Formerly egg white, skim milk, and even beef blood were used as proteinaceous fining agents. More purified and predictable proteins are generally used today, gelatin and casein being the most common in California. A solution or fine suspension of the protein is made up in some of the wine and then is well mixed into the rest of the wine at the rate of about 1 ounce per 100 gallons. Tests on small portions should be made to determine the optimum dosage for a particular wine. The protein forms a coagulum which settles over a period of several days to a few weeks and leaves the supernatant wine clarified. A major factor in the coagulation and precipitation of proteins from wine is reaction with tannins. If insufficient tannin is present or too much protein is added, clarification may not be satisfactory. Ordinarily red wines contain sufficient tannin to clarify well, and removal of some of the astringency of the tannin may be a desirable effect of the fining. With white wines addition of an equivalent amount of tannin before fining with proteins may be necessary. The removal of some color with the fining precipitate may reduce the intensity of red wine color and may lighten the color of white wines.

110

The most commonly used adsorbent fining agent is the clay-like mineral bentonite. This is added as a finely powdered and well-hydrated slurry at the rate of about 4 pounds to 1,000 gallons of wine, again based on preliminary tests. Bentonite adsorbs finely dispersed substances and clarifies as it settles to the bottom. It is particularly effective in removing protein which might cause turbidity in wine. Its use may thus supplement the use of protein fining agents and even correct the results of overfining with too much protein.

A metal-removing fining agent not permitted in the United States, but in use in Germany and other countries, is potassium ferrocyanide. The process is known as blue fining because a blue precipitate is formed. This procedure requires careful control, but is very effective in clarifying wine and is particularly valuable in removing small amounts of copper, iron, and other metal ions that cause troublesome precipitates and catalyze oxidation. In the United States certain trade-named substances are permitted which accomplish similar effects.

Various other agents have special uses or are being studied for use in wine clarification. Among these are activated charcoal for selective removal of color or odor, pectin-splitting and other enzymes for clarification (particularly of fruit wines), and fining agents derived from plastics such as polyamide powder and polyvinylpyrrolidone. Since wine making is a "permissive" industry, the use of all these agents is closely controlled by governmental regulations, and a new agent must be approved before it can be used commercially. In some cases samples taken before and after treatment are submitted to a federal Alcohol and Tobacco Tax Division (A.T.T.D.) laboratory for each lot of wine treated before it can be released for marketing.

TARTRATE STABILIZATION

Potassium bitartrate, the potassium half-salt of tartaric acid, is familiar to the housewife as cream of tartar. Grape juice contains considerable amounts of this compound. As the juice is

111

fermented the solution becomes supersaturated, since alcohol lowers its solubility. As a result, this salt crystallizes slowly from the wine and forms argols or crusts in the wine tanks. If all excess is not removed by proper stabilization procedures it may continue to form deposits in the bottled wine. Although no real harm is done by this crystallization, and the crystals are often sparklingly pretty, the American consumer dislikes what seems to him to be "sand" or even glass splinters in his wine. Two common procedures are in use to see that the wine is stable with respect to tartrate deposition: cold stabilization and ion-exchange treatment. Cold stabilization involves hastening and completing the precipitation of all the potassium bitartrate which would come out of solution at any normal storage temperature by chilling the wine nearly to its freezing point (lower than water's freezing point, 32° F., because of the presence of alcohol). The wine is held at this temperature until the precipitable tartrate (and incidentally some other insoluble substances) has crystallized out; it is then filtered while cold to remove the precipitate and to prevent it from redissolving as the wine warms. This is a controlled form of the effect of winter temperatures upon wine in European cellars.

The other stabilization practice, ion-exchange treatment, is more modern. Minerals or resins such as those used in water softening are converted to the sodium form. This means that the insoluble substances are loaded with sodium ions; when a fluid such as wine or hard water is passed through a bed of these particles, other positively charged metal ions may be taken up and the sodium ions released. Thus the potassium of wine is taken up and at least part of the potassium bitartrate is converted to sodium bitartrate. The sodium salt is more soluble in wine than the potassium salt, and therefore the precipitation of tartrate from the wine can be prevented. The ion-exchanging materials can be regenerated and reused and the process can be precisely controlled. Variations in the process can be used to produce other modifications in the wine's composition, and troublesome ions such as those of calcium, magnesium, iron, and copper may be removed by ion-exchange treatment. As with any beverage process, ion-exchange treatment must be properly done and closely supervised to prevent undesirable taste and quality effects.

IRON AND OTHER METAL IONS IN WINE

The undesirable effects of certain metal ions have been mentioned. The inorganic fraction of grape juice, the ash that would be left upon complete combustion and evaporation, is a complex mixture which contains at least trace amounts of most of the common elements found in the soil, including potassium, iron, copper, calcium, magnesium, sodium, aluminum, manganese, phosphorus, sulfur, and boron. With the exception of potassium, the natural constituents may, but do not usually, amount to enough to cause trouble. Wine is slightly acidic, however, and if *allowed to do so* will readily pick up iron and copper from metal equipment, and calcium from concrete tanks. Iron at more than about ten parts per million and copper at one part per million or less is likely to promote oxidative and other reactions and produce changes in color, flavor, and clarity in wine. For this reason brass and mild steel equipment has been largely replaced by stainless steel, glass, and other materials in the wine industry. Calcium ions produce turbidity in wines because their salts with tartaric and other organic acids are relatively insoluble. Calcium ions may be picked up from the asbestos pads and diatomaceous earth filter-aids used in filtering wines. This is usually avoided by washing these materials with citric acid solutions before use or perhaps by discarding a little of the first wine through a filter. Pick-up of calcium from concrete storage tanks is avoided by acid cleaning and by use of coatings, usually waxes or plastics.

OTHER FINISHING OPERATIONS

Care is needed at each step in the fermentation, aging, clarification, and stabilization procedures for wine production. Fortunately, wine is *not* subject to all the problems and hazards

113

of many other foods, but its quality can be damaged at any point along its relatively prolonged production path. A tank with brass fittings may contaminate the wine with a trace of copper. A pump may be operated improperly and the wine become aerated and eventually oxidized. If such errors are not prevented, the wine will be ruined.

The final acts in the drama of wine production—preparation for market—are no less important. If the wine is to be blended this should be done well in advance so that a "marrying" period can reveal any further need for treatment (fining, etc.). Wines ready for marketing are usually given a final "polishing" filtration on the way to the bottling machine. The potentially harmful effects of oxidation by air in the headspace of the bottle and dissolved in the wine are minimized or prevented by various procedures. The wine may be stripped of dissolved oxygen by passing bubbles of nitrogen through it. Bottles may be purged with nitrogen or carbon dioxide and filled so as to displace the gas without introducing air, and may be sealed under vacuum.

The bottles used by wineries in this country are invariably new owing to legal requirements and for reasons of sanitation, uniformity, and convenience. The appropriate size and shape of bottle for the type and brand of wine are used. Since many types of wine are damaged by sunlight, the bottles are usually of colored glass, commonly dark green or brown. A small amount of sulfur dioxide is often added just before bottling. Other antioxidants such as ascorbic acid (vitamin C) might be substituted or other microbial inhibitors may be used. The wine may be pasteurized or filtered so as to be effectively sterile as it is bottled. The bottles are often capped with screw caps, except for wines which are to be aged in the bottle. For these natural corks have been preferred. If wines are to be bottle-aged at the winery they are ordinarily "binned"—stacked in the cellar—without labels. Otherwise they are usually labeled immediately and, after a short period of observation to check for unexpected problems, shipped to the market.

114

Operations in Wine Making

Many more details of wine making could be discussed. Some will be covered in later chapters; others require explanations which would be tedious in a book of this sort. If possible you should visit some wineries. Most of them welcome visitors. They often give conducted tours and offer samples for tasting. Not only is this a good way to increase your understanding of the process of wine making, but also it offers an excellent opportunity to find and purchase wines which suit your taste.

Summary.—The home winemaker may not be particularly dismayed if some of his production is poor or is even a total loss. The commercial winemaker cannot afford such results. He must control each step of the vinification process so that possible deficiencies are avoided or minimized and each wine's quality is maximized. Chemical analyses, microbiological examinations, and systematic tasting are helpful and usually are necessary for rational control and consistent success in modern wine making.

The wine grapes must be picked at the proper time and handled quickly and carefully. They are crushed, destemmed, sulfured, and fermented. According to the requirements of the wine type, the wine is drained and pressed from the pomace. Approximately 175 gallons of wine may be obtained from a ton of grapes. Dry wines should ferment to an alcohol content about 0.55 times the original Brix of the must. Temperature control during fermentation, avoidance of metal pick-up, particularly copper and iron, and the proper minimum of access of oxygen are positive quality factors with most wines. Appropriate aging and treatments to achieve stable clarity are followed by bottling.

The consumer can influence the quality of wine by learning what experts consider to be important quality factors, adding his own preferences, and then selecting types and styles of wine which please him and do not violate accepted quality standards. By this selectivity he gets better wine now and encourages the conscientious producer for the future. The consumer can participate more directly in improving the quality of wine by experimenting with bottle-aging of commercial wines. He can add to his enjoyment and range of experience by making some of his own wine at home and may produce high-quality wines if he follows good commercial practices.

Chapter 8

MAKING TABLE WINES

The term "wine growing" is often used. Grapes are more perishable and difficult to transport than wines. The grower of wine grapes has historically made them into table wine which he later sold. His agricultural produce left his farm in the form of bulk table wine. The product of many small winegrowers was often collected by brokers and blended and processed by vintners (wine merchants, especially wholesale) before reaching the retail market in the cities. This cottage-industry type of wine making still exists in several parts of the world. Under this system the average quality of the blended wine is likely to be low because of some very poor lots resulting from ignorance or errors made by some of the growers. The price received by the grower tends to the least common denominator, and this will dissatisfy the grower who produces good wine.

This unsatisfactory situation has led to the development of modern wine making in several directions. The former broker-vintner may operate a modern central winery and buy grapes from growers, thereby avoiding the poor-quality wine produced by the careless maker of wine on the farm. Several grape growers may join forces to build and staff a coöperative winery to produce and market quality wine either directly to the consumer or through a bottler with an established wholesale-retail trade.

The large centralized winery makes possible the production of good wines in large volume and, particularly with wines which require expensive equipment such as brandy stills, results in more efficient and economical production. If, however, only dry table wines are to be produced, these call for relatively little expensive equipment and can be produced economically in small wineries. Thus a place remains in the table wine industry for the small producer. Of course, these small wineries need a certain minimum production if they are to be money-making operations. The most successful have concentrated upon producing premium quality table wines, usually vintage-labeled varietal wines, and a sizable part of their production is often based upon their own vineyards. Since high-quality vintage varietal type wines are almost of necessity produced in lots no larger than a few thousand gallons, the small winery may compete effectively in this area with larger organizations.

An interesting and world-wide phenomenon in the wine industry is the wine producer who has been successful in another line of work and then taken up winery operation as a serious vocation or avocation. The story of one such winery illustrates the possibilities. The late Mr. J. D. Zellerbach, former United States Ambassador to Italy, knew and liked fine table wines. After retirement from his duties with the Crown-Zellerbach Paper Company and the United States Department of State, he planted a vineyard and erected a model winery in the Sonoma Valley of California. His objective was to produce Chardonnay and Pinot noir table wines as fine as or greater than any in the world. With the guidance of a scientifically trained enological biochemist and the most modern techniques, his winery, at his untimely death, was selling wines which proved his goal to be realistic.

Part of the charm and fascination of wine and winegrowing lies in the fact that it is possible to find, tucked away in some valley, a little winery producing very fine wines which may be in demand all over the world. It is also part of the fun that the products of many fine wineries are not known outside a certain district because production is limited and most of it is snapped up by local connoisseurs as soon as it is released. This lends zest to the search for unfamiliar labels and special lots of wine. If one educates and trusts his own palate rather than the pronouncements of wine snobs, one can drink better wine at lower prices by such searching.

It is not intended to leave the impression that only small wineries are capable of producing high-quality table wines. It is almost impossible to obtain a bad bottle of wine with the label of a large American producer and if one is found it undoubtedly was the result of an accident after it left the winery. The same statement cannot be made about all small producers In producing wine in large volume to a standard of uniformity as well as quality, however, the large company may be forced to blend its smaller lots of superlative wine with the rest, whereas the small producer may sell his wine selectively lot by lot. The resultant great diversity of wine by producer, by lot, by season, and of course by type is a dividend to the consumer and sets wine apart from most of the foods in this age of mass production.

WHITE TABLE WINES

It is possible to make white wines from red grapes except for the few varieties which have red flesh (Teinturier types), since the red pigment does not readily or quickly escape from the cells of the skin unless the grape is overripe, damaged by mold, or beginning to ferment. This practice is not widely followed for table wines because it has no particular advantage and extra work is necessary to ensure that no red color appears in the wine. A few varieties commonly made into white table wine (e.g., Gewürztraminer and several eastern varieties like Delaware) have a faint red or pink blush on the ripe berries, but this causes no problem. The grapes which are commonly made into white table wine and are likely to be named on the label of wines produced in California include Chardonnay (Pinot Chardonnay), Chenin blanc (White Pinot), Emerald Riesling, Folle blanche, French Colombard, Gewürztraminer, Grey Riesling, Malvasia Bianca, light muscat (specific variety not usually named), Pinot blanc, Sauvignon blanc, Sémillon, Sylvaner (Franken Riesling), and White Riesling (Johannisberg Riesling). The wines of a few of these (Folle blanche, French Colombard, Grey Riesling) may not be distinctive enough to enable one to name the variety in blind tasting, but they often are good, well-balanced, fruity wines. The varieties Delaware and Catawba may be found as white table wines (as well as rosé or red) with distinctive *labrusca* flavors. Other white grapes used in producing table wines which are not usually labeled as varietal wines include Aligoté, Burger, Clairette blanche, Green Hungarian, Palomino (Golden Chasselas), Saint-Émilion, and Thompson Seedless. In addition to a relatively neutral flavor, these grapes may have properties which make them less suitable or more troublesome for wine making. For example, Palomino tends to have low acidity and to make a flat-tasting wine. Owing to the presence of existing plantings and good viticultural properties—particularly high yields—they are used, however.

High-quality white table wines in general, and the dry ones particularly, are not easily made. When well made they have a delicate fruity yet vinous odor (with the appropriate varietal notes) and a light straw to bright medium golden color with no muddiness or brown and no off-flavors. Overripeness must be avoided by picking the grapes at 20–23° Brix. By our estimate of Brix × 0.55 the wines should then be 11–12.6 per cent alcohol by volume. This level is enough for preservation and good quality; a higher level in dry white table wines indicates overripe grapes. The acidity should be determined and the harvesting adjusted as much as possible to keep acidity up in a warm climate or down in a cold one to about 0.8 per cent calculated as tartaric acid.

Making Table Wines

Once the decision to harvest has been made, the grapes must be handled with care at every step. White wines are particularly susceptible to damage by oxidation and browning, and any off-flavors permitted to develop will be noticeable over the desired delicate aroma and taste. Precautions must be taken to avoid browning. Sulfur dioxide should be added to the must as soon as possible at the rate of 75–150 parts per million, depending upon the tendency of the variety to brown and the condition of the grapes. The separation of the juice from the pomace and the inoculation of the juice with yeasts ordinarily should be accomplished as soon as possible, but this general rule may require modification. A short period of holding (2–5 hours) of the sulfured must may be necessary for adequate juice yield. Settling and partial clarification of the must before fermentation may be desirable to aid in complete clarification later. The sweet pomace may be diluted and fermented for distillation or for blending, but it is not used directly in white table wine production.

Improved quality results if white table wine fermentations are carried on at a relatively low temperature. Fermentation at 80° F. or more is undesirable, causing loss of grape aroma and perhaps the development of "hot fermentation" off-flavors. The recommended temperature for fermentation is 50–60° F. In California and in large containers this low temperature requires cooling of the must before inoculation and during fermentation. The fermentation is slow at this temperature and takes four to six weeks to reach completion. The longer time, slower carbon dioxide evolution, and greater susceptibility of the wine to damage by the oxygen of the air makes it preferable that the fermentors for white table wine be closed and fitted with a suitable air-restricting fermentation vent.

After fermentation the wine is racked, fined, and cold-stabilized or ion-exchanged, as previously described, except that with these wines extra precautions are necessary to keep air contact low and minimize pick-up of metals. The use of casein or casein plus tannin fining is often helpful in keeping

121

the color light by removing part of any brown pigment which may have formed. Some producers both in Europe and in California no longer use wooden cooperage for dry white wines. Others believe that storage for a few months in previously conditioned used wooden casks produces a desirable minimal degree of oxidation and improved flavor. Barrel aging should not be so prolonged as to contribute a noticeable woodiness or oxidation flavor. Since the flavors of most of the wines in this class emphasize light grapy aromas, they are usually finished and sold relatively young—within two years after vintage. All white table wines receive some "rest" in the bottle to recover from the effects of bottling. The lots and types of wine with less delicate more full and rich flavors may be stored in bottle an additional one to four years or even more. This practice can produce very desirable bottle bouquet and other subtle flavor changes which result in a more interesting and complex wine.

The consumer can do this for himself by buying several bottles of the same wine and keeping them. Each bottle should be stored on the side so the cork is moist. Storage should be at a uniform, cool temperature, preferably 50–55° F. A bottle should be served occasionally to observe progress and avoid too long storage and eventual decline in quality. It is an exceptional white dry wine that will improve after three to five years of such storage (or a total age of 4–7 years) and many should not stay that long. The lighter, more neutral wines are probably best when purchased and are unlikely to benefit from such treatment. They have probably been treated with sulfur dioxide and perhaps other antioxidants just before bottling and as these diminish to a low level with time, undesirable changes may occur. Owing to the useful effects of sulfur dioxide in bleaching brown pigments and resisting oxidation, the tendency is to use too much of it. A not uncommon defect in white table wines is excessive free sulfur dioxide. The odor is not only easily noticeable in these light wines, but tends to anaesthetize the nose and prevent enjoyment of the desirable aromas.

Making Table Wines

White table wines may be made sweet by various procedures such as arresting fermentation by clarification and filtration to remove the yeasts or adding sugar (illegal in California), unfermented juice, or concentrated grape juice. Such wines do not have sufficient alcohol to prevent further fermentation and are by nature subject to biological instability. They can be rendered stable for marketing by adding a high level of sulfur dioxide, 250 parts per million or so, and then aging them until the free sulfur dioxide decreases and becomes less objectionable by gradual oxidation and fixation in the form of reaction products. Pasteurization, sterile filtration, and newer inhibitors such as sorbic acid and diethylpyrocarbonate may also be used to prevent yeast growth in these wines after bottling. Natural sweet wines result from botrytised or otherwise dehydrated grapes whose musts are so high in sugar that the yeasts are unable to ferment it all before the alcohol level becomes inhibitory. These are more readily stabilized, but the same considerations apply. The longest-lived white table wines fall in this class; some improve for two to three years in wood and five or more years in bottle.

PINK OR ROSÉ TABLE WINES

Rosé table wines are much like white wines in their preparation and properties. They should have a bright pink to light red color without excessive orange or purple shading. They should be light, fruity, and quick-maturing. They contain more tannin and are therefore slightly less subject to oxidation, browning, and clarification problems than white wines. Rosé wines are usually made from grapes which have insufficient color to make a normal red wine. They can be made from red grapes by limiting the time the skins are in contact with the fermenting must. Rosé wines can also be made by blending red and white grapes or red and white wines. The best of these procedures is the use of red grapes and a short fermentation on the skins. If the grapes are very low in red pigment content

123

or if a blend of a high proportion of white grapes is used, the wine is likely to be tannic and unbalanced, since longer contact with the skins is required. If the grapes are low in color from being grown in a hot region, they are likely to make low-tannin flat wines. The usual practice is to use varieties of grapes which produce the desired bright color and fruity flavor and are moderate in the amount of red pigment. The variety Aramon and Grenache are used in France. Grignolino is employed in Italy and occasionally by a few growers in California. Grenache and Napa Gamay are also favored for rosés in California. These varieties contribute distinctive varietal qualities to the wine and often are named on the label. Obviously, the wines should truly have a varietal character. Other varietally distinctive red grapes can be used, such as Cabernet Sauvignon or Pinot noir, but this is not common, for they are likely to be in demand for red wine production. Muscat-flavored pink (Aleatico) and light red varieties (Muscat Hamburg) are commonly made into dessert wines rather than into pink light muscat-type wines. Rosés are also made from standard nondistinctive red wine grape varieties.

Grapes for rosé wines should have a composition similar to that of white wine, with moderate sugar (20–23° Brix) and reasonable tartness (at least 0.7 per cent titratable acid). Freedom from bruised or damaged grapes, rapid sulfuring (75–150 parts per million of sulfur dioxide), inoculation with wine yeast, and a brief fermentation on the skins (24–36 hours) are desirable. As the preferred degree of color extraction is reached, the wine is separated from the skins by draining or pressing. Since some sugar and red pigment remain in the pomace, it may be added to fresh must and used to make ordinary red wine. It is probably more appropriate, if the winery also distills wine spirits, to convert this sweet pomace and that from white wine production to alcohol by dilution with water and fermentation. The resultant dilute wine and the other residues such as lees can be distilled to recover the alcohol.

Rosé wines are ordinarily not aged in oak containers; if they are so aged, they are stored for only a few months. They are not ordinarily aged very long in bottles either, and are stabilized, finished, and marketed as fresh fruity young wines, often the same year they are produced and rarely more than three years later. For the American market a rosé with some residual sugar (1–5 per cent) has proved popular and the stabilization practices mentioned for sweet white table wine are necessary. It is unfortunate that the dry and slightly sweet rosé types are not easily distinguished by the labels.

RED TABLE WINES

Grape varieties commonly used for dry red table wines that are distinctive enough to warrant a varietal label, and are usually so labeled, include Barbera, Cabernet Sauvignon (often labeled just Cabernet), Ruby Cabernet, Concord, Gamay, Pinot noir, and Zinfandel. Many other varieties of grapes can make distinctive red wines, when all conditions are favorable. A few of the less common which may be found on California varietally labeled red table wines include Grignolino, Petite Sirah, Pinot St.-George (Red Pinot), Charbono, and Nebbiolo. Some widely planted distinctive varieties, notably Zinfandel and Grenache, go also into nonvarietally labeled red table wines along with less distinctive varieties such as Alicante Bouschet, Carignane, and Refosco.

Red grapes for table wines are ordinarily picked when they are slightly higher in sugar (21–23° Brix) than grapes for white or rosé wines. They should retain a moderate acidity—at least 0.6 per cent titratable acidity. The requirements for good red wine processing are perhaps a little less stringent, since the product is more robust in constitution and flavor than white wine, but many of the same considerations apply. The grapes must reach the winery in good condition. About 100–150 parts per million of sulfur dioxide are added as the grapes are crushed, or immediately afterward. The must, consisting of the

125

entire crushed grape mass, perhaps even including the stems in very warm regions to raise the tannin level, is then inoculated and the fermentation begins. The fermentation temperature, the cap management, and the aging procedure distinguish red wine production from that of white and rosé wines.

The fermentation temperature should be kept from rising above 85° F., but should be above 70° F. during the tumultuous fermentation. The evolution of the carbon dioxide causes the skins to rise to the surface of the wine and form a dense "cap" there. This cap is partly exposed to the air, since red wine fermentors are usually open-topped, and frequently is covered with foam, Figure 14. Owing to the rapid fermentation occurring within it and its insulating nature, the cap is as much as 15° F. warmer than the body of the fluid. These factors favor development in the cap of organisms other than yeasts, particularly heat-tolerant and aerobic bacteria which may produce off-flavors and high volatile acidity (acetic acid). Also, extraction of red color from the skins is not obtained unless there is contact between the fluid and the cap. These ill effects are avoided by keeping the cap wet and periodically mixing it with the body of the fluid. This can be accomplished by "punching down" the cap with a suitable plunger by hand at least twice and preferably several times during a 24-hour period. Punching down the cap is too laborious for a large winery and a similar result can be achieved by "pumping over." The fermenting fluid is drawn off below the cap and is pumped and distributed or sprayed over the cap. This also is repeated several times a day. Several types of special fermentors with screens or other arrangements are designed to hold the grape-skin mass below the surface or to use the carbon dioxide pressure from the fermentation to force wine over the cap. None of these are in wide use because of expense of construction, difficult cleaning of equipment between lots, and sanitation problems.

When the desired level of red pigment and tannin has been

FIG. 14. Sampling fermenting red wine must for hydrometric testing. Note cap. Source: The Wine Institute.

extracted, the skins and seeds are removed by draining and pressing. The apparent Brix at this time is usually 6°–10°, Figure 14. The fermentation and the cap manipulation cause the breakdown of the pulp; the recovery of the wine is easier and the yield better than is the juice recovery for white wine. Today's consumer is interested in lighter, early-maturing wines and unfortunately seldom does any aging in his own private wine cellar. To meet this changing demand the winemaker

127

the world over has been cutting down the time the wine is in contact with the pomace in order to extract less tannin. Prior to the Second World War, a fermentation period of fifteen days on the skins was not uncommon for premium wines which were to be aged. At the present time a period of three to six days on the skins is probably typical for most producers, both in California and abroad, particularly in the Bordeaux region. For popular-priced wines, heat treatments to release the red color before fermentation rather than extraction by alcohol during fermentation may be used and therefore the contact time cut to hours rather than days. However, heat treatments developed so far tend to produce some browning, undesirable flavor changes, and clarification difficulties.

After the wine has been separated from the pomace the fermentation is allowed to go to completion at moderate temperatures (60–70° F.) and with the usual precautions of closed fermentors, a fermentation bung, and so on. For the "mellow" reds a small amount (1–5 per cent) of residual sugar may be retained in ordinary red wines to be marketed and consumed young. As the yeast and other lees settle out, the wine is racked periodically. If the malo-lactic fermentation is desired, it may be encouraged by leaving the wine in contact with the yeast longer than usual and continuing storage at a relatively warm temperature. The relatively high tannin level of red wines promotes good fining with proteinaceous agents such as gelatin; if the tannin is excessively high and the wine too astringent the level can be reduced by such fining. The wine may be cold-stabilized or ion-exchanged to control tartrate precipitation. During these treatments the wine is ordinarily stored in large tanks; the surface-to-volume ratio is such that even if they are wooden not much effect from the wood as compared to other tank materials can be noted in the wine. If the wine is to command a premium price it is usually placed after the initial clarification and stabilization treatments, in smaller white oak containers (50–500 gallons).

Some European wineries use new barrels for aging red wine. In most American wineries the oak flavor produced by new 50-gallon barrels is considered too strong even if the new barrels have been washed out with mild alkaline solutions such as sodium carbonate (soda ash) and then hot water. Such barrels may be "broken in" by using them for a season or two for aging wines to be blended into standard wines before use with premium wines. Aging in barrels may also be for only a limited time and then the wine may be transferred to larger casks for further aging, Figure 15. The wines are carefully watched during the aging process. The ullage is made up as often as necessary (at about 1–3 week intervals). Representative samples from each wine lot are carefully tasted and ana-

Fig. 15. Ovals and tanks for aging wines. Source: The Wine Institute.

Fig. 16. Stacking bottles of table wines for aging. Source: The Wine Institute.

lyzed by the winemaker periodically—certainly twice a year and preferably more often. The wine is ordinarily racked and as a result slightly aerated about twice a year to promote clarification and aging. When the desired stage of aging in wood is reached and the wine is mature or ripe to bottle, it is given additional clarification and stabilization if needed. Often this consists only of a final polishing filtration as the wine is bottled.

Care should be taken during bottling that the wine is not agitated in the presence of air or permitted to take up too much oxygen. The bottles should be stored for at least six months after being filled and corked; such storage, binning, is practiced by some wineries for two to four years for their premium red table wines, Figure 16. Many rich red wines will improve for as long as a dozen years in bottles and survive in good condition for much longer. Naturally such aging is expensive, involving hazards and tying up capital. Again the consumer can add much interest, save part of the cost, and probably raise the average quality of the red wine he serves at his table by buying some well in advance of his immediate needs. If long bottle aging is practiced, some "crust" will probably form as tannins and pigments gradually precipitate with time. There are no known stabilization procedures which will prevent this and still retain the desirable features of the wine. The wine can be decanted clear for serving and the crusted bottle placed on the table as a conversation piece. If you prefer the brighter red and more fruity, zestful and hearty flavor of younger red wines, of course, they can be consumed as purchased. If the brick-red color and the more complex and mellow flavors appeal to you, buy older wine or age your own wine. And, if you enjoy wine frequently with your meals, you will probably learn to vary your menu by enjoying both. After a little experience with wines of various types and ages served with different dishes, you will be able to recognize the light simple wine that deteriorates rapidly with age and must be consumed young. You will also come to recognize the richer wine which may be too young, harsh, or strongly flavored for your taste now and can be profitably aged longer.

Summary.—The production of table wines demands knowledge, skill, and attention, but not necessarily a large or expensive establishment. Most white table wines are produced from grape juice in such a manner as to emphasize a light color and delicate, fresh, grapy flavors. Red table wines are generally more intensely flavored and more astringent owing to fermentation and extraction of certain materials from the crushed whole red or purple-skinned grapes. Rosé wines are intermediate in that a light, bright pink color and usually a fresh, fruity flavor result from brief fermentation on the skins of light red-colored grapes.

Table wines are traditionally dry, although some naturally sweet table wines, especially the botrytised type, have a long and illustrious history. Slightly sweet wines have become rather popular on the United States market for moderate-priced standard white, rosé, and red table wines, but their sweetness is not uniform and might be disadvantageous in that quality defects can be masked by sugar. Furthermore, unless the sugar level is indicated by the label, those preferring dry wines may be disappointed.

Other important quality variables in table wines include the grape-varietal flavors (which may or may not be present) and the flavors resulting from age. Relatively few white and rosé table wines currently on the American market exhibit much aged bottle-bouquet flavor; longer aging could bring a gain in complexity of flavor and only a small loss of their young-wine freshness. Red table wines exhibiting a reasonably wide range of the flavors developed by short or long aging both in wood and in bottle are available in American wineshops. Since aging is costly, the inexpensive red wines generally receive less aging than the premium-priced wines.

Chapter 9

MAKING SPARKLING WINES

Wines which are not still, those which contain excess carbon dioxide, are called sparkling wines. A layman's definition would be that sparkling wines pop when opened and give off copious amounts of carbon dioxide bubbles when poured into a glass from a freshly opened bottle of the cool wine. The legal American definition for tax purposes is that wines containing more than 0.277 gram of carbon dioxide per 100 milliliters are subject to tax as sparkling wines. This amount is equivalent to less than one-half of an atmosphere of carbon dioxide pressure. It was chosen as about the maximum carbon dioxide content without appreciable visual or flavor effects in wine served cool (55° F.). It is possible for white table wines (if fermented very cool, or under pressure and bottled without much aging or other opportunity for the carbon dioxide of the original fermentation to escape) to retain small amounts of carbon dioxide. If a malo-lactic fermentation occurs in the bottles or just before bottling, as in the *vinho verde* wines of Portugal, considerable carbon dioxide may remain in the wine. If these wines do not exceed the legal limit, they, along with wines that have been stripped of air with carbon dioxide gas or have otherwise contacted carbon dioxide at low pressure during processing, would be classified as still wines. This is important, for the federal tax on still table wines is 17 cents per gallon and the tax on sparkling wines is $3.40 per gallon. It follows that sparkling wines cannot be inexpensive, since the federal tax alone is 68 cents per bottle on top of all the processing costs, distributing expenses, state and local taxes, and retailing costs.

Champagne and champagne-type wines are the classic and important group of effervescent or sparkling wines. The carbon dioxide pressure in these wines is high, about 4 atmospheres, or 60 pounds per square inch of bottle surface as found in the market. Wines of less than 2 atmospheres of carbon dioxide, sometimes called "pearl" wines, are popular in Germany, South Africa, Australia, and some other countries, but have not been marketed to any great extent in the United States. These high levels of carbon dioxide can be introduced into wine in two major ways: by yeast fermentation in a closed container to prevent loss of carbon dioxide, and by artificial carbonation, as for carbonated soft drinks.

Artificial carbonation is accomplished by passing the proper amount of carbon dioxide gas under moderate pressure into the wine at about 24° F. and then bottling it immediately. The carbon dioxide, like most gases, is much more soluble in the wine at low temperature and high pressure. As the bottled wine warms up, the pressure, as determined by the amount of carbon dioxide taken up, increases: 2 atmospheres at freezing become about 7 atmospheres at room temperature. This type of wine must be labeled as artificially carbonated, and is subject to a federal tax of $2.40 per gallon. In spite of its tax advantage over the fermented sparkling wines this type of wine has decreased in sales in the United States. Several factors have contributed to the near-disappearance of carbonated wine from American usage. (Note that the term "carbonated" should be reserved for this relatively rare type of wine.) The consumer seems to feel that, since champagne is a luxury, he wants the best or none at all, and is repelled by the labeling requirements for

134

artificially carbonated wine. Perhaps as a corollary to this, the producer has tended to try to stay in the market by shaving costs and cutting prices. Although good wines can be made by artificial carbonation, generally the best base wines have not been used. Moreover, most artificially carbonated wines tend to lose their carbon dioxide more quickly than do effervescent wines produced by fermentation. The prolonged display of bubbles and the tingling taste of sparkling wines are highly desirable parts of their appeal.

Several known factors and perhaps some unknown ones promote the desired retention of carbon dioxide with prolonged slow evolution of bubbles. One factor is the complete lack of haze or particles in the wine which would serve as nuclei for bubble formation; brilliantly clear sparkling wine is, therefore, important for this reason as well as appearance. The presence of nitrogen or other dissolved gases also initiates bubble formation and hastens the loss of carbon dioxide. Traces of surface active agents promote bubble emission and an undesirable persistent foam on the wine in the glass. This could conceivably result from the use of detergents without completely rinsing them from winery equipment, but winemakers are careful to avoid this and the glasses in which the wine is served are the more likely source. The presence of agents such as glycerol, sugar, and soluble peptides appears to favor the formation of smaller bubbles and slower carbon dioxide loss. The peptides and amino acids arising from yeast autolysis seem to have this effect. Complexes or reaction products which slowly form during aging have been said to exist between the wine constituents and the dissolved carbon dioxide. These presumably revert to carbon dioxide more slowly than if carbon dioxide were merely in solution. More remains to be learned about these effects.

The production of artificially carbonated wine at home by using dry ice is a dangerous practice and should not be attempted. The gas will evolve from the solid carbon dioxide faster than it can dissolve in the wine. The resultant high pressure is likely to convert a closed container into a bomb. If an open container

135

is used, little carbonation results and oily or metallic off-flavors are likely to be introduced by impurities in the dry ice. The flavor differences between the same base wine carbonated and naturally fermented can be considerable and they have only the carbon dioxide in common.

The discovery of champagnization of wine by fermentation in a stoppered bottle is attributed to Dom Pérignon, who was Cellarer in the Benedictine Abbey of Hautvillers in France near Reims from 1668 to 1715. He is also said to be one of the first, and possibly the first, to use corks from Spanish cork oak to close wine bottles. The better seal provided by natural cork must have been an important factor in the first accidental production of champagne. Wines bottled too soon from a vintage which, owing to cold winter weather, had not completed fermentation of all the sugar could begin to ferment again in the spring. The bottles which had the fortune to survive the increased pressure may well have inspired the reported cry of the discoverer: "Come quickly! I'm drinking stars!" The details of the matter are obscured by time, and it is quite probable that the good monk would be horrified at the immodesty of the role attributed to him. Be that as it may, the district of France called Champagne gave its name to this sparkling wine. Through the art and technology of many wine-makers, first in France and later elsewhere as well, the controlled process of fermented-in-the-bottle sparkling wine production has developed. It remains one of the prevalent methods of champagnization; the other common method is the bulk or tank fermentation method.

Making sparkling wine includes, first, careful making or selecting of the base wine. This is essentially a dry white table wine. It should have a moderate alcohol content (10–12 per cent), a good acidity (0.7–1.0 per cent titratable as tartaric acid), and no more than a light straw or low-yellow color. It must be "clean," meaning properly made, with no noticeable defects or off-flavors, and should have less than ten parts per million of

136

free sulfur dioxide content. This is an important consideration because the evolution of the carbon dioxide bubbles carries odors to the nose and enhances any defects in odor as well as the desirable aroma and bouquet. Excess sulfuring may show up as objectionable sulfur dioxide odors, or the yeast fermentation may cause the reduction of some forms of sulfur to hydrogen sulfide—the rotten-egg odor.

Sparkling wine stock is ordinarily a blend, and varietal designations, with the exception of muscat, are not often noted on the labels. Chardonnay and Pinot noir are used in Champagnes of France. The red or "black" Pinot noir is converted to white wine for this use by special selection of the clusters and berries used and immediate pressing of the grapes in shallow presses, usually without prior crushing. Sparkling muscat wines are a famous product of Italy—the *spumante* of Asti, for example. California and other regions which produce sparkling wines make sparkling muscat wines as well as champagnes (the name is now considered generic in the United States when not capitalized) and pink or red sparkling wines, often called sparkling burgundy, by essentially the same processes. The base wines are frequently chosen for their rather neutral fruity-vinous quality rather than for pronounced varietal distinctiveness. However, many of the better varieties for white table wine, such as Sylvaner, Saint-Émilion, Folle blanche, Chenin blanc, Chardonnay, or French Colombard, are ordinarily included in the blend to achieve the necessary acidity, balance, and fruitiness for a good sparkling wine. Popular sparkling wines are made in New York, Ohio, and Canada by blends including some *labrusca*-flavored varieties, particularly Delaware and Catawba, and often also a neutral wine to prevent the flavor from being excessively strong. Since the escape of the carbon dioxide enhances the aroma of the wine, light and delicately pleasant odor is desired in the base wine, and strong or heavy odors are avoided. An intense muscat grape aroma is not objectionable in sparkling muscat wines.

137

Making Sparkling Wines

The wines prepared or selected for champagnization are racked, blended, clarified, stabilized, and fined beforehand. The descriptive terms used in sparkling wine production have come mostly from the French language, for obvious reasons, and the lot of stable, clear, blended wine for a particular run of sparkling wine production is termed the *cuvée*, literally "tubful." The fermentation of this wine for the second time requires the addition of more yeast, more fermentable sugar, and (occasionally) yeast food in the form of ammonium phosphate (0.5–1.0 grams per liter). If the alcohol level is higher than 12 per cent or if the sulfur dioxide level is appreciable it may be difficult to referment the wine—an additional reason for holding these low. The yeast starter is grown up in the usual fashion in some of the *cuvée* wine, and the sugar and other additives, if any, are prepared as a concentrated solution in some of the same or very similar wine. The yeast is specially selected for the purpose. Two desirable traits of such yeasts are the ability to ferment under these conditions (low temperature particularly) and the production of an agglomerated "granular" sediment of yeast cells when the fermentation is finished.

The yeast starter and the sugar solution are added in the proper amounts to the *cuvée* and the whole is well mixed to ensure even distribution. Generally 2 to 3 per cent by volume of active starter is used. The *cuvée* wine is usually dry, but if fermentable sugar remains it must be taken into account or excessive pressure will result. As a rule of thumb, 4 grams of sugar per liter of wine will produce one atmosphere of carbon dioxide pressure upon fermentation. Therefore, for a total of about 6 atmospheres (about 90 pounds per square inch), 6 x 4 grams per liter = 24 grams of sugar per liter should be present at the start of the refermentation, or about 20 pounds of sugar per 100 gallons. It is usual to aerate the wine slightly to encourage yeast growth. The mixture, consisting essentially of base wine, yeast cells, and sugar, is then drawn off to the next stage—the *tirage*. Up to this point the process is essentially the same whether bottle or bulk fermentation is to be used.

138

Making Sparkling Wines

FERMENTATION IN THE BOTTLE

For bottle-fermented sparkling wine, the wine is kept well mixed to prevent the settling out of the yeast and is filled into champagne bottles. The bottles are corked with the large wired- or clamped-on corks, especially made for sparkling wines, or today often with cork-lined crown caps. The sealed bottles are then stacked horizontally in a cool place (not over 60° F.) to ferment. The bottles are made of heavy glass and the push-up or punt at the bottom gives added strength, but if the temperature is too high, fermentation too rapid, sugar addition incorrectly high, or the bottles defective, breakage and loss will be excessive. Since scratched bottles may burst, handling is careful and the bottles should not be reused ones.

Complete fermentation and pressure generation are slow and may take from a few weeks to as long as three months, but the *tirage* should remain undisturbed for at least a year to allow the yeast to settle and die, Figure 17. This is important because much of the special flavor and bouquet of bottle-fermented champagne develops as the wine ages at this stage. It is believed to result from the autolysis of the thin film of yeast cells on the walls of the bottle followed by complex reactions of the liberated chemical compounds.

At the completion of aging on the yeast sediment, the bottles are placed neck down in racks and the riddling process begins. The yeast which has deposited on the walls of the bottle must be prepared for removal. Each *tirage* behaves somewhat differently and each person develops his own technique of riddling by experience, but the objective is to cause all the sediment to collect in a thin layer upon the cork, leaving the wine and the walls of the bottle absolutely clear. In order to break the "mask" of sediment loose from the bottle it is given a short sharp spin of an eighth of a turn or so and then dropped back into the rack, neck down, with a jolt calculated to move the sediment toward the cork. A skillful riddler or "turner" can manipulate as many as 20,000 to 30,000 bottles a day. Each

Fig. 17. Champagne aging in a cellar. Source: The Wine Institute.

bottle is turned once a day (in opposite directions on alternate days) and if the wine is easily clarified a week may suffice for completion of the riddling operation. A month or more may be needed to collect all the sediment from a different lot.

The next operation is disgorging—the removal of the collected yeast-cell sediment from the bottle. For this operation the bottles are handled carefully so as not to disturb the sediment. They are refrigerated to nearly the freezing point to lower the pressure and a small plug of ice is then frozen in the neck by immersion of the cork and two or three inches of the neck in a subfreezing bath (about 5° F.) which includes all the sediment in the ice. Care is necessary in these operations to avoid an abrupt temperature change which would crack the thick glass. The bottle is then turned about 45° from upright and opened; the gas pressure pushes out the ice and the sediment with it. Properly completed, these operations leave the bottle and its remaining contents brilliantly clear. Some carbon dioxide is lost during the time the bottle is open and, if the disgorging is not skillful or the wine foams out of the bottle when the pressure is released, considerable wine may be lost also. The wine must be cold (35–45° F.) to retain as much of the carbon dioxide as possible and work must be rapid and efficient. Only a few bottles are open at a time. Between operations they are held in an apparatus with a spring-loaded stopper to minimize escape of the sparkle-producing gas. The *dosage* is then added (Figure 18), the level of wine is replenished if necessary from another bottle, and the bottle is recorked with its final natural or plastic cork, which is wired in place.

The *dosage* (like *tirage*, this rhymes with garage) operation consists of adding a syrup to adjust the sweetness of the wine. Although most people would say they liked their sparkling wine absolutely dry, the fact is that without a little sugar they would find it unpleasantly tart (or, as they might say, sour). The designation of sweetness levels is by no means uniform, but the common terms and their approximate meaning in percentage of sugar are: *brut* 0.5–1.5 per cent, *sec* 2.5–4.5 per cent, *demi-sec* 5 per cent, and *doux* 10 per cent. The required amount of sugar to reach these levels is added to each bottle as a measured amount of concentrated syrup in the *dosage* operation. This *dosage* syrup usually consists of about 60 grams of cane sugar in 100 milliliters of a mixture of about 90 per cent well-aged,

141

Fig. 18. Champagne dosage machine.

high-quality white table wine and 10 per cent fine brandy. It may be aged for some time before use.

Why does this *dosage* sugar not ferment? Most of the yeast cells are dead and few remain in the wine after the aging and disgorging operations. Even though some carbon dioxide is lost, the pressure remains at about two to four atmospheres (30 to 60 pounds per square inch) and inhibits fermentation. Nutrients other than sugar are likely to be depleted by the first two fermentations and the alcohol is raised slightly by the second fermentation and by the brandy of the *dosage*. These and other factors combine to make a third fermentation unlikely. However, if the bottle fermentation is conducted at a relatively warm temperature and the aging in the bottle is less than six months, viable yeasts may be present. This routine speeds production and lowers costs, but there is a risk of fermentation of the *dosage*. To prevent this, sulfur dioxide may be

142

added with the *dosage*. The quality of the resultant wine is reduced.

The bottles of finished wine are generally stored horizontally for a brief period to set the cork into the familiar mushroom shape and to allow detection of leakers. Further aging at this stage appears to have no great advantage. The bottle is now dressed in its labels, foils, and furbelows and sent off to grace elegant occasions, launch ships and brides, and otherwise make all this trouble worth while. Since an estimated 120 hand operations go into each bottle of fermented-in-the-bottle champagne and its production requires skill and involves an appreciable risk of loss it will always be a costly product. The process is not particularly amenable to improvement or economy by large-scale operation and therefore the small family-type champagne cellar can compete successfully. Sparkling wine does have an advantage over other wines in that it can be made from the stock wine at any time of the year and thus the use of equipment and labor can be spread more evenly and planned more efficiently.

Ways of saving labor and decreasing the cost of sparkling wine include the transfer process, Figure 19, for bottle-fermented wine and the bulk or tank fermentation process, which is essentially the use of a large "bottle." In the transfer process the wine is fermented and aged in individual bottles as just described. Instead of riddling and disgorging, however, the bottles are discharged by machinery into a large tank. The tank and the filtering system used to remove sediment and yeast from the wine are maintained under counterpressure with air or nitrogen because the use of carbon dioxide other than that naturally present in the wine might result in carbonation and is illegal if the product is to be labeled as bottle-fermented. Meanwhile, the bottles are washed and after addition of the appropriate *dosage* the wine is filtered into the washed bottles, corked, and finished as for the hand-processed product. The transfer process not only saves labor but gives a more uniform product, since the natural bottle-to-bottle variation even within a single

143

cuvée of bottle-fermented wine can be fairly high. However, there can be some contact between the wine and air, and the highly reduced condition of the wine may be modified, with consequent darkening of color and change in flavor, in the direction of oxidation. Transfer-processed wines can be labeled as bottle-fermented.

BULK-PROCESS SPARKLING WINE

The wines produced by fermentation in bulk must so state on the label to prevent them from competing unfairly with the more costly bottle-fermented wines. These wines are also referred to as tank-fermented or Charmat process sparkling wines after the inventor of the widely used type of tank. The selection of the *cuvée* and its preparation for champagnization are nearly the same for bulk as for bottle fermenting. The fermentation tank is made of inert, nonreactive materials such as stainless or glass-coated steel. It is relatively small as wine tanks go, holding about 500 gallons, so that temperature and pressure can be controlled more economically. The tank is constructed to withstand 200–250 pounds per square inch as a safety factor. It is outfitted with pressure and temperature gauges and safety pressure release valves, and is equipped for temperature control by circulation of refrigerant in a jacket. Since excess pressure can be allowed to escape, the sugar control need not be as precise as with bottle fermenting. Some tanks contain a collapsible plastic-bag liner which makes possible filling and emptying without air contamination. Since these tanks are expensive, reasonably rapid turnover is desired. About two months per cycle or five to seven *cuvées* per year are probably typical.

A single tank may be used, but it is more usual to have two or three arranged to accommodate different stages in the process. The fermentations may be conducted at about 55° F. and should be completed in about two weeks. The large volume of wine produces a relatively thick layer of yeast cells as they deposit after fermentation. If the wine is allowed to stay in contact with this thick sediment, off-flavors, particularly hydrogen sulfide, may be introduced as the yeast cells begin to decompose. This is ordinarily prevented by limiting the time of contact between the wine and the sedimented yeast. Some of the desirable features of bottle-fermented champagnes arise during the breakdown of yeast cells during the aging period. Thus a difference in flavor between the two types may result from the lesser aging with yeast in the bulk process. The degree of difference depends, of course, upon the aging received by the bottle-fermented wine being compared, and may be minimized

FIG. 19. California sparkling wine cellar. (The wine is fermented in the bottles, lower left, disgorged into the transfer tanks, and later filtered into new bottles.) Source: The Wine Institute.

by transferring the wine to another tank for aging with some but not all the yeast or by agitating the bulk-process wine for a period to prevent the formation of a thick layer of sediment.

The bulk-processed sparkling wine is ordinarily given a cold-stabilizing treatment to remove the excess tartrates after the secondary fermentation, and is filtered cold and under pressure to remove the remaining yeast cells and precipitated tartrates. This filtration is an important step because viable yeast cells remain which might referment the *dosage*. Therefore this last polishing filtration should be under essentially sterile conditions to render the product free of yeast cells. The wine is filled into bottles with the appropriate *dosage* and the bottles are finished for marketing. It is still usual to include sulfur dioxide in the *dosage* to prevent growth of any viable yeast cells that may have escaped filtration.

Bottle-fermented wines have little chance of contacting air and picking up oxygen unless the transfer process is used. Sparkling wines fermented in bulk, however, are likely to absorb some oxygen in the course of transferring, bottling, and filtering, particularly because it is illegal (to prevent carbonating the wine artificially) to use carbon dioxide as the source of counter-pressure or for bottle purging. As a consequence, bulk-processed sparkling wine may darken in color and partially oxidize from contact with air. A small amount of sulfur dioxide at bottling may be added to counteract this problem and incidentally to make more remote the possibility of yeast or other organisms growing in the finished wine. Free sulfur dioxide is very noticeable, however, even at relatively low levels in sparkling wine and thus easily becomes objectionable.

Red and pink sparkling wines are processed in a manner very similar to the methods described for the white. The higher tannin content and frequently higher alcohol of these wines make them more difficult to referment. To start the yeast, more aeration of the *tirage* wine may be necessary, and a slightly warmer fermentation temperature may be helpful. The red wines are more difficult to clarify completely and hence are more likely to gush, that is, foam over explosively when the pressure is released. For these reasons bulk fermentation, with its greater opportunity for correction of difficulties, is more commonly used than bottle fermentation for pink champagne and sparkling burgundy. The relatively strong flavor of these wines makes the delicate bouquet of bottle-aging less noticeable.

Summary.—Sparkling wines are relatively expensive, owing to high taxation as well as processing costs. High quality cannot be attained without care in the selection of the table wine to be champagnized. Directly carbonated wine has not achieved wide acceptance by the public, and most sparkling wine is produced by secondary fermentation directly in the bottle or by the bulk process.

The bottle-fermented sparkling wine is usually clarified by expensive and tedious hand processing, whereas in the bulk process the methods of production and filtration are less costly. The bulk processor usually achieves high quality in his sparkling wines by emphasizing fruity-grapy qualities. The bottle-fermented sparkling wines may be produced so as to emphasize age-derived flavors by allowing time for yeast autolysis and aging reactions. The transfer process involves bulk filtration and consequent cost reduction for bottle-fermented champagnes, but may produce a slightly different product owing to such effects as air pick-up during this process.

The sparkle, carbon dioxide, of wines in this class constitutes an important part of their appearance and flavor. They are properly served very cool to retain the bubble display and the dissolved gas. Although, owing to the low temperature and the sting of carbon dioxide in the nose, these wines are not "sniffed" in the glass, the evolution of the gas tends to make more pronounced both good and bad odors. Considering the difficulty and expense of learning to judge and appreciate sparkling wines, it is not surprising that the full range of their qualities and variations is recognized by few consumers.

147

O for a beaker full of the
warm South,
Full of the true, the blushful
Hippocrene,
With beaded bubbles winking at
the brim,
And purple-stainèd mouth.
—John Keats

Chapter 10

MAKING DESSERT WINES

In this chapter we consider the making of wines which require the addition of ethanol distilled from wine. These are often referred to as fortified wines and may be defined as that group of wines produced by the addition of wine spirits. As a rule their final alcohol content is 18–21 per cent by volume (federal requirement) or 19.5–21 per cent (California requirement). Certain special wines such as altar wines and wines in this class imported from other countries may have 14–18 per cent alcohol. The term "fortified" is avoided by the industry because it suggests that the extra ethanol serves no special purpose other than raising the alcoholic potency of the wine. This is not true. If a yeast fermentation is coaxed along by gradual addition of sugar ("syruped fermentation") or by other means, it is possible to produce maximum alcohol levels of 16, 18, or even as high as 20 per cent by volume depending upon the yeast strain. Fortification is not only more convenient than syruped fermentation, but also the latter process creates special tax problems and often the wines have a "mousy" flavor.

Fermentation by all yeasts and growth of nearly all other

organisms are either nonexistent or too slow to be a problem at 20 per cent or more alcohol. Thus the wines containing 20 per cent by spirits addition are barely above the limit for biological stability and can be aged, shipped, and left in half-finished bottles with much less danger of spoilage from microbial action than table wines with their legal (tax bracket) limit of 14 per cent alcohol. Addition of wine spirits before the sugar is all fermented arrests the fermentation and preserves the remaining sugar, giving a stable sweet wine. Although residual sugar in wines of lower alcohol is now commercially possible, it requires special treatment and care.

The third and perhaps most important reason for the addition of wine spirits to wine is that it makes possible special types of wine. These wines owe a good part of their special and distinctive flavors to the type of wine spirits used, the manner of its addition, and the special properties and reactions resulting from or made possible by its presence. These wines include a broad spectrum from sweet (dessert) wines to dry (appetizer) types typified by the extremes available in port and sherry. For convenience we shall refer to the entire group as dessert wines to avoid the cumbersome term "wines produced by the addition of wine spirits" or the connotations of "fortified wines."

In some wine-producing areas of the world famous for dessert wines the winegrower is still a small vineyardist-winemaker. Even in such highly developed wine-growing regions as California there are a few small but well-known producers of dessert wines. However, the necessity for the production of neutral wine spirits for addition to these wines places a special burden of expense for equipment and operational skill on the small operator. This may be avoided if the small operator obtains the wine spirit from a central distiller rather than producing it himself. However the typical California dessert wine plant is a large operation, Figure 20. In some countries beverage alcohol is produced by or for a governmental agency which then controls its distribution and use in dessert wine production. The

149

more usual development in our free enterprise system has been that the wineries which produce dessert wines have become large (in terms of gallons processed) in order to benefit from the efficiency and economy of a centralized, integrated operation.

The dessert winery operation to be described is typical of several of the large organizations with nationwide distribution of their brands. In the modern agricultural business vernacular, these companies are integrated both vertically and horizontally. They have multiple facilities to produce wines in various regions and thereby have a broader-based business and product line. They may, for example, develop some of their wineries to produce premium table wines, others for standard table wines, still others for standard dessert wines and distilled brandy, and so on. They may then collect and blend wines from these different wineries to give them a quality and price range as well as a wide range of types under their various labeled brands. These larger wine coöperatives and companies may tie together under one management vineyards, wineries, distilleries, aging cellars, bottling plants, retail stores, and even glass factories and cooperage works. By no means all the dessert-wine producers are as large or diversified as this, but even the smaller producers are very efficient and cost-conscious because of the equipment and facilities required.

The production of dessert wines is more adapted than that of table wines to the relatively hot regions where grapes are grown. Ripe grapes with more sugar are desired for dessert wines and moderately low acidity is not as detrimental for these wines. Varietal flavors are less in demand for dessert wines (except muscatel) and high-yielding standard varieties are often used. Since about half of the total sugar of the grapes processed is diverted to the production of the spirit used for fortification, grapes and residues unsuitable for direct use as wine may be utilized. The best juice from the best available grapes may be used for the base wine to which the spirits will be added, and the spirits may be prepared from the grapes with too many

Fig. 20. Aerial view of dessert wineries (still tower and water cooler in center). Source: The Wine Institute.

raisins, too low acidity, little sugar, or browned juice. In this country the spirit used for dessert-wine production must come from grapes and is prepared by distillation at 185 proof or higher. Since 1 per cent ethanol by volume measured at 60° F. is two degrees proof, 185 proof is $185 \div 2 = 92.5$ per cent ethanol. The remaining 7.5 per cent or less is mostly water which distills with the ethanol. The high-proof spirit for addition to wine is usually neutral or "silent" in that it is so purified that very little flavor-bearing congeneric substances are present and it contributes relatively little direct flavor other than ethanol. The indirect effects on flavor are great, however, and the typical dessert wine flavor does not develop in low-alcohol wines. A few American-made wines and several imported dessert wines are made with fortifying brandies which do contain appreciable amounts of flavoring substances in addition to ethanol. Pot-distilled brandy in particular may give a characteristic flavor which is a quality feature of some wines.

151

The operations of wine making described in Chapter 7 are applicable to dessert wines with emphasis on the scale of the operation. The grapes are usually crushed in a Garolla-type crusher-stemmer. These large units crush up to 150 tons of grapes per hour, and a large winery may have as many as four in one installation. During the six weeks or so of the crushing season, such an installation may produce a million gallons of crushed grapes per nine-hour working day and process 25,000 tons of grapes in a five and a half day work-week. Each day's million gallons of crushed grapes must be processed to make room for the next day's million gallons. A million gallons would fill about thirty family-sized swimming pools!

The preferred method of collecting white juice or red wine is by settling and draining off the free-run, followed by processing of the wet pomace to recover the remaining sugar or wine for blending or distilling. The total volume of wine is reduced by the distillation of part to be added back to the rest. The yield of finished dessert wine should be 75–100 gallons per ton of grapes processed, depending upon the alcohol-recovery procedures, sweetness of the grapes, and type of wine being produced.

WHITE SWEET WINES

The white sweet wines include muscatel, white port, and angelica. Angelica, a product which originated in the early days in California, is a medium golden-colored, fruity, very sweet dessert wine. White port as made for the United States market is rather similar to angelica, but is typically somewhat lower in sugar, has less color, and, possibly, is more neutral in flavor. Both are marketed as such, but also are useful blending wines to adjust sweetness (e.g., of sherry) or as base wines for flavored specialty wines. Since wine which is to be used as white port must be so designated before it is produced, most of the wine marketed as angelica is selected from stocks carried on the inventory as white port.

Muscatel is a white sweet wine made from muscat-flavored

white grapes, predominantly Muscat of Alexandria and Muscat blanc, and is full-flavored, with the typical muscat aroma and a light to medium golden-brown color. Muscat of Alexandria is used to make sun-dried raisins. Most of the muscats tend to raisin easily. Raisin flavors are undesirable, however, in muscatel and so should be avoided by early and selective harvesting. Muscat varieties tend to be pulpy and difficult to convert to a high juice yield.

White port and angelica may be made of any of the standard varieties of light-colored wine grapes. Thompson Seedless and other viniferous table grape varieties are often used also. A few varieties such as Fernão Pires and Verdelho produce more distinctively flavored white dessert wines, but are not widely planted in California.

Low-colored red varieties such as Mission may be used for white dessert wine production, but the musts tend to be darker even under the best conditions; considering the present standards for white port, they are more suitable for darker wines such as sherry.

Grapes for sweet wines are usually harvested at about 23–25° Brix. If it is necessary to make use of less sweet grapes, such as rejects from table-grape shipments, they are diverted to wines for distilling.

Sulfur dioxide is almost always added, in the proportion of about 100 parts per million at or immediately after crushing. It is preferable to inoculate with 1–3 per cent of a separately grown yeast starter, but if the fermentations are clean and progressing well a portion of the preceding lot of wine may be used. The free-run juice is separated before inoculation and fermentation for angelica and white port. For muscatel it is not uncommon to ferment for a short period (24–48 hours) on the skins to extract more of the characteristic flavor. A short period of heating by passing through a heat exchanger (2–3 minutes, 180° F.) may be used to produce the same effect, but tends to give darker and cloudy wines. In order to achieve

153

the desired light color for white port, low-colored grapes with no raisins and little enzymic browning, a low contact with air, the use of sulfur dioxide, and fermentations not over 80° F. and preferably lower are emphasized. Dessert wines are made in hot areas, at the hot time of the year (100° F. in the shade is common); large capacity refrigeration systems are needed to cool the musts and fermenting wines. Angelica is usually handled similarly. Angelica can be essentially fortified grape juice, and color control is less of a problem, although it is required by law that the must be fermented to at least 0.5 per cent alcohol before angelica is fortified.

White port and muscatel ordinarily receive their addition of wine spirits after fermentation has lowered the temperature-corrected hydrometer reading to about 15° Brix, Figure 21. Addition of neutral high-proof spirit at this point to 20 per cent ethanol by volume gives a new corrected hydrometer reading of about 7° Brix after the wine has been well mixed. Thus a typical wine may be spoken of as 20 x 7, meaning 7° Brix by the hydrometer stem and 20 per cent alcohol by volume determined by distillation of a sample. Dessert wines as marketed generally range from 6° to 8° Brix or about 10 to 14 per cent sugar with angelica and muscatel on the high side, and ports on the low, of this range.

To avoid complications the wine spirits are added after pomace separation for muscatels and, of course, for the other white sweet wines. The addition of the spirits is carefully controlled by government regulations to protect the tax and legal interests of the federal government. The fermentation stops as soon as the alcohol is mixed in, but it may be necessary to allow for the small degree of fermentation that occurs during the addition and mixing with large, rapidly fermenting lots. The wine is allowed to settle for as little as one day to as long as thirty days to allow the precipitation of lees and initial clarification to occur. Early racking may prevent development of off-flavors if the lees are copious. The wine is usually fined with

154

Fig. 21. The consumption of sugar during rapid fermentation of a white dessert wine must is followed by testing frequently with a hydrometer. Note concrete storage tank in background. Source: The Wine Institute.

155

bentonite at about 5 pounds per thousand gallons, settled, racked, and filtered. Wines may be blended at this point to adjust the composition. The blend may then be passed through heat and cold treatments for stabilization. The heating (usually one minute at 180–185° F.) pasteurizes the wine, aids clarification by coagulation of proteins and other colloids, and helps mature the wine. Refrigeration to 16–18° F. for about a month with at least one filtration while cold and perhaps cycling of the temperature between 16° and 32° F. promote the complete removal of the precipitable tartrates and colloids.

White port is not usually placed in wooden tanks, and may be treated with activated charcoal to keep its color low. It is ready to market after these treatments and sufficient storage to allow the harsh taste of the freshly added spirits to mellow and marry with the wine. "Marrying" is a term used by flavorists and perfumers to describe the poorly understood but observed effect of increasing harmony of a blended mixture of flavors after they have been allowed to react together for a time.

Dessert wines are not immune to bacterial spoilage, particularly by *Lactobacillus tricodes*, also called cottony "mold" (incorrectly) because of the fluffy tufts of cells which it produces by growing in dessert wines. Therefore white port and most other dessert wines are given about 50–70 parts per million of sulfur dioxide and/or a pasteurization treatment at bottling. The use of sulfur dioxide in white port is more important for antioxidant effects and color control than for its antibacterial action.

White dessert wines do not improve much after bottling and may become sherry-like after a long time; so bottle-aging is not practiced. These wines are intended for reasonably immediate consumption and are usually marketed in easily resealed bottles with metal screw caps or occasionally wooden-topped replaceable cork stoppers. The relatively small amount of white port

156

produced in Portugal is aged in the manner of red port, and is a somewhat different product from that usually produced in America. Angelica formerly was aged for a period in well-leached wooden tanks, and still may be found slightly more colored than the typical very light colored white port. However, the final processing of the two is essentially the same. Muscatel, on the other hand, should be aged for three years or longer in puncheons or tanks of wood, preferably oak. These should be "topped" at least every few months to make up the ullage and prevent excessive oxidation. The muscat-grape aroma will persist during this aging and the wine will become more smooth and mellow as the yeasty, new-wine flavor and harsh rawness of the freshly added brandy disappear.

PINK DESSERT WINES

California tokay is a pink dessert wine prepared by blending approximately equal parts of ruby port, California sherry, and angelica. It has no relationship to Hungarian Tokay, which is not fortified and has a golden or amber color. Other dessert wines may be prepared from grapes with a low red color content incapable of giving a red wine. Aleatico, a muscat-flavored variety, has been used to produce a pink muscatel. However, production practices for such wines do not differ appreciably from those for red dessert wines and they are not common products. Dessert wines which might be considered pink, based upon their red color content, but which have an appreciable brown or orange hue arising from color modification of red wines are called tawny. Tawny port arises from either long aging (4–6 years) of port in barrels with occasional racking and aeration or from a quick-aging treatment involving baking at 120–140° F. for a few days. The latter treatment tends to develop a more pronounced caramel flavor than does the former and is therefore forbidden in Portugal and is not used by the better American producers.

157

Making Dessert Wines

The classic red sweet wine is port and unless qualified by other terms (i.e., tawny or white) is red. Ruby port implies port which is bright red and relatively young and fruity as distinct from aged ports of more complex but less fruity flavor. The port of Portugal was developed by Englishmen for the English trade. It is interesting to consider the production of this rich, full-flavored, generous wine in a hot climate for consumption in a chilly, clammy one. This warming, comforting, sweet beverage serves as a sort of shippable "bottled sunshine" to transfer some of Portugal's (or California's) excess to wintry areas. The only other California red dessert wine of importance, red muscatel, is made using Muscat Hamburg or Aleatico grapes and combining the techniques of port and ordinary muscatel production.

The grapes used for port production in California naturally include all red varieties widely planted in the warmer regions of the state. Since the red color content of the grapes is reduced by growing them in a warmer climate, some light red varieties (e.g., Mission and Grenache) are too light-colored for conversion to port without blending and in fact may be made into sherry or even white port. Other varieties such as Carignane and Zinfandel can be made into good port, but red pigment content may be a problem. Some varieties can produce high quality port with distinctive odors and flavors which deserve varietal labeling. These include Tinta Madeira, Touriga, and Souzão. To bring the red color up to desired levels the red-pulped varieties Salvador and Alicante Bouschet may be used. Since these two do not have very desirable characteristics other than high color, it is hoped that new varieties such as the recently introduced Royalty and Rubired can replace them and give better quality as well as high anthocyanin pigment content.

Grapes picked for port should have a moderately high sugar content (23–25° Brix) but few raisined berries. The presence of many raisins will give their characteristic flavor to the wine, which is undesirable and off-type in port. The grapes should not be allowed to become overripe because of the excessive loss of acid and the danger of raisining. The increase in pH resulting from too low acidity in overripe grapes gives a bluish shade to the wine and a flat flavor, whereas normal acidity helps keep the color a brighter red and improves the flavor. The anthocyanin, red pigment, content is relatively low for grapes grown in warm, port-producing regions. Care in picking and handling the grapes to prevent damage and loss of the red color by sunburn, raisining, and enzymic changes after bruising is important, and harvesting too late is likely to give less rather than more red pigment in the finished wine.

The grapes are stemmed, crushed, and sulfured as for white port, but the starter yeast is added to the whole crushed mass. From this point on, the port maker is racing to get the red pigment extracted from the skins and the fermenting wine pressed off the skins before it must be fortified to retain the desired sugar. Even if the musts are refrigerated and the fermentation conducted below ambient temperature, say at 75–85° F., the Brix will usually drop from 24 to 15° Brix in 24–48 hours and the wine must be separated from the skins and the wine spirits added. The winemaker is probably using low-colored grapes and must make the best use possible of this time to ensure the transfer of all the extractable color from the skins to the wine. He is likely to have crews working almost continuously at punching down the cap in these large installations or, more probably, continuously pumping the wine over the cap. In so doing the disintegration of the pulp, the death of the grapeskin cells, and the release of the pigments to the wine are hastened. The same purpose is accomplished in Portugal by the process of treading the grapes. Although this is very effective, it does not appeal to American producers or consumers.

Even continuous pumping over may not be efficient enough in recovering the red color from the skins, and other procedures

159

are in use or under test for improving this process. Storage of the grapes for a few days under carbon dioxide pressure before fermenting has been used in Europe. The grapeskin cells die and then the anthocyanin pigment readily diffuses out. Another procedure has been to add the fortifying spirits or a completely fermented wine to the freshly crushed grapes. The alcohol serves to kill the cells and extract the color. This leads to either loss or more reprocessing of the alcohol, however, and complicates the excise supervision. The most common practice is short-term, high-temperature treatment. Properly done, the color is quickly released and little "cooked" flavor introduced. An example might be pumping the must through a heat exchanger at 180° F. for two or three minutes followed by cooling back to fermentation temperature. This also pasteurizes the wine so that the necessary yeast starter provides a clean fermentation. The use of 100 parts per million of sulfur dioxide in the freshly crushed must aids in releasing the red color and helps avoid loss of it by enzymic browning reactions.

As soon as the color has been extracted as much as possible and preferably while the wine tests about 17° Brix, the free-run is drained off and the pomace pressed. One of the more gentle presses (basket, Willmes-type, etc.) is preferred, but speed and capacity often dictate the use of screw presses. The pressed wine is usually more highly colored than the free-run and may be blended back to raise the color and tannin level. These fluid-recovery processes take time and the Brix will continue to drop as fermentation goes on. A drop of 2° Brix during draining and pressing is common. At about 15° Brix by hydrometer, the wine spirits are added and the fermentation is halted.

The California port cellar must be balanced so that the wine may be marketed as a 20 x 7 standard port with the desired color level. This poses a problem and a different one each vintage season, because of variation in the grapes and the wine lot by lot and season by season. To achieve the desired blends, the winemaker adjusts his production practices for each lot accordingly. If he has several very sweet lots, he may ferment some lots nearly to dryness on the skins, as if they were to be table wines, before adding the wine spirits. If several lots have been low in sugar, he may produce red juice by heat treatment, ferment only slightly, and fortify. He may use concentrated red juice for sweetening. Some lots of Salvador or other very highly colored grapes can be made into dark red port. By judicious combining of these products he can produce the main lot or lots of young port wine to be further processed for sale as the type or types of port his winery markets.

If the winery is marketing an early-maturing ruby port, the wine is passed through the usual cold or ion-exchange tartrate stabilization, bentonite fining, pasteurization, and so on, and bottled. Such wines are stored in large lined concrete tanks, Figure 22, and can be on the market within a few months of their production. If the company desires to market a more "aged" type of port, it may give the wine one or more cycles of heating (either similar to pasteurization or more prolonged and at temperatures of about 120° F.) followed by refrigeration. This process and the related rackings and pumping give definite but limited oxidation which modifies the wine's flavor, color, and quality. Sometimes a period of contact with small chips of seasoned white oak heartwood may be used to give a portion of the wine a slight oaky taste reminiscent of the barrel flavor. These quick-aging procedures give to the wine many of the same attributes of prolonged aging—a richer, more harmonious, and more complex flavor. However, the preferred practice is still considered to be the traditional type of storage in wooden cooperage for four to six years. The wine is ordinarily blended and stabilized before filling into the aging barrels. Some producers, especially the large port shippers, have developed into a fine art the preparation of complex fractional blends of young wines plus some very old wines to produce a range of standardized distinctive port type wines for their own and their wholesale customers' brands. "Vintage" or "crusty"

161

port, a type produced with limited age in wood, but six to twenty or more years in bottles, is not often found on the market today. Rich ports may improve considerably with age in the corked bottle, but this practice is prohibitively costly for most wineries, and few wine merchants take the time. By choosing his wine carefully and "laying down" a stock the consumer can experiment with this effect himself. At one time a proud father would store away some port when his son was born to be used at the son's coming-of-age celebration. Certainly a pleasant custom worthy of revival.

SHERRIES AND RELATED WINES

We have emphasized the prevention or control of even limited oxidation, but, in the preparation of wines now to be described, oxidation is produced deliberately, but still in a controlled manner. Whether one starts with a red wine or a white wine, the final product of oxidation by air contact is a rather dark, slightly reddish-brown or amber wine with a characteristic flavor. Because of the resulting color, red wines are seldom used as starting materials. Oxidations in wine are of more than one kind, and produce different types of flavor and compositional change. The major over-all flavor change has been described as maderized (purists insist on the spelling "madeirized," since the word derives from Madeira Islands, but the first syllable is accented and the spelling given is comparable to that used in French, Italian, etc.), *rancio*, sherry-like, and plain oxidized wine. Nutty, raisin-like, or caramel flavors may be associated with the maderized flavor, but are not the same. *Rancio* (incorrectly translated as "rancid") is reserved by some for the maderized flavor when it arises in red wines. Maderization may be produced by prolonged aging or by heating.

The wines in this group are all of somewhat elevated alcohol; produced in the United States in the dessert wine range (19.0 or 19.5–21 per cent by volume). A fairly high level of alcohol (over 15 per cent) is necessary for the wine to survive oxidative

162

processing without becoming vinegar through the action of
acetic acid bacteria. Since these bacteria are inhibited by alcohol more easily than are yeasts, some wines in this class from
other countries are marketed at only 16–19 per cent alcohol.
Since most wines in this class have either long age in the presence of air or heat treatments before bottling, other microbes,
especially the anaerobic *Lactobacilli*, are less often a problem.

The three types of product we are to discuss are prepared by
spirit addition to white base wine and production of oxidized
flavors either by heating, by prolonged aging in the presence
of air, or by growing yeasts aerobically on or in them—the
flor yeast process.

163

The method of heating is used for most of this type of wine sold on the American market. The three M's, Málaga, Marsala, and Madeira, are grouped in this class. Málaga is traditionally a muscat-raisin, caramel-flavored, very sweet fortified wine. It can be prepared by making an angelica-type sweet wine from partly raisined grapes. It is not a large item in the United States wine trade. Marsala, a somewhat similar type, has a cooked-caramel flavor which may be produced in the United States by concentrating white grape juice by boiling down to a syrup. This syrup is then used in blending with baked sweet wine to produce the desired effect. Madeira-type wines include a range of sweetness and are also produced today by heating or baking the wine. Little wine made in the United States is labeled madeira, but actually a great deal of such madeira-like wine is produced. A large part of the wine produced in California, New York, and other states which is labeled sherry has more in common with imported Madeira than with Spanish sherry. It is interesting to note that baked wines are called "madera" in the Soviet Union. American-produced baked sherry is made by "baking" the fortified wine at 120–140° F. for 45 to 120 days. During this period some contact with oxygen is allowed. The only contact may be between the surface of the wine and the air above it in the tank during heating, or bubbles of air or oxygen gas may be passed into the wine during heating. The term "baking" should not be taken too seriously, since the temperature inside a room used to bake sherry is livable even if uncomfortably like standing in the sun in Death Valley. The best product results from the lower temperature and longer time of treatment in the range given.

The origin of this process in the United States and the reason why the product is called sherry rather than madeira are obscure. It may have represented originally a quick-aging procedure. A few producers combine heating with aging by placing the barrels of sherry wine in the sun. For a time greenhouse-type glass structures were used for heating the wine with better control and this developed rapidly into the present system. Today such wines are baked in wood, concrete, or metal tanks. The high temperature may be maintained by placing the tanks in a heated, temperature-controlled room. Alternatively, coils heated by circulating hot water may be placed in the tank or the wine may be pumped through a heat exchanger and back to the tank. A large body of fluid does not heat up or cool off rapidly and one must avoid excessive localized heating at the heated coil or other surface. If the heating surface gets too far above the desired temperature, true cooking, scorching, or charring will produce undesirable harsh flavors.

The wine to be converted to sherry is called sherry material or shermat. This is usually produced as a white wine fermented "dry" ($-1°$ to $0°$ Brix) and then adjusted by addition of wine spirits to the desired alcohol content. Since the characteristic flavor results from the processing, varietal-flavored grapes have no advantage. In fact, a varietal flavor is usually not desired in the product. Eastern producers use *labrusca* varieties, but the processing (often by the oxygen process patented by Tressler) removes the "foxy" flavors completely or nearly so. Other varieties in use include most of the common white and low red-colored standard dessert wine varieties such as Mission, Thompson Seedless, Emperor, Malaga, Flame Tokay, and Palomino. The Palomino and Pedro Ximenes varieties are the most common of several grown in Spain for sherry. The Palomino is a pulpy grape difficult to crush and press, and is noted for a low acidity and high pH. A moderate total acidity and rather low pH are desirable features of must for sherry, and better varieties should be developed.

One way of lowering the pH of the must for shermat is to "plaster" it. The addition of the mineral gypsum (calcium sulfate), or in Spain "yeso," an earth with a high gypsum content, will lower the pH and increase the apparent acidity. Two molecules of potassium bitartrate of the wine and one of calcium sulfate react to produce calcium tartrate, which precipitates out of the solution and leaves one molecule of potassium sulfate and one of free tartaric acid. This process is permitted in the United States for *flor* sherry. The residual potassium sulfate may contribute a slight salty taste to the product. If most of the potassium bitartrate has already precipitated, as in an aged or stabilized wine, calcium sulfate will not have much effect, and it may be necessary to add tartaric acid or perhaps citric acid to lower the pH.

The preparation of the base wine, shermat, except for the more complete fermentation, is essentially as described for white port. The wine may be settled and racked to separate the yeast lees before adding the wine spirits and again afterward. Usually a small amount (1.0–2.5 per cent) of residual sugar is desired during baking; if not present in the initial shermat, it can be added by blending in the appropriate amount of angelica or white port. The "cream" (7.5–10 per cent sugar) and medium (2.4–3.5 per cent) sweet baked sherry may be brought up to their final sugar level by the same method, preferably after baking. Some aging of the shermat in wood cooperage before baking is desirable, but for economic reasons is not universal. Treatment with white oak heartwood chips at about 5 pounds per 1000 gallons may accomplish part of the same effect and may be applied before or during baking. It is usual to fine the shermat with bentonite and rough-filter it before baking. It may be fined again with bentonite or with gelatin or casein and tannin after baking. During baking the progress is followed by critical tasting, and by analyzing color development (it darkens), aldehyde content (it rises), and furfural derivative production (they increase as sugars react) to determine the desirable point for termination. For premium quality the baked wine may be aged for one or two years more in wooden containers. It is stabilized by refrigeration to about 17° F. for two to three weeks and filtration, or by ion-exchange treatment, to prevent tartrate precipitation in the bottle. It may receive a small amount of activated charcoal to lighten the color in view of the preference today for paler sherry. After a final polishing filtration the wine is bottled and is ready for sale. Sherry of most types may be kept for a long time in the sealed bottle with no appreciable improvement or deterioration, although some of the lighter types, particularly *fino* or *flor* sherries, do seem to lose quality after a few years in sealed bottles and rather quickly in opened bottles.

Sherry is produced also by long aging of the shermat in wooden cooperage, Figure 23, without any baking. The smaller the container the more rapid is the change. If well-conditioned white oak 50-gallon barrels are used, two to four years is probably long enough. In some wine cellars the barrels of sherry are not filled full and the ullage is not replenished to hasten oxidative changes. This type of aging is costly, but can produce high quality wines or wines very useful for blending. Much care and art should go into the blending of any wine, and sherries are particularly suitable for improving quality and uniformity by fractional blending. A series of trial blends should be made up and adjusted by critical tasting and evaluation in comparison with samples from previous lots under the same label before the commercial-sized lot is blended.

Flor sherry is produced by a very different process. The dry shermat for *flor* (Spanish for flower) sherry is initially fortified only to 14.5–15.5 per cent alcohol by volume. If it is lower, acetic spoilage may occur and if higher the *flor* yeast will grow poorly. The wine is then inoculated with yeast for the "flowering" process. In this process the aerobic growth of yeast produces a special flavor, the *flor* or *fino* odor. This flavor involves the production of acetaldehyde by the oxidation of part of the ethanol and other complex changes. The aldehyde content is increased in most sherries to some degree, but may reach 500 parts per million or more in *flor* sherry. This aerobic yeast growth is accomplished in two ways: surface growth of a film of yeast cells, or submerged growth with aeration and agitation of the solution. A film-forming yeast such as *Saccharomyces beticus* appears to constitute a physical modification which can form a floating film, rather than a metabolically special organism, for the *flor* aroma can be produced by aerobic submerged culture with most fermenting yeasts.

If the surface-film method is used, the wine is kept in a fairly shallow layer with access to air, as in a nearly half-empty barrel. The film-forming yeast grows and develops a rather heavy, wrinkled creamy white film over the surface. The film is aerobic, but the wine under the film is actually at a rather low oxidation-reduction potential and remains rather light in color. With time the film occasionally breaks (especially if allowed to get too hot in the summer or cold in the winter) and falls to the bottom. Autolysis of some of the yeast occurs, but the living film usually regrows over the surface. This process may be allowed to continue for several years. In dry climates the relative loss of moisture through the side of the cask and perhaps via the film slowly increases the concentration of the alcohol and of the nonvolatile constituents of the wine until eventually the *flor* is unable to grow. It is obvious that withdrawing part of the wine at different stages can give a whole range of products with more or less wood-age, yeast autolysis, and *flor* contributions to their flavor. Submerged culture *flor* production in modern controlled fermentors has the advantage of speed and controllability, but does not give sherry with the wood-aged, yeast-autolysate complexities of the film process. It is a useful blending material and can be used to impart a *fino* aroma to a baked sherry base, giving a very interesting yet inexpensively produced wine. The *flor* sherry or *flor* blend is finished by further fortification if necessary to bring it to the desired final alcohol content (19–21 per cent in this country) and is finished in essentially the same manner as are the other sherry types.

Summary.—Production of dessert wines and sherries lends itself well to the economics of large-scale operation. Grape varieties capable of moderate to high production are used for

Fig. 23. Imported barrels for aging sherry in a California cellar. Source: The Wine Institute.

these wines and the vineyards are characteristically in the warmer grape-growing districts. Many of the products emphasize flavors developed by processing and aging, rather than the distinctive flavors of specific grape varieties, although this is not true of muscatels and need not be true of ports.

The spirit used in fortifying these wines contributes directly to their quality and composition. By arresting fermentations with fermentable sugar remaining, stabilizing wines against microbial and other changes, and by making possible special reactions during aging, the added spirits indirectly modify the wine's quality. In the United States most producers are emphasizing highly purified neutral spirits to avoid heavy, hot, or harsh flavors requiring long aging to become smooth. The resultant wines can be very bright or light-colored and have a fruity flavor. If less purified, richer, or stronger-flavored brandy is used, pot-distilled for example, longer aging may be required and a different type of wine is produced. Long aging in wooden containers can be an important quality factor in some muscatels, ports, and sherries, giving a richness, complexity, and smoothness to the product. Bottle-aging seems less important in these wines than in the lighter wines, but certain types of port profit from bottle-aging for a long time.

Sherries are prepared in three major ways: by the *flor* process, by baking, and by long aging in partly full containers. All these processes involve oxidative changes which largely determine the final flavor of the wine. Many styles and flavor gradations of sherry are available on the market and anyone who does not "like sherry" is betraying the fact that he is not aware of or has not tried the wide range of sherries available to him. The same is probably true of the rest of the dessert wines described in this chapter, though all the others are sweet, whereas sherry need not be.

Chapter 11

DISTILLATION AND BRANDY

Distillation was apparently discovered by the Chinese at a very early date, certainly in the pre-Christian period. It was not extensively used for wines in Western Europe before the end of the Middle Ages. From the alchemist's laboratory it was first used for commercial distillation of wines in the sixteenth century. The equipment used was very primitive: a pot to which heat could be applied, an air-cooled space above the pot where some volatile materials condensed, and a pipe surrounded by water where condensation of the remaining vapors to liquid occurred. It is obvious that the more volatile constituents of the wine are found in increased concentration in the condensate from the vapor and the less volatile in increased concentration in the liquid residue.

Ethanol (ethyl alcohol) and water are miscible in all proportions. Ethanol is lighter than water (specific gravity 0.79384 *in vacuo* at 60° F.) and boils at 172.9° F. at sea level (760 mm. pressure). When ethanol is mixed with water a rise in temperature and an increase in volume occur. When the mixture is returned to the original temperature the volume decreases. The maximum contraction occurs when eight molecules of water and one of alcohol are mixed. A hydrate is probably formed. At about 97.3 per cent, ethanol forms a constant boiling-point mixture (an azeotropic mixture) with water. It is not, therefore, possible to raise the alcoholic content of the condensate above this percentage by simple distillation.

Ethyl alcohol is by far the most important volatile constituent of wines as far as brandy production is concerned. Methyl alcohol is present in small amounts in wines made from grapes: a little less from varieties of *Vitis vinifera* than from V. *labrusca* and more in spirits from fruit wines or in brandies distilled from the pomace (skins and seeds). Methyl alcohol may be important in the formation of odorous constituents. In spirits distilled from grape wines it is present in too small quantities for toxic effects.

Alcohols containing more than two carbon atoms are present in small amounts in wines and other fermented beverages. These include *n*-propyl, isopropyl (3 carbon atoms), *n*-butyl and isobutyl (4), *n*-amyl and isoamyl (5), and *n*-hexyl (6). In normal brandies the sum of the higher alcohols (also called fusel oils) does not exceed 1 per cent of the total alcohol present. The total amount of higher alcohols present in the brandy depends on the composition of the wine and on the methods of distillation. The volatility of the higher alcohols varies with the alcohol content. Thus amyl alcohol (one of the chief components of fusel oil) is less volatile than ethyl alcohol if the ethyl alcohol content is above 40–45 per cent (by volume) and more volatile if below. In the first case the higher alcohols tend to concentrate in the residue (tails, or "feints"); in the second case, in the "foreshots," or heads.

The higher alcohols all have very pronounced odors and if present in too high a concentration are definitely undesirable. Up to a certain point they may contribute to the desirable odor of the product.

Acetaldehyde, the most important aldehyde produced by fermentation, is always present in wines and brandies; being more volatile than water or ethyl alcohol, it distills off first. If present in too high a concentration in the distillate it has un-

172

desirable sensory properties, but normally the amount is too small to detect. It may be important in reactions with alcohol to produce acetal.

When wines, especially those containing yeast cells and distilled in direct-fired stills, are heated some furfural may be produced. Although it boils at 243.1° F. small amounts are found in the distillates. In larger amounts its odor is undesirable.

Wines and brandies contain a number of ethyl and some methyl esters. Fermentations with certain undesirable yeasts seem to produce excessive amounts of some esters. Distillation of wines containing higher amounts of yeast cells also seems to result in a higher ester content in the distillate. Ethyl acetate is present in detectable amounts only in spoiled wines. It appears in the heads during distillation.

Both acetic and lactic acids are slightly volatile, but insufficient amounts normally distill to give an odor to the product.

Other volatile materials include those found in the grapes or those produced by fermentation of defective musts. Varieties of the V. *labrusca* type contain the very distinctive ester methyl anthranilate, but little distills over. Musts containing free sulfur (from that sprayed on the grapes to control powdery mildew, oïdium) often result in wines containing hydrogen sulfide or mercaptans—both undesirable if present in sufficient amounts. Musts or wines to which excessive sulfur dioxide has been added are also less desirable for distillation. Moldy musts are usually settled prior to fermentation and special care is taken in distillation of their wine.

STILLS AND DISTILLATION

When the temperature of a liquid is gradually raised one reaches a temperature when the liquid boils, i.e., molecules escape from the surface as vapor. The amount of heat required to raise the temperature 1° varies markedly for the same amount of different liquids.

173

Distillation and Brandy

In an alcohol-water mixture (of below 97.3 per cent ethanol) the vapor leaving the surface contains a higher percentage of alcohol than the original liquid. This is the basis of fractional distillation, which permits brandy production from wine. As the distillation of an alcohol-water mixture continues, the alcohol content of the liquid is gradually lowered and hence the alcohol percentage in the vapor also decreases.

If the wine is placed in a closed pot provided with an outlet arranged to cool the vapors, one has a pot still, Figure 24. Heat may be applied by direct fire (as in Cognac) or with steam (as in California). The simple pot still has been greatly modified. A simple or more complex system of partially cooling the vapors is usually provided. This partial condensation is called rectification. The wine to be distilled is often used to partially cool the vapors. This is a desirable economy measure. A typical pot still is shown in Figure 24.

As the temperature of the pot increases the more volatile constituents tend to be present in higher percentages in the first fractions that come off. When distilling wine the non-alcohol components of the distillate are high early in the distillation when the alcohol content of the distillate is over 50 per cent. Furfural starts to distill over when the alcohol content of the distillate reaches approximately 40 per cent and continues down to about 25 per cent. The higher alcohols are not distilled over when the alcohol content of the distillate from a pot still falls below about 30 per cent.

When distilling not from wine but from previously distilled distillate (as in Cognac) somewhat different results are obtained. The aldehydes are then primarily found in the heads, but the esters, at this higher alcohol percentage, distill over a wider range of alcohol content, even during the distillation of the tails fraction. Increasing the speed of distillation increases the rate of distillation of the volatile acids and esters. It is believed that a slow distillation gives a product of higher quality.

174

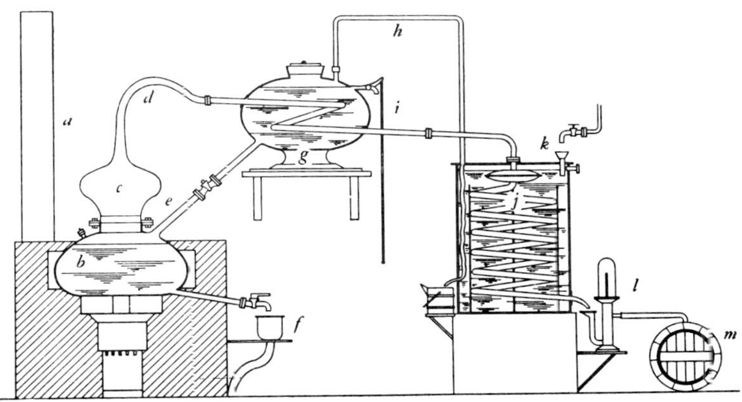

FIG. 24. Pot still (g, preheater; j, worm condenser; 1, simple try box; m, barrel for receiving the brandy).

However, the quality of the product of a pot-still distillation is partially (if not largely) controlled by the sensory examination of the distillate which is made during distillation. Depending on the quality of the distilling material and the quality of product desired, more or less heads or tails are removed by the distiller. The percentages removed obviously greatly influence the quality of the product. This removal, when combined with the amount of heads or tails returned for a secondary distillation, further influences the composition of the product.

The advantage of the pot-still procedure for production of brandy may be assigned primarily to this control over the composition and quality of the product by the distiller. Even when the raw product is of poor quality, the distiller, by controlling the amount of heads and tails retained, influences the quality of the product. The disadvantage of the pot-still procedure is primarily its higher cost of operation. This is true not only of the brandy production but also of whiskey production

Because of the high cost of operation of pot stills the continuous procedure was introduced in the nineteenth century—

first for industrial alcohol and whiskey and later for brandy. The continuous still is essentially a series of interconnected pot stills, Figure 25. The column type of continuous still is a cylindrical tube divided into sections by a series of plates. Each plate functions as a separate pot still. Down pipes between plates provide for return of liquid from one plate to another. The down pipes are on opposite sides of the column for alternate plates. The upper part of each down pipe extends above the plate to allow a liquid layer on the plate. The lower end of the down pipe is inserted in a cup in the lower plate to form a liquid seal. In the typical column still the hottest part is the bottom of the still where the steam is introduced. The lowest temperature and highest percentage of alcohol are found at the top of the column still.

The plates in the column still are perforated, usually with the opening covered by bubble caps. The perforations on the lower plates of the column are open to permit distilling materials with a larger percentage of suspended solids to pass. The upper or bubble-cap plates function as the rectifying (i.e., purification) part of the column.

In the typical column still the wine is introduced at some intermediate plate on the column. Heat is supplied from steam introduced at the bottom of the column. The alcohol percentage decreases as the wine flows down the column and increases at each plate as the more volatile alcohol vapors rise up the column. To conserve heat, as with the pot still, the dealcoholized liquid from the bottom of the still is used to heat the wine which is to be introduced into the still.

Column stills are said to function continuously, but eventually the plates need to be cleaned. In normal practice the column still is shut down and washed out once a week.

The product from the top of a column still, like that from a pot still, must be cooled to condense the vapor to a liquid, and from a liquid down to room temperature.

176

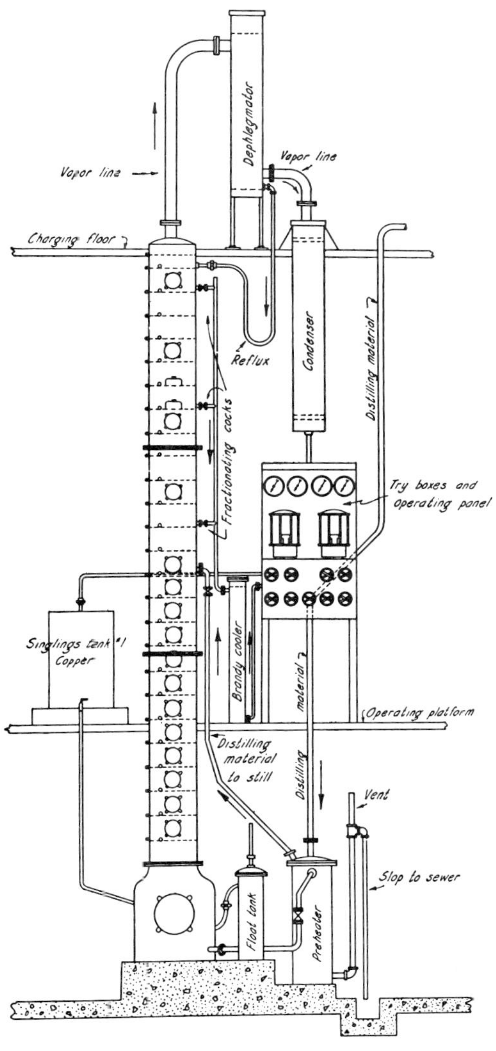

Fig. 25. A modern column still. Source: Joslyn and Amerine (1941).

177

Distillation and Brandy

Two special problems of column-still operation are the removal of higher alcohols and of aldehydes. The higher alcohols gradually accumulate on an intermediate plate of the column —usually at a plate with an alcohol content of about 135° proof.* It is possible to draw off the higher alcohol layer from a plate on which it accumulates if the column is operating to produced high-proof (over 170° proof) spirits.

To remove aldehydes a special aldehyde column is attached to the still. The aldehydes removed are best utilized by introducing them into a rapidly fermenting must where the yeast reduces the acetaldehyde to ethyl alcohol.

Continuous stills, like pot stills, must have condensers to condense the vapor and to reduce the temperature to normal. Two condensers are usually used—a dephlegmator which condenses only part of the vapor and returns this fraction to the column and a brandy condenser which condenses the remaining vapor which is withdrawn wholly or partially as the product.

In California the column still is used both for the production of beverage brandy and for fortifying brandy for dessert wine production. The fortifying brandy is usually distilled at 190° or higher proof. Brandy for beverage purposes must be distilled at 170° proof or lower. Separation of fusel oils is difficult when using a column still to produce beverage brandy, for the plates on which the higher alcohols accumulate are only one

---

* "Proof" is an old English term for measuring the alcoholic strength of distilled beverages. Black powder and the beverage were mixed and a flame applied. If the mixture exploded the beverage was "proof." When physical methods for determining alcohol percentage were developed, "proof" was found to be slightly over 50 per cent alcohol. Legally, English 100 per cent proof spirit contains 57.1 per cent by volume of alcohol, and alcoholic strength is usually expressed as under or over proof. In the United States proof (or 100° proof) spirit contains 50 per cent by volume of alcohol. Hence 200° proof spirit is absolute alcohol. Most brandies, whiskeys, rums, and liqueurs are sold at between 84° and 102° proof, i.e., between 42 and 51 per cent alcohol by volume.

Fig. 26. Control panel for a brandy distillery. Source: The Wine Institute.

or two plates lower on the column than those from which the 160° to 165° proof brandy is to be withdrawn.

Continuous stills are not only more efficient than pot stills in their energy utilization, but also their operation can be automated. Automatic controls for feed, product flow, and temperature control of the condensers are easily applied to continuous stills, Figure 26. These lead to more uniform distillates and less expensive operations. However, pot-still brandies are generally higher in nonethanol flavor constituents and in some countries, Portugal for example, are preferred for fortification.

Many modifications of the simple pot and column stills described above are being used. In California, column stills with mechanical movement of fermented pomace in the still are used to remove the residual alcohol from the pomace. Distillation under vacuum seems to result in fruitier products, but the equipment is expensive and whether the product justifies the expense has not been determined.

Aging of brandy for beverage purposes is an expensive operation. Not only is the product tied up for two to ten or more years, but there are losses of alcohol during aging. In this country the federal government allows a certain amount of evaporation for each year of aging and within this allowance taxes are paid only on the aged product remaining for bottling. The present tax on brandy and other distilled alcoholic beverages in this country is $10.50 per 100° proof gallon, more than $2.00 per bottle, if sold at 100° proof.

TYPES OF BRANDY

Brandies are usually classified by region of production. This may be due to the influence of soil conditions or the variety of grapes used. However, the biggest differences in quality appear to originate from the method of distillation and the aging practices.

The most important French brandies are produced in the Charente district north of Bordeaux. The product is called

Cognac from the town of the same name. The soil of the district is highly calcareous and the best brandies are produced in the district containing the highest calcium carbonate content in the soil, called the Grande Champagne. A neighboring district with less soil calcium carbonate is Petite Champagne. Other districts are Borderies, Fins Bois, Bons Bois, and Bois Ordinaires. The product of the first two districts is usually sold as Grande Fine Champagne or Fine Champagne Cognac. The word "Champagne" in this usage has nothing to do with the sparkling wine of this name.

Brandies of different parts of the Charente district and of different ages are used to produce the other commercial types of Cognac. Usually these are sold as "3" or "5" star (for the cheapest), VSOP (for a better quality) and under proprietary brands of varying quality and price.

The predominant grape variety of the Charente is Saint-Émilion (called Trebbiano in Italy and Ugni blanc in the south of France). In the cool Charente it ripens poorly, in most years producing a wine of only about 8–9 per cent alcohol and 1.5 to 1.7 per cent total acidity.

Immediately after the vintage, distillation of these wines is begun. The wines are not clarified; indeed, distillation of the yeast deposit with the wine is one of the factors favorably influencing quality. The traditional pot still is exclusively used for the distillation. The stills are direct-fired. Two distillations are made: the first at only about 54° proof. Heads and tails fractions are collected separately. The still is then emptied and a new charge is made. The tails of the first distillation are usually added. A third charge is distilled again with the tails of the previous distillation. The three main distillates are combined and redistilled to between 140° and 150° proof. Heads and tails fractions are separated.

The product is cut to about 100° proof with distilled water and aged in new oak casks. These are made of the hard Limousin oak and vary in size from 50 to 200 gallons. Cognac

181

decreases in alcoholic strength during aging. During aging the Cognac improves in quality for a number of years; some are aged for as long as twenty-five years. Eventually, aging in the wood must be discontinued because too much woody flavor is extracted and the alcohol content becomes too low. Some of these old brandies are especially useful for blending purposes. Some brandies are transferred from the new cooperage to used cooperage to reduce the extraction of tannin.

Most of the younger Cognacs (the "3" star quality, for example) are slightly sweetened before sale. Connoisseurs prefer drier Cognacs with a moderate but clean aged odor. One should beware of imported brandies which are offered for sale in odd bottles implying long aging. Napoleon brandies have long since disappeared from the market and if bottled would be no better now than when bottled. If left in the wood for more than about twenty-five years they would be spoiled or undrinkable. The regulations of the Internal Revenue Service require honest labeling as far as age is concerned, and since about 1960 most of the exaggerated claims of excessive aging on imported brandies have disappeared. The best Cognacs are sold as Grande Fine Champagne, though the blended Cognacs of some of the better firms are very fine—and expensive.

Armagnac is produced in much smaller quantities than Cognac and is less exported and less well known. It is produced in a delimited district in southwestern France. The wines are distilled in a semicontinuous fashion at only about 126° proof in pot stills with a small stripping column. Only one distillation is made. The product is aged in oak casks. The odor of Armagnac is considered by experts to be less complicated and fine than that of Cognac, even when well aged. Armagnac criteria of quality are certainly less standardized than those of Cognac, and commercial products of very variable quality are often found on the market—some in fancy bottles which obviously have nothing to do with the quality of the contents.

Much cheap brandy is produced in pot and column stills in

the south of France. Some of this, at highly competitive prices, may be found on the American market as "French brandy." We have been, perhaps, unlucky in finding many of these to be newly distilled brandies with added color, sugar, and flavor.

If the pressed skins and seeds from the fermentation are placed in a pile and aged for one to several months they undergo changes in flavor—anaerobic changes which have not been well studied or elucidated. If the surface of this pile of pomace (or *marc*) is then removed and the remainder placed in a pot still very pungent distillates will be obtained. These are usually not aged and reach the market as clear liquids. In France these are called *eaux-de-vie-de-marc* or marc brandy. The best are produced in small amounts in Burgundy. They are expensive and the odor is so pungent that one must cultivate a taste for them—which, truthfully, hardly seems worth the effort. Some use them in coffee, but their cost hardly recommends this use.

During the Second World War some Portuguese brandy was exported to this country. It was often excessively sweetened and flavored and sometimes was noticeably high in higher alcohols. After the war the importations decreased and show no signs of again increasing.

In contrast there is a continuing and fair demand for Spanish brandies in this country. This is surprising because they tend to be rather hot-tasting and lack a fruity or wine-like odor. Some of the cheaper products are clearly sweet. Some Spanish brandies are aged by a fractional-blending system (or in a *solera*) and sell at premium prices. Aging alone, however, cannot produce a high-quality product. Use of wines of better quality would improve the product and give a better result after aging. One clear test of the lack of quality of many of these brandies is the difficulty of consuming them straight or even in a highball. They do taste better in coffee.

The few Italian brandies that we have tasted in the United

States have been both flavored and sweetened. Some French wine is imported into Germany for brandy production. Even French oak casks have been used for aging in Germany. In spite of this and excellent stills, highly trained operators, and skillful blending, the products usually taste somewhat artificial.

At least one Greek brandy has enjoyed some popularity in the United States. We wish that we could recommend it. South African brandy has been found to be more interesting. It has a cleaner grape (not raisin) odor and is less sweetened. Unfortunately, it is apparently available in few localities. We have tasted brandies made in the Soviet Union. The younger brandies are frankly hot in taste, but the more expensive have obviously been aged.

Peruvian *pisco* brandies are sold as clear brandies, so obviously have no wood aging. Their almost exclusive use in sweet fruit-flavored punch seems appropriate and significant. The Mexican brandies tasted here and in Mexico have not been memorable, except for a noticeable added flavor of "oil of cognac" in some. "Oil of cognac" is a highly flavored product produced by distilling, in a pot still, a yeast suspension. It is usually high in ethyl heptanoate and other esters.

California brandy has enjoyed increasing popularity since the Second World War. Virtually all of it is produced by column stills. After distillation at about 170° proof it is cut with water to about 102° proof, a small amount of caramel syrup is added, and it is aged in new barrels (54 gallons) made of American oak. The cheaper sorts are aged from two to four years, but some eight-year-old California brandy is now available.

California brandy is carefully distilled so that obvious excesses of higher alcohols are rare. In fact, some seem to be so highly rectified in distillation that they lack grapiness.

Two general types of California brandy are found on the market—those containing sweetening and flavoring materials and those without. If the latter are aged for four years or more at over 100° proof and are not reduced below 100° proof when bottled they may be labeled "bottled in bond." * Only a small amount of brandy is bottled in bond. The distillation and new-oak aging procedures used in this country do not favor production of a product which can be drunk straight as bottled-in-bond whiskey.

Most California brandies are therefore reduced (cut) to 84° to 88° proof with water before bottling. The best brandies can be consumed without further dilution, but most are served in highballs with soda or, preferably, water. A good California brandy has an unmistakable wine-like odor, a distinct oak or vanillin-like smell, and a clean, nonhot dry taste. It should be light-amber in color with no greenish tint (due to excessive iron).

Some pomace brandy, produced by distilling fermented pomace in a pot still, has been produced in this state. It has been called grappa and is sold as a colorless beverage. It is often used in coffee, which seems as good a use as any.

The use of gigantic snifters for serving brandy (California or imported) is almost pure affectation. The snifter tends to volatilize too much of the brandy. Where an off-odor is suspected, a snifter may be useful to professionals. When the snifters are ostentatiously warmed it is positively reprehensible. The warmth of the hand on the bowl of a small glass is sufficient to bring out the odor of a fine brandy.

Judging brandies requires experience. However, the occupational defects of sweetness, higher alcohols, hotness, and added flavor are relatively easy to identify and avoid. The great desideratum is a complex but balanced odor and a clean and soft taste. Cognacs should have the characteristic Cognac odor, but not too concentrated. Marc brandies should have a pungent odor, but not an offensive one. California brandies should have a pleasant wood or vanillin odor. They, as well

---

* Identifiable by a green tax stamp across the top of the bottle. The date of distillation and bottling is given on the stamp.

185

as most other brandies, including the cheaper cognacs, are best served as highballs. Only the very finest brandies can be appreciated pleasurably when served undiluted.

Summary.—Distillation separates and concentrates ethanol and other volatile materials from wine. Pot stills have certain advantages, particularly the possibility of controlling the quality by sensory examination of the product during distillation. Continuous stills are cheaper to operate and are now used for brandy production in most countries.

The most important single type of brandy is Cognac. It is a pot-distilled product which is produced in a variety of types and qualities. Armagnac is the second most important type of French brandy. The increasing popularity of California brandy seems to be due to its careful distillation and to the aging in oak barrels. Other countries produce brandy, some of which is sweet or hot in taste or flavored.

The sensory qualities and proper use of brandy are outlined.

Chapter 12

SPECIALTY WINERY PRODUCTS

BY-PRODUCTS OF THE WINERY

The residues obtained in winery operation may be converted to by-products. These include the fusel oil recovered incidental to large-scale wine distillation for eventual use in lacquer solvents, and tartrates from pomace, lees, and distillery wastes recovered to give cream of tartar for baking, tartaric acid salts for use in photography, and tartaric acid for acidification of wines and other foods. Although the latter was done in this country during the world wars, tartrate recovery from winery wastes has not been economically attractive here in normal times because of the low price of tartrates imported from countries with larger wine production and lower production costs. Grape residues are, however, the major world source of tartaric acid, and this useful acid may become worth recovering as labor costs rise in other countries and wine production in the United States becomes more centralized in fewer and larger modern wineries.

In general, the same situation prevails for the other two potential processed by-products—tannin and oil from the seeds in winery pomace. Grape-seed tannin is produced in Australia and Europe and sold world-wide primarily for use in adding to and fining wines. The production and demand are rather small compared to the total possible production. Grape-seed oil is a good semidrying oil suitable for food uses as well as for paints. Beyond a small amount produced for special uses, particularly raisin "polishing" to decrease sticking and give improved appearance, this oil is not usually recovered except under wartime or food emergency conditions. The nonprocessed residues such as pomace and still bottoms usually constitute more of a disposal problem than valuable by-products. The value of winery wastes for cattle feed and soil improvement agents is minimal, but they may be so used owing to availability, low cost, and need for disposal.

Some other products of wineries are more properly termed accessory products. Juice from wine grapes is sold to be used in production of grape juice drinks, baby foods, jellies, and many other food products. This may be white or red juice. If it is to be red, the color must be released from the skins by appropriate short heat treatment or other means. The juice is clarified and processed at low temperature with minimal air contact to avoid browning and flavor changes. High sulfur dioxide levels (1,000 parts per million or so) may be used to prevent fermentation, and the free sulfur dioxide may be removed later by treatments such as stripping under vacuum. Such unfermented sulfited juice is called muté in the winery. Today it is more common to process the juice by concentration under vacuum to a high sugar level (60–70° Brix). This red or white concentrate is stored under refrigeration until needed. The extremely high sugar content resists fermentation, and cold storage away from air contact helps prevent browning and other changes. Concentrated juice is not only a product marketed to other food processors, but also is useful in the winery for sweetening wines and may even be diluted and fermented to wine after the usual vintage season. With the modern type of high-vacuum, low-temperature, and perhaps essence-recovering concentrator a very high quality product is obtained. Dealcoholized, concentrated wine to be used for

188

flavoring can be prepared by similar processes as an accessory product. The alcohol is recovered for other uses. Wine vinegar may be another accessory product of wineries. Unlike the situation in former times, it is seldom produced accidentally.

In addition to these by-products, accessory products, and the primary products of table wine, sparkling wine, dessert wine, and distilled wine spirits, there are numerous specialty wine products which are often made by only one producer by a secret process. Two classes of these specialty wines—flavored wines and fruit wines—are worthy of discussion of the general principles of their production.

VERMOUTHS AND OTHER FLAVORED WINES

The production of flavored wines is a very ancient practice which appears to have gained historical impetus primarily from two directions. The ancients' wine was often poorly flavored or partly spoiled owing to acetification and other contaminations. It often kept poorly owing to low alcohol, lack of sulfur dioxide, and ignorance of the process of making and keeping good wine. The addition to wine of substances to correct, cover up, or resist such spoilage was a matter of trial and error. The addition of sea water to wine, particularly that for slaves, was a Greek and Roman practice. Besides preventing excessive intake and brightening the color of the red wine, no doubt this helped cover the off-flavors of low-quality wine. Addition of pine resin, as still practiced to some degree in Greece, may have arisen similarly. From the effort to cover bad odors and tastes it is a short step to the practice of adding desirable flavors and letting the wine serve as the vehicle and to some extent the preservative for the added flavor. Just as spices for foods and perfumes for the person developed originally to cover bad situations and evolved to give extra interest and pleasure after conditions improved, so did spiced, perfumed, and flavored wines develop and survive.

The second line of development of flavored wines was medicinal and mystical. The medicines, narcotics, and love potions of the day were mostly botanicals chosen for known or supposed efficacy. Potions were prepared partly on the basis that any plant with an unusual or strong odor or taste must be good for something and a little bit of everything should make a fine cure-all. Formulas were ritualistic and complicated. Wine was the solvent of choice for the ancient would-be pharmacist because the alcohol made it a better solvent and lent its own euphoric talents. It was a happy marriage because the mild antibacterial and preservative value of the essential oils and other materials extracted from these herbal medicaments helped keep the low alcohol more or less sweet wine from spoilage and the alcohol of the wine in turn helped preserve the medicine, tonic, or magic potion. Many of the botanical medicines which have real value are bitter, quinine for example. A bitter taste came to be desired and preferred in these products. This acquired taste for bitterness survives today and many of the traditional types of flavored wine have a noticeably bitter aftertaste.

After the development of distillation, fortified wines and brandy became the base chosen for flavored wines and liqueurs. The extra alcohol improved the solvent power and the ease of preservation particularly after opening. It is interesting that the traditional class of flavored wines—the vermouths—retains much of the ancient character, even though few people still believe that vermouths have medicinal value or magical properties.

The name vermouth derives from German *Wermut* (literally, man's strength) and is related to wormwood, a common herb, *Artemisia absinthium,* used in many formulations. The name of the herb derives not from any infestation of its stem, but rather because one of its medical uses was as a vermifuge —which may or may not make it seem more attractive to you. Vermouths today are prepared with familiar flavors and spices such as allspice, anise, bitter orange peel, cinnamon, clove, coriander, fenugreek, ginger, marjoram, nutmeg, rosemary, sage, savory, thyme, and vanilla. Exotic botanicals are also used: angostura, blessed thistle, cascarilla, cinchona bark, horehound, hyssop, dittany of Crete, European centaury, galingale, hart's tongue, hops, lemon balm, rhubarb, saffron, valerian, yarrow, and zeodary. The list of materials which have been used is very long and the ingredients and amounts employed by any one producer are seldom made public. Although there are class similarities, the flavoring specialist strives to produce a blend of flavors which is so complex and harmonious that his product is distinctive and yet is not readily "analyzable" by either tasters or chemists. The use of fifteen or more different ingredients in one formulation is usual.

There are two general types of vermouth, the French and Italian styles sometimes referred to as dry vermouth and sweet vermouth. The dry or French type is characterized on the American market by a very light straw color, about 4 per cent sugar, a light but definite aromatic herbal flavor, and a slightly bitter aftertaste. The traditional level of herb addition is about 0.5 to 0.75 ounce of the mixture of dry herbs per gallon of wine. This type of wine served cold or perhaps over ice or with soda is a delightful preprandial libation for social or private gatherings. Unfortunately, Americans generally have not learned this, although vermouth is so used in Europe. A major portion of American vermouth is used in mixed concoctions such as the martini (dry vermouth) and the manhattan (sweet vermouth). Since it has become fashionable to make the martini almost straight gin and yet economics (and in our opinion desirable flavor) dictates a sizable portion of vermouth, the market has favored almost colorless and lightly flavored dry vermouths.

Italian style or sweet vermouth has a much darker color and richer flavor. It usually is prepared with from 0.75 to 1.5 ounces of dry herb mixture per gallon. Caramel coloring may be used to give the typical medium dark brown color. The base wine is or includes some muscatel, and citrus, anise, or vanilla

191

as well as herbal notes are often recognizable in it. The after-taste is still basically bitter, but the sugar level (about 15 per cent) contributes sweetness and body to Italian style vermouth.

The base wine for dry vermouth is prepared by blending white port or angelica, dry sauterne, and high-proof spirit to the proper sugar content. It may be treated with activated charcoal to ensure a low color and a neutral odor. Angelica, white port, muscatel, and, rarely, sherry may be blended in California for the sweet vermouth base. The alcohol content of American-made vermouths is in the dessert wine range, 18–20 per cent by volume. Those made in Europe are often lower, 16–18 per cent. The base wine is usually colored with caramel or de-colorized with carbon as the type of vermouth requires, clari-fied, and stabilized before addition of the flavoring substances. The base wine may be aged in wooden cooperage before and again after flavoring for a total of three to five years; however, this is no longer generally done for sweet vermouths, and dry vermouths are usually finished and marketed within a year.

The preparation and use of the flavoring mixture is a critical part of the production of these wines. The whole plants, fruits, seeds, barks, roots, flowers, and other botanicals that make up the herbs and spices to be used are often expensive materials which must be collected from many parts of the world. Like all natural products they are variable by source and season and are subject to damage and deterioration. The vermouth producer must depend upon reputable suppliers and must be selective for genuineness, quality, and freshness in his purchases. To compensate for unavoidable variation in the strength and char-acteristics he must adjust his formulas to maintain a uniform flavor in the finished wine.

The dry herbs may be added to the wine and steeped therein, perhaps at slightly elevated temperature, for some weeks or a few months. This is termed the infusion process. Small trial lots are prepared for comparison with the previous production of the winery, and the selected proportions are carefully weighed out for the production lot. The materials are preferred whole or only coarsely ground. They must be dry, clean, and mold-free, and are stored carefully to retain their odors—usually in a refrigerated room. The herbs are not left in the wine too long lest undesirable flavors or clarification problems result from excessive extraction. For the same reason the herbs are not pressed when removed from the wine. As long as stirring and circulation of the wine are provided, a convenient method is to submerge the flavoring materials in the wine in an open-mesh cotton cloth bag.

A second method of adding the flavoring to the wine is to prepare a concentrated extract in wine spirits, water, or wine, which is then added to the production lot of vermouth. It is possible to buy such concentrated flavoring from supply houses. These may be of individual flavoring substances or the total flavor mixture for standard or your selected vermouth specifications. Producers with appreciable sales of vermouth are believed to prefer some modification of the extract process, but prepare their own extracts, wholly or in part.

After the wine has been flavored, it is filtered. Fining with bentonite, refrigeration, filtration while cold, and pasteurization may be necessary to achieve stable clarity, but excessive processing is avoided to prevent loss of the added flavors. The flavors are usually allowed to "marry"—stabilize and harmonize their flavor values—for a few months and then the wine is bottled for sale. A final polishing filtration and a small addition, 50 parts per million or so, of sulfur dioxide are usual precautions at bottling.

In addition to the traditional vermouth types, there are many proprietary flavored wines. Byrrh, a product of France, is a "secret formula" branded wine which is quite bitter and made from red wine. Dubonnet, both red and white, is another which is made under license in this country. There are many others, both native and imported (e.g., mint-flavored wine, coffee-flavored wine, etc.), but most of them are not widely distributed in this country.

Owing to a reinterpretation of the laws on flavored wines, a

193

new class of wines has appeared on the American market. The prototype of these "special natural wines" was given the proprietary brand name of Thunderbird and was first marketed in 1957. This and a number of similar products now account for nearly 10 per cent of the total wine produced in the United States. They are called "special" because each individual named brand has a specific formula of added flavors which is approved by and filed with the Internal Revenue Service (but not made public). They are "natural" in that the flavoring substances must all be isolated or prepared directly from natural sources and not chemically synthesized. Most of these wines are prepared from a neutral white port base wine, but a few are made from red dessert wines. It is believed that the extracts and essential oils for these wines are purchased from flavor supply houses, added in the proportions called for by the formula to the base wine, and finished for marketing as are other dessert wines.

FRUIT WINES

A special natural wine could be prepared by adding neutral spirits to a neutral white grape must and then adding flavor concentrated from raspberries except for the legal restriction that fruit juices cannot be used to give wine from one fruit the flavor of another. Ignoring a few other legal and labeling requirements, it would be possible to prepare a similar wine by adding neutral spirit to raspberry juice. Still a third wine-like beverage could be prepared by direct fermentation of raspberry juice. The first type could not be labeled raspberry wine; the second type could be so labeled if the added alcohol was derived from raspberries. The wines labeled with raspberry or other fruit names are usually made by a modification of the third process.

The wines made from fruits and similar products other than the wine grape—cider (apples), perry (pears), blackberry wine, mead (honey), plum wine, and a host of others—are impor-

194

tant home products and some are important commercially, especially in colder climates where wine grapes cannot be grown. North-central Europe and Scandinavia are noted producers and consumers of such wines and wine-like alcoholic fruit beverages. England and northern France also have important cider and perry production. Fruit wines and mead have a long history and are worthy of study in their own right, but their commercial production is relatively limited and their perishability such that most of them are not stored long or distributed widely. This group would include products of the home winemaker (e.g., rhubarb wine, dandelion wine, etc.) which involve steeping or fermenting the named material in "wine" resulting from sugar syrup, yeast, and yeast nutrients. The wine grape is virtually the only fruit which commonly reaches a high enough sugar and the proper acid balance for a good-flavored and stable wine. Other fruits including *Vitis labrusca* grapes and many fermentable substances such as honey require adjustment of either sugar or acid or both to produce a satisfactory wine-like product. Most fresh fruits such as berries, cherries, Concord grapes, citrus fruit, and so on are rather high in acidity; so, if all the sugar is fermented, the dry wine is unpleasantly sour. The law permits, for such wines, the reduction of the concentration of acid by dilution with water to a minimum of 0.5 per cent calculated as malic acid for apples and citric acid for other fruits if the volume added is not more than 35 per cent of the total ameliorated volume of juice or wine. Wine from loganberries, currants, or gooseberries, owing to the very high natural acidity, may receive additions to 60 per cent of the diluted total volume. If the fruit to be used is below 0.5 per cent acid, citric or other approved food acid may be added to that level. Acid may also be added at the discretion of the winemaker if the total added is not greater than 0.2 per cent and if the juice or wine is not then diluted with water. The sugar content of most of these fresh fruits is too low for stable wine, and is lowered still further if the acidity is ameliorated by addition of

195

water. It is therefore permitted to add sugar (sucrose, glucose, invert syrups, simple syrup, etc.) under strict control. The rules are complex, but in general the juice before fermentation may not exceed 25° Brix; after fermentation and perhaps sweetening for sale or adding wine spirits prepared from the same kind of fruit, the alcohol should not exceed 14 per cent or the solids content of the wine exceed 21 per cent by weight. The permitted practices with respect to wines from dried fruit (raisins, dates, etc.), honey, and other fruit products are similar to those just described for fruit wines, except that those with high sugar content may be adjusted with water to not less than 22° Brix before fermentation in most cases.

These fruit-type wines are subject to the same considerations as are table wines. They are marketed as fresh fruity products with as much as possible of the characteristic flavor and color of the specific fruit. The fermentation may take place in the presence of the whole macerated fruit mass, but if so the pulp is pressed off and removed within two or three days. Since the presence of berry seeds and such parts in the later stages of fermentation may allow the extraction by the alcohol of bitter or haze-producing substances, such contact should be limited as much as possible. The release of the juice before fermentation by pressing, usually after heating for a short time to disrupt the cells, is often practiced. It is usually necessary to add an inoculum of wine yeasts and particularly with highly ameliorated (sugar and water added) fruit musts, yeast, yeast nutrients such as ammonium phosphate, and yeast extract are likely to be beneficial. Since the juices of most of these fruits are highly susceptible to oxidative browning reactions and other deterioration, moderately high levels of sulfur dioxide (100–200 parts per million) and minimal contact with air are employed.

Most of these wines are marketed with residual fermentable sugar and therefore require a final pasteurization or sterile filtration to maintain them biologically stable after bottling. The tannin level is ordinarily low in fruit wines and they are not as

196

stable to air or as easily fined or clarified as the wines from wine grapes. Bentonite fining is used. Pectin-splitting enzymes and other complex enzyme mixtures are often used to aid in fruit-juice recovery and clarification. These wines are seldom aged; they are finished and marketed young with essentially the same techniques and considerations as for any sweet white or rosé table wine, except that only *Vitis labrusca* wines in this group require stabilization with respect to potassium bitartrate, for fruits other than grapes rarely contain it.

Summary.—By-products of the winery such as tartrates, seed tannin, or seed oil are usually of marginal profitability and recovered only in special situations or war emergencies. Accessory products such as concentrated grape juice are becoming more and more important both for sale to other food processors and for use within the winery as a means of prolonging the fermentation season or making other products.

A major class of the specialty wines are the flavored wines, both vermouths and others with specially formulated natural-flavor mixtures. The formulas used for these wines can be generalized to some degree, but for specific products are seldom revealed. The taste of the blender and of the consumer can have free rein.

Fruit wines and other nongrape wine products are often subject to special production problems such as dilution to lower the acid concentration, and addition of sugar and yeast foods to make proper fermentation possible. The products are at their best when they resemble an alcoholic fresh juice of the fruit concerned.

Chapter 13

THE WINES OF FRANCE

France is the most important wine country in the world, not
because of the amount of its production (because in recent
years Italy has sometimes produced more grapes and wine than
France) but for the following reasons: the French per capita
consumption is larger than any other country; France produces
more kinds of important wine types; and aesthetic production
and appreciation of wine have been brought to a higher degree
in France than in any other country.

Vines are grown in all except the northern departments of
France. The most important wine districts are those of Alsace,
Burgundy, the Rhone, the Midi, Bordeaux, the Loire, and
Champagne. (See Figure 27.) In discussing each of these districts and their wines we shall emphasize the factors which
influence the quality of the wine produced in the district, the
types of wine produced, and the use of the wine.

Some French wines are "classified" and certain wine-producing regions are "delimited." In France the *appellations contrôlées* are the most respected (often abbreviated A.C.). However, *vins delimités de qualité supérieure* are of distinctive
character (usually abbreviated V.D.Q.S.). Since this subject is
important in most European wine-producing countries and a
constant bone of contention between European and non-European countries it deserves full consideration.

Fig. 27. The main wine and brandy districts of France.

199

The Wines of France

Certain regions in Europe (e.g., Burgundy) have been famous for the quality of their wines for centuries—so famous that when new wine-producing countries started to produce wines (e.g., California) they labeled their wines after the famous wine districts of Europe. The exclusive right to an appellation of origin has been officially claimed since the Madrid agreement of 1891. The Lisbon agreement of 1958 also reaffirmed this right. Although the right was most often expressed against foreign countries in the twentieth century, it also began, and is still, exercised against wines incorrectly labeled within a single country. The best example of this was in the Champagne region of France where importation of white wines from the south of France so lowered the price of Champagne grapes as to threaten economic ruin. This led to the Champagne riots of 1910 and the promulgation of an early type of *appellations d'origine* for Champagne in 1911.

This, and all later such laws, assumes that the climate, soil, variety (or varieties), and local methods of wine production produce a unique wine type which deserves to be protected by the government. Gradually most of the important wine-producing districts of France have been classified and delimited and the practice now extends to the Douro and other regions in Portugal, to the sherry district near Jerez de la Frontera (with perhaps less rigidity), to many regions in Germany and, recently, to certain Italian districts.

In general, the laws first delimit the district, sometimes on the basis of soil types and geological formation, and sometimes on historical precedents. The variety or varieties which may be used are specified and often their maximum production, the theory being that when a variety is overcropped it no longer has the typical flavor. Restrictions may be placed on minimum per cent alcohol, methods of wine production used, and so on.

It would be naïve to believe that this had solved the problem of authenticity for all wines labeled Burgundy, port, and so forth. The extensive enforcement organizations which have had to be set up and the plethora of lawsuits would indicate that legislating vinous honesty is no easier than legislating any other kind of honesty

Nevertheless, these laws constitute an answer to the non-French "burgundy" producer as to how it should be done, theoretically at least, in France and, of course, a quasi-legal case that, since it is not so done elsewhere, the wines do not have the right to the appellation.

Our own Federal Alcohol Administration Regulation No. 4 expressly prohibits American wines and brandies from using appellations such as Château d'Yquem, Saint-Julien, Saint-Estèphe, and Cognac. Unfortunately, it permits generic use of foreign geographical names such as burgundy and rhine.

The whole subject of *appellations d'origine* is in a state of evolution. There is an obvious disadvantage from the prestige point of view for a California wine to be labeled "burgundy." If California producers developed unique local names, protected by proprietary or regional regulations, and eschewed all foreign appellations, the public might soon forget the foreign appellations. According to this theory the label "California burgundy" simply advertises that the "real thing" is produced in France. There have been some efforts to use regional and coined names in California, but except for the use of varietal appellations most California wines are sold with generic names.

Californian (and Australian and other) producers do not believe that the problem is this simple and have officially resisted any limitations on the right of American producers to use whatever foreign appellations they please. Even the comparatively innocuous limitation of Federal Alcohol Administration Regulation No. 4 was vigorously fought by the official representatives of the California wine industry.

In view of the intransigent positions of both protagonists further discussion does not seem necessary. However, it does weaken the position of all producers of *quality* wines to say that the geographical appellations are without meaning.

201

The Wines of France

ALSACE

From 1870 to 1918 Alsace was occupied by Germany and most of the wines were shipped from Alsace to Germany to blend with German wines. They were sold as ordinary table wines without any indication of origin. Consequently, there was very little demand for quality wines from Alsace, and only a small amount of the wine was bottled. When Alsace was returned to France some decision had to be made in regard to the viticultural industry. Since Alsace had become a part of Germany the great Algerian wine industry had developed to supply blending wines for the low alcohol wines of the Midi. There was thus very little demand for cheap blending wine in France. In fact, France had a surplus of wine in the late 1920's. Consequently, with their higher cost of production there was very little place for ordinary Alsatian wines in the French economy. The decision was made in 1920 that Alsace should produce better-quality wines, wines worthy of being bottled and which would command a sufficiently high price to recompense the growers. The district had no regional designations that were important enough to use as the basis of labeling, and consequently Alsace is the only district of France in which varietal labeling is widely practiced.

Alsace is a cool viticultural area mainly in Region I (p. 46). White varieties are used primarily; the most important traditional variety is Chasselas doré, but since 1920 it has gradually been supplanted by White Riesling, Sylvaner, Gewürztraminer, and small amounts of Chardonnay and other varieties. The wines are fermented in the normal process, but after the fermentation they require a malo-lactic fermentation to reduce the total acidity. The best wines are probably those of Gewürztraminer, although a number of fine Rieslings are produced in the warmer years. The particular vintage is not as important as in Germany, but the best wines are produced in the warmest years.

202

The wines of Alsace are pleasant and fruity, with characteristic grapy varietal flavors. They perhaps are not as crisp and as distinctive as similar wines made in Germany, but they are very good drinking wines for all that, and are, we think, particularly adapted to being served at lunchtime.

Alsace is a good example of how a wine district can improve its quality and achieve recognition. The wines of Alsace are now distributed throughout the world and are a tribute to the attention which the French have been able to give to the production of quality wine.

BURGUNDY

Although the Burgundy region proper is confined to the slopes of the Côte d'Or, it is customary to include Chablis and the districts to the south of the Côte d'Or in the "Burgundy" classification. (See Figure 28.) This is especially true as far as listings in wine lists are concerned.

Chablis is one of the smallest classified wine regions of France and it may be a disappearing wine district. The reason is that vines are grown in a chalk soil in Chablis and the culture of the vine at best is difficult. A series of poor years owing to frost and hail has made the growing of vines in this region more expensive. The sole variety grown is Chardonnay and it ripens only moderately well in Chablis. The exception to this was in 1949 and 1959 when the vines of Chablis ripened their fruit so well that their wines resembled those of Burgundy more than the traditional Chablis.

Characteristically the wines of Chablis are rather high in total acidity, with a crisp and very fruity tart flavor. They are what the French call "fish wines" and are properly served with fish, for their high acidity helps to reduce the fishy flavor. The best wines of Chablis are always labeled with the name of the vineyard following the word Chablis. However, such wines are expensive and are found less and less on the market. Wines labeled simply "Chablis" are of markedly lower quality.

203

The Wines of France

The Côte d'Or is one of the most famous wine districts of
the world and its fame is an ancient one. Vines were certainly
planted in this region during the Roman period and many famous monasteries had vineyards here during the Middle Ages.
It is properly divided into three parts: the Côte de Dijon, the
Côte de Nuits, and the Côte de Beaune, extending about 30
miles from Dijon to just south of Beaune. The Côte de Dijon
is the smallest and least important of the three. The Côte
d'Or is a gentle slope facing to the east, and the soil is generally
calcareous. The climate is about equal to that of Region I, and
consequently only early-ripening varieties can be planted here.
The best ripening is achieved on the well-drained warmer
slopes. There is no reason to believe that the calcium content
of the soil per se has anything directly to do with the quality
of the wine. More likely the higher quality is related to the fact
that calcareous soils are well drained and the temperature of
the soil (and of the microclimate directly above the soil) is
higher in well-drained soils. Grapes grown in a similar soil on
the lower slopes or in the valley do not ripen nearly as well as
those on the well-drained slopes above. Since this is a cool region, the extra ripening of the warmer soils is of very great
importance so far as the composition of the musts and the
quality of the wines are concerned.

The best red wines are all made from the variety Pinot noir
or from selections (clones) thereof, but on the lower slopes some
Gamay is grown. There are many different clonal selections of
the Pinot noir variety, some of them differing appreciably in
the amount of color in the skins. The wines of Burgundy thus
vary considerably in color. They also vary in color because more
attention may be given to the extraction of color from the skins
during alcoholic fermentation in some cellars. In several cellars
the musts are warmed after crushing and before fermentation,
and in others the cap is manipulated so that more color is extracted from the skins.

The sole variety planted for the best white wines is Chardon-

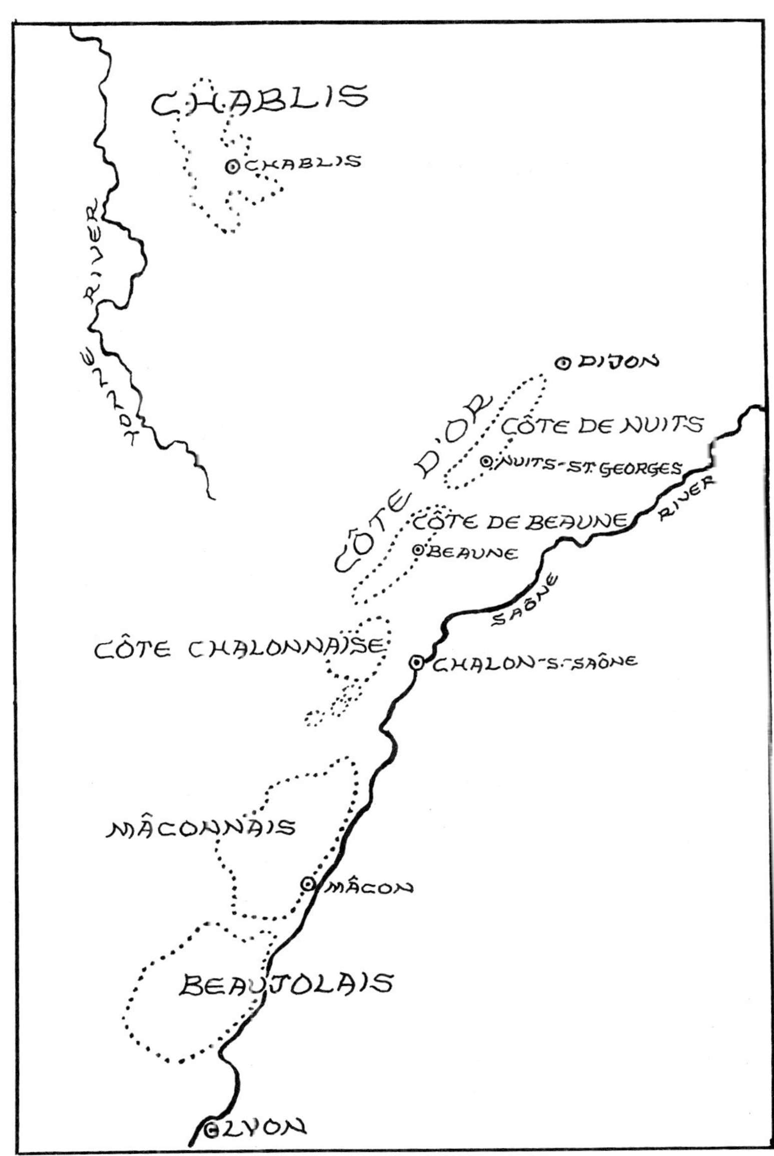

Fig. 28. The Côte d'Or and related districts in France.

nay, but on the lower slopes there are some Aligoté vineyards. Aligoté makes a pleasant wine, but the climate of Burgundy is too cool for it and it rarely ripens sufficiently to show its best quality. Because of the cool climate it is often necessary to add sugar to the musts of Aligoté, to those of Chardonnay occasionally, and to those of Pinot noir about two or three years in five. Some producers add sugar almost every year.

After pressing of the whites the fermentation is carried out in relatively small cooperage, 50–250 gallons. The reds may be fermented in 500- to 2,000-gallon open vats. Following pressing the final fermentation takes place in relatively small cooperage. The wines are usually aged in 50-250-gallon barrels.

The nomenclature of Burgundy wines can be rather complicated. The best wines come from small vineyards and are usually given the name of the vineyard. Thus we have, in the Côte de Nuits, Clos de Vougeot, and in the Côte de Beaune, Pommard. However, many of the vineyards have been subdivided. The famous vineyard Romanée has been subdivided into La Romanée, Romanée-Conti, and Romanée-Saint Vivant. The same is true of Pommard, which has the vineyards Les Épenots, Les Rugiens, Les Argillières, etc.

Sometimes a village appropriates the name of its most famous vineyard and the wines of the village are sold with this hyphenated name: for example, Chassagne-Montrachet and Vosne-Romanée—the towns of Chassagne and Vosne having appropriated the name of their most famous vineyard. In the case of Montrachet which lies between two villages both have attached the name—Chassagne-Montrachet and Puligny-Montrachet. Some wines are sold just as Bourgogne, without village or vineyard appellation. These are certainly of lesser quality and are sold at a lower price. Occasionally one finds Burgundy labeled Hospices de Beaune. This is a charity hospital in Beaune which owns a number of fine vineyards. The Hospices make these wines and usually bottle them with the name of the person who gave them the vineyard. Many of these vineyards are in the Côte de Beaune.

Most experts consider the red wines of the Côte de Nuit to be the best. Most of the great white wines come from the southern part of the Côte de Beaune—from Meursault and Montrachet.

The red wines contain considerable alcohol, frequently as much as 13 or more per cent. They are soft, that is, not high in acid or in tannin, and they have a most intriguing ripe grape odor from the Pinot noir grapes. The occupational disease of the reds is to have been sugared too much so as to raise their alcohol content and to increase color extraction. In some wines the musts have been heated too much to facilitate color extraction and the wines have acquired a special (undesirable) odor. Occasionally the wines have undergone too prolonged a malolactic fermentation, so we find bottles on the market which are gassy. Formerly some old Burgundies developed a bitter taste, but in recent years this seems to be rare, probably owing to the discreet use of sulfur dioxide. Good recent vintage years have been 1959, 1961, 1962, and 1964.

The whites likewise are high in alcohol. Many of the 1959's had about 14 per cent and some did not ferment completely dry. In any year they are very rich wines with the characteristic ripe almost fig-like odor of Chardonnay grapes, particularly in the warmer years.

While the red Burgundies may last for five to ten or more years, in recent years the white Burgundies have shown a tendency to go "off" in three to five years. This is usually evidenced by darkening of the color and the development of a distinct oxidized odor. Whether this is a permanent development involving changes in winery practice or only reflects the climatic conditions of the last few years we do not yet know. For the first time white Burgundies have begun to appear on the market with noticeable sulfur dioxide.

South of the Côte d'Or are a few Pinot noir vineyards producing good wines under Region II climatic conditions. The slopes are not as definite to the east and the soil is not as highly calcareous as in the Côte d'Or. For this reason the grapes do not ripen quite as well and the wines do not have as much quality. A little farther south, in Beaujolais, the main red variety is Gamay and not Pinot noir. Here it makes an early maturing, very fruity red wine which is one of the most popular luncheon or above-average-quality wines of France. Some Chardonnay has been planted at Pouilly-Fuissé. A Pouilly-Fuissé can be a very good bargain indeed because it does not have the snob appeal and exaggerated price of the high-quality white Burgundies of Montrachet or Meursault. However, it must be admitted that it does not have the vinosity or over-all quality of a fine white Burgundy.

THE RHONE

A number of important red and pink wines are produced in the viticultural districts south of Lyon. The climate becomes progressively warmer toward the south of the Rhone Valley. Conditions in the northern vineyards are as cold as in Region II, but many of the southern vineyards are in Region III and in certain years as warm as in Region IV. The first district, with an *appellation contrôlée* is Côte Rotie. The vineyards of Côte Rotie are planted to Viognier (a white variety) and Petite Sirah (a red). These are blended in the vineyard as well as during fermentation. The wines are high in color and rather tannic, and age slowly in the cask for three or four years and in the bottle. Wines fifteen or twenty years old from the Côte Rotie may just be coming to their peak maturity. The wines throw considerable sediment during the aging in the bottle, but are not difficult to decant off the sediment prior to serving.

The Hermitage district farther south is likewise a red wine district, although a very small amount of white wine is produced. The variety used for the red, Petite Sirah, produces a wine of fine color and marked tannin. Old red wines of twenty and thirty years of age from this district may be tasted at their peak quality. The tannin obviously acts as an antioxidant during the aging of these wines and helps to maintain them free

Fig. 29. Vineyard in Beaujolais. Source: Amerine and Cruess

of oxidation for long periods of time. Usually the wines are decanted before shipment if they have thrown much sediment. In addition, it is usually necessary to decant them before serving. The whites are Marsanne and La Roussette (a variety of Marsanne which is replacing the old variety Roussanne).

The region near Avignon called Châteauneuf-du-Pape has an ancient viticultural reputation, but the district fell into bad planting practices after the invasion of phylloxera. By 1911 it was no longer considered one of the better wines of France. Thanks to the efforts of the growers the varietal planting has been greatly improved and the wines of Châteauneuf-du-Pape have now achieved a very sound reputation for quality. The most important variety is Grenache, although several other varieties are permitted by the regulations of *appellations d'origine*. Other varieties include Clairette blanche, Terret noir, Picpoule and Carignane. The reason for continuing the mixed planting is that Grenache does not have a high color, and to

209

produce a good red wine some better-colored varieties are necessary. Although the wines of Châteauneuf-du-Pape are not high in color or in tannin, they do age very well, although perhaps not quite so long as the wines of Côte Rotie and Hermitage. A little white Châteauneuf-du-Pape is also produced. The wines of this region have considerable robustness and alcoholicity and can be very good indeed when they are about ten years of age.

Across the Rhone River from Châteauneuf-du-Pape, near the town of Tavel, Grenache is grown by itself and is used to produce a pink wine. It is well known in France and is occasionally exported to the United States. Unfortunately, the Tavels are rather highly sulfured to reach the American market in good condition and they have a tendency to oxidation and development of a slight bitter aftertaste. They are better drunk in France than in this country, and even there tend to be a little alcoholic for a rosé.

PROVENCE AND THE MIDI

In spite of the contrary opinion of local enthusiasts, the wines of Provence barely rate mention. The varieties are undistinguished, the climate hot, and the rosé wines passable. There are exceptions to most rules and a few better wines can be found, but the very few wines entitled to an *appellation contrôlée* indicate the opinion of the French.

Quantitatively the Midi is by far the most important grape-growing district of France and probably the most intensely cultivated grape-producing area of the world, with the possible exception of Fresno County in California. Over one-third of the wine produced in France comes from the four departments of Aude, Hérault, Gard and Pyrénées-Orientales. All the way from Marseille west to the Spanish border one sees nothing but vast vineyards of Aramon, Carignane, Alicante Bouschet, and other *gros producteurs*. It is a district of high yields—8, 10, and 12 tons to the acre, of low alcohol content (7, 8, and 9 per cent are common) and generally undistinguished wines. Only a few of the vineyards in the whole of the south of France are allowed a geographical *appellation contrôlée*. Among these are the muscatel from Frontignan and the various red sweet wines from the Pyrénées-Orientales department, especially Banyuls from the region near the Spanish border. Minervois and Corbières are examples of wines entitled to the lesser *vins delimités de qualité supérieure* and in the Aude and Pyrénées-Orientales a fair amount are produced. But these are only a drop in the bucket to the ocean of ordinary red, pink, and white wines produced in the departments of Hérault and Gard. The economic importance of Algeria to France was that the high-alcohol wines of Algeria were imported specifically to blend with the low-alcohol wines of the Midi in order to produce the 9, 10, and 11 per cent alcohol wines which the French worker drinks every day with his lunch and dinner. Recently there have been efforts to improve the quality of wines of local regions in the Midi, but few of these have yet appeared on the American market. Because of the moderating influence of the Mediterranean, it is not a region of very warm climates. But the exposure is to the south and the vineyards on the upper slopes develop a higher percentage of alcohol, and warm conditions reduce the acidity.

BORDEAUX

When Eleanor of Aquitaine married the Duke of Normandy and Count of Anjou (later Henry II of England) in 1152 she brought with her as her dowry all the southwestern third of France. For 300 years the British ruled Bordeaux and left many imprints on the region. A large and important wine trade developed between Bordeaux and the British Isles. The British taste for clarets has dominated the Bordeaux wine picture for many centuries. The English law of inheritance by the eldest son has been applied in Bordeaux and therefore the large holdings have been maintained more or less intact. It is not a small

211

region viticulturally, with over 250,000 acres of grapes and a production which varies from about 50 million to 130 million gallons per year.

The location of the important districts are indicated in Figure 30: Médoc, Graves, Sauternes, Saint-Émilion, and Pomerol are the most important for quality. These are all entitled to an *appellation contrôlée,* and the names of the districts are found on the labels on the French as well as the American market.

The Médoc is the most important red wine-producing district of the Bordeaux region and one of the most important in the world. It is a region of rolling hills and the exposure and soil conditions are not critical, although there are local prejudices in favor of some vineyard areas and against others. The unique feature of the Bordeaux district is the relatively large size of the vineyards—many of 15 to 50 acres and some of 100 and even 200 acres. Whether large or small, the vineyards are commonly called "châteaux."

The Médoc itself is divided into a number of communes—Saint-Julien, Saint-Estèphe, Pauillac, Margaux—and wines produced within these communes also are entitled to an *appellation contrôlée.* Many wines are bottled under the label of the commune. Saint-Julien was so well known in California before Prohibition that some California producers actually called their wine St. Julien because of a fancied resemblance to wine of the Bordeaux district.

Within the communes are many individual vineyards. The *appellation contrôlée* applies to the commune, not to the vineyard, name.

In 1855 the wines of the Médoc were classified for the last time officially and this classification is still often quoted. It divided the best vineyards into five categories: first, second, third, fourth, and fifth growths, or *crus.* The classification obviously was related to the prices paid on the Bordeaux market for the wines in 1855.

Since that time some of the châteaux have increased their

212

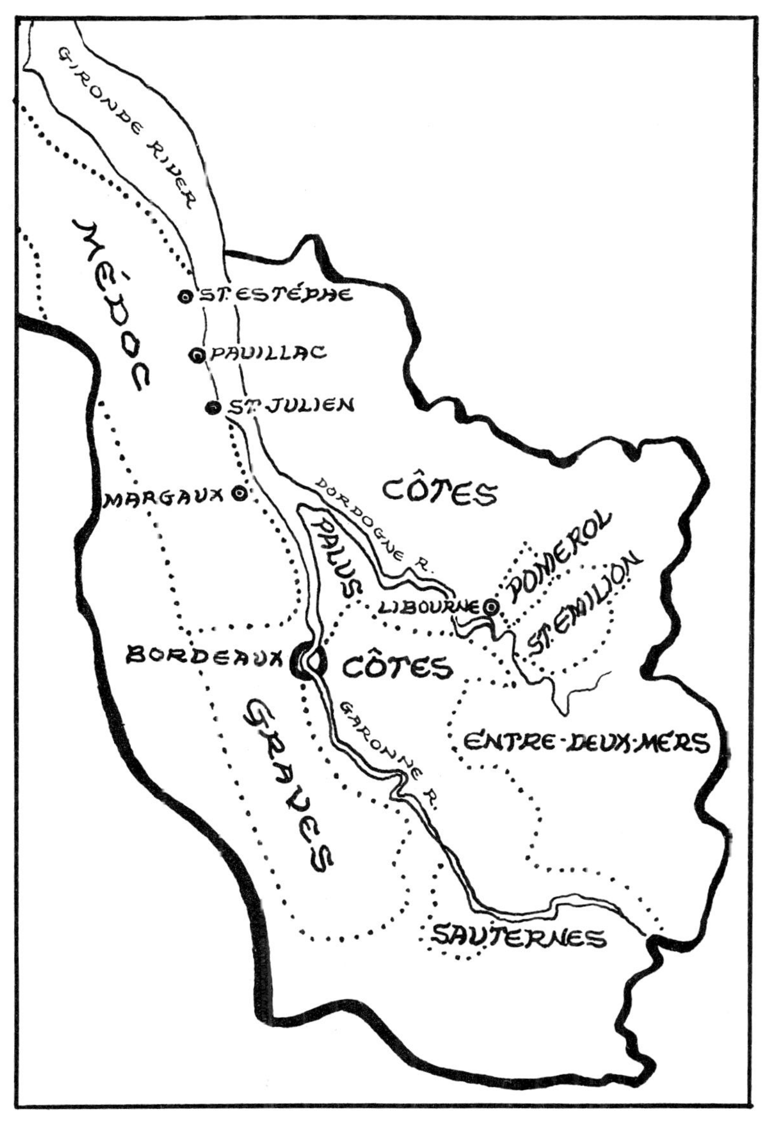

FIG. 30. The Bordeaux district in France.

plantings, phylloxera caused many changes in the varietal selection (*encépagement*), the owners have changed (some several times), wine-making procedures have been greatly modified (especially in some châteaux), and the ability of the managers of the châteaux has certainly varied. Wines of certain châteaux which may have achieved a relatively high price in 1855 may sell today at a lesser relative price, and thus may not really be entitled to a rank above wines of other châteaux of the district. The merchants in Bordeaux would like to change the classification, but châteaux which now have a high classification are not willing to see any change made. Certainly the classification of 1855 is only a rough guide to the quality of the wines of Bordeaux and the wine merchants' prices more clearly reflect the quality of the wines than the classification of 1855. Nevertheless, the first four big growths of that classification, Château Latour (largely English-owned), Château Margaux (to be distinguished from the wines from the commune of Margaux), Château Lafite-Rothshield, and Château Haut-Brion still produce some of the best wines. Strictly speaking, the latter château is in Graves, but was classified with the Médocs because of its great character. It is now essentially American-owned.

Formerly the major châteaux bottled their wine at the château only in the best years. Recently the demand for these wines has been so great that they are bottled at many of the châteaux in poor as well as in good years. The cult of château-bottling may have been desirable when the quality of the wines differed so much from each other and from year to year. Even then a certain amount of sound château wine was exported for bottling abroad. Finally, a few châteaux do not bottle at the château and are thus not entitled to magical *mis en bouteilles au château* or *mise du château*. What such "label drinkers" forget is that it is the quality of the wine that counts: as long as the Bordeaux châteaux insist on bottling their wine at the château in good and poor years the practice is meaningless.

214

The Graves is best known for its white wine, but actually more red than white is produced in this region. The reds are usually sold as Graves or sometimes with the château name. They are not of exceptional quality, however, and they are certainly not as good a buy as the wines of the Médoc with the exception of a few especially fine vineyards. The white wines of the Graves are widely distributed simply as Graves, although many château-bottled white wines are sold. The whites are produced from Sémillon and Sauvignon blanc in the ratio of about 1 to 2. These are dry to slightly sweet white wines which tend to be rather high in sulfur dioxide. One can usually find better bargains in white wines elsewhere in France than from Graves. In fact, one could predict that the enological practices of Graves will probably improve during the next decade to reduce the sulfur dioxide and to improve clarity.

Sauternes is the most famous sweet white table wine of France. It is probably best exemplified by the wine of its premier vineyard, Château d'Yquem. In Sauternes the same varieties as in Graves are planted, Sémillon and Sauvignon blanc, but the ratio here is about 2 to 1 in favor of Sémillon. This greater planting of Sémillon exists because it is somewhat more subject to a fungus, *Botrytis cinerea*, which is necessary for the production of the sweet wines (p. 63).

The effect of *Botrytis* is to loosen the skin and hasten moisture loss from the berry. This results in a decrease in the volume of the berry and hence in an increase in the concentration of the sugar. The shriveled berries also have a high concentration of odor and tannin because of the larger surface-to-volume relationship of the shriveled berry. There is a special flavor due to *Botrytis*. From these musts wines of 12 to 14 per cent alcohol and from 5 to 15 per cent sugar are produced. The production of Sauternes is a climatological phenomenon because the growth of *Botrytis* depends upon having a high humidity for short periods of time to secure infection. These periods of high humidity must be followed by dry periods so that moisture loss

215

will be encouraged and the berries can shrivel. Similar conditions exist in many years in vineyards on the Loire and in most years in Germany.

Saint-Émilion is a wine district which has only recently been classified. Its wines have markedly improved their quality in the twentieth century. The two best vineyards, Château Cheval Blanc and Château Ausone, are now as well known and as expensive as any of the premier châteaux of the Médoc. The same varieties are planted here as in the Médoc, namely, Cabernet Sauvignon, Cabernet franc, Malbec, and Merlot. But these varieties are all of the Cabernet family and have similar varietal aromas. The Cabernet franc, planted more here than in the Médoc, tends to make the wines a little softer, but the difference in tannin is not great. The wines of Saint-Émilion are a little softer than those of the Médoc, since the grapes are more protected from the cool Atlantic breezes which reach the Médoc. But it is not correct, as is frequently claimed, that the wines of Saint-Émilion resemble those of Burgundy. If they resemble any other French red wines it is the wines of the Médoc or the other red wines of Bordeaux.

Next door to Saint-Émilion is Pomerol, a region whose production of quality wines also seems to be on the increase. The wines, however, greatly resemble those of Saint-Émilion, but because they are less well-known they are likely to be better buys for the immediate future than those of Saint-Émilion. Château Petrus, however, is by no means inexpensive.

Large amounts of ordinary red and white wine are produced throughout the Bordeaux district. If sold inexpensively, say about $1.00 or less per bottle, they may be worth investigating.

THE LOIRE

All along this river there are vineyards, some of considerable extent and vinous importance. In the east near Sancerre and Pouilly-sur-Loire, vineyards are planted to Sauvignon, which seems not to be the same as Savignin blanc of the Jura, but rather similar to the Sauvignon blanc of Graves and Sauternes. These are white wines of moderate quality and are usually dry. When they are not too highly sulfured and in years when their alcohol content gets as high as 11 or 12 per cent they can be quite nice wines. But by no stretch of the imagination can they be considered high quality wines.

A little farther west are the vineyards near Vouvray which are the best known vineyards of the Loire. They were planted to Chenin blanc, which here is often called Pineau blanc de la Loire.* The wines of Vouvray can be either dry or sweet; some are slightly but naturally sparkling, called *pétillant*, and others are made sparkling by fermentation in the bottle (and are sold as Vouvray *mousseux*). The *pétillant* wines are said not to travel well, for they lose this gassiness when they are shipped through warm regions or held under warm conditions. It is probably true that the best wines of Vouvray are to be drunk in Vouvray. In the very best years, when it is humid and then warm, a considerable amount of *Botrytis* will cause the berries to reach high sugar, and naturally sweet Vouvrays are produced. Some of these age very well and reach qualities which approach those of a good Sauternes.

Still farther west are the vineyards around Saumur and Angers. Here again the Chenin blanc is the predominant variety and the wines are generally dry and white, but occasionally one finds a sweet white wine in the best years.

A little to the south are the wines of Chinon and Bourgueil where some rather light red wines are produced from Cabernet Sauvignon or Cabernet franc. They are by no means as good as even the wines of the lesser districts of Bordeaux.

Finally, at the very end of the Loire near Nantes are the wines produced from the variety Melon and known as Muscadet. They have no connection, however, with muscat wines, as they are dry and white and have a very pleasant, but non-

---

* This is the origin of the mistaken idea in California of labeling the Chenin blanc as White Pinot.

217

muscat, character. They are rather good buys at the present time because the district has only recently been delimited and the wines have not yet achieved sufficient reputation to demand excessive prices.

CHAMPAGNE

The Champagne district south of Reims is the coldest district where grapes are grown in France. It is also one of the most famous single wine districts in the world. The wines originally produced in this district were dry white and red wines of no particular merit. However, about 150 years ago the commercialization of the wines of the district began, and the present type of sparkling wine gradually developed in the nineteenth century.

The industry was an extremely hazardous one in the early years until methods of determining sugar could be developed, and it was not until the latter part of the nineteenth century that the industry entered into its prosperous period. Before this many of the wines had been bottled with too much sugar and the bottles broke during fermentation in the bottle. However, the development of accurate methods of determining the sugar content made it possible to add the exact amount of sugar, and breakage was reduced to only 1 or 2 per cent.

At present about two-thirds of the vineyards are planted to Pinot noir and one-third to Chardonnay. The district is strictly delimited; in fact, it is the prototype of the classification of districts under *appellation d'origine*. This delimitation took place following the Champagne riots when growers rebelled against the importation of white wines from the south of France for the production of wines to be sold as Champagne.

Because it is necessary to produce a white wine from dark grapes, the grapes must be completely free of damaged or moldy fruit. In such fruit the pigments from the skin will get into the juice and it will not be possible to produce a white wine. The red grapes must be hand sorted to remove the undesirable berries. Also, it is not possible to crush the fruit in the usual type of crusher, since any contact of the crushed fruit with the juice will lead to an increase in the color of the juice. Therefore, the black grapes are pressed in large flat presses directly without crushing. The black grapes are tolerated only because they ripen a little before the Chardonnay and thus give the wine a little more alcohol than if it were made completely from white grapes. This balancing of the wines of the white and the red grapes is one of the secrets in preparation of Champagne. Nowadays the primary fermentation is carried on in large containers and the wines are clarified by fining and filtration so that they are ready for the secondary bottling by the spring of the year following the vintage.

The Champagne companies produce two basic types of wine. The so-called vintage Champagne must be at least 80 per cent from the wines of the given year. The blending involves more or less wine from white grapes and the blending of wines from vineyards in different parts of the Champagne district. Each company has its own blending formulas for assembling the *cuvée* of a vintage Champagne. It should be emphasized that a vintage wine is not made every year but only in the years when at least 80 per cent of wine of superior quality can be assembled from that particular year. The other 20 per cent is wine blended in from other years to increase the alcohol or adjust the acidity or for adjusting the flavor.

The second main type of Champagne produced today is the nonvintage type, a blend of wines of both white and red grapes from various parts of the Champagne district and from several different years. Here the wines are not, of course, of as high a quality as the vintage Champagnes, but they are assembled with great care so that the nonvintage Champagne of a given company will have a characteristic and uniform flavor from one year to the next.

Whichever type of wine is being produced, the appropriate amount of sugar and multiplying yeast is added and the wines

219

are then bottled and properly corked. The secret of making high-quality Champagne is that the wine should remain in the bottle in contact with the yeast for at least one year. The development of the so-called "Champagne nose" depends on the autolysis of the yeast cells and the development of new types of odorous materials from the products of autolysis. It is believed that the amino acids account in part for the development of these new nuances of odor. The wines are then placed on racks to bring the sediment down onto the cork, are later disgorged, and the appropriate amount of *dosage* is made in order to produce the various types of Champagne: *brut, sec, demi-sec, doux*. The *dosage* is prepared from a sweetened wine and Cognac.

Champagne, then, is a blended wine produced by careful secondary fermentation in the bottle and finally given its proper cachet by the addition of the appropriate amount of *dosage*.

The appeal of Champagne is partly psychological—Champagnes are almost synonymous with the *nouveaux riches*, with high society, and perhaps with proposals, weddings, christenings, and anniversary celebrations. However, the appeal of Champagne is not merely psychological, but involves the special character of the Champagne nose referred to above. It is not difficult to detect the difference between a Champagne wine and sparkling wines produced from other districts where the varieties of grapes, the climate, and the processes used are different.

Summary.—The reputation for the high quality of some French wines is certainly justified. The important factors contributing to quality include variety of grape, exposure of vineyards, soil temperature, wine-making procedures, and proper aging of the wines. The maintenance of this reputation for quality depends on the honesty and idealism of individual producers and on the strict French laws which delimit the grape-growing regions, control the varieties which may be planted (and their maximum production), determine the minimum percentage of alcohol, and to a certain extent standardize wine production.

Among the external forces which have greatly influenced the French wine industry is the export market, particularly of Great Britain, Belgium, Switzerland, and lately the United States. The standards of the English market have been particularly influential in the Bordeaux wine industry. Unfortunately, the recent increase in demand has forced prices upward.

But the greatest factor has probably been the French people, who consume over thirty gallons per capita and whose pride in the quality of French wines helps immeasurably in maintaining high quality. Many poor wines are, of course, produced in France, and some are even exported. But France also produces some of the finest—wines whose fame have made them the prototype for similar wines produced in other countries.

Chapter 14

THE WINES OF NORTHERN AND EASTERN EUROPE

Most of the wines of Germany, Switzerland, Czechoslovakia, Austria, and Hungary are white wines, and they bear a family resemblance to each other because of the cool climate under which they are produced.

GERMANY

Germany is not a large grape-growing or wine-producing country, but it is important because of the high quality of its wines. Probably a larger percentage of the wines of Germany are prepared for bottling than those of any other country. This is all the more remarkable when we consider that in nearly every year most of the musts of Germany need to be sugared so that the wines will contain a normal amount of alcohol. The alcohol content of German wines tends to be low—usually only 9 or 10 per cent. Because of the cool climate the natural acidity is always excessive and malo-lactic fermentation is invariably practiced to reduce the excessive tartness.

The most important wine districts of Germany are along the Rhine River (Figure 31). In the south, opposite Alsace, there are wines in Baden. In spite of local enthusiasm they are not of memorable quality, with occasional exceptions. Much Chasselas doré is still planted, which limits the quality obtainable.

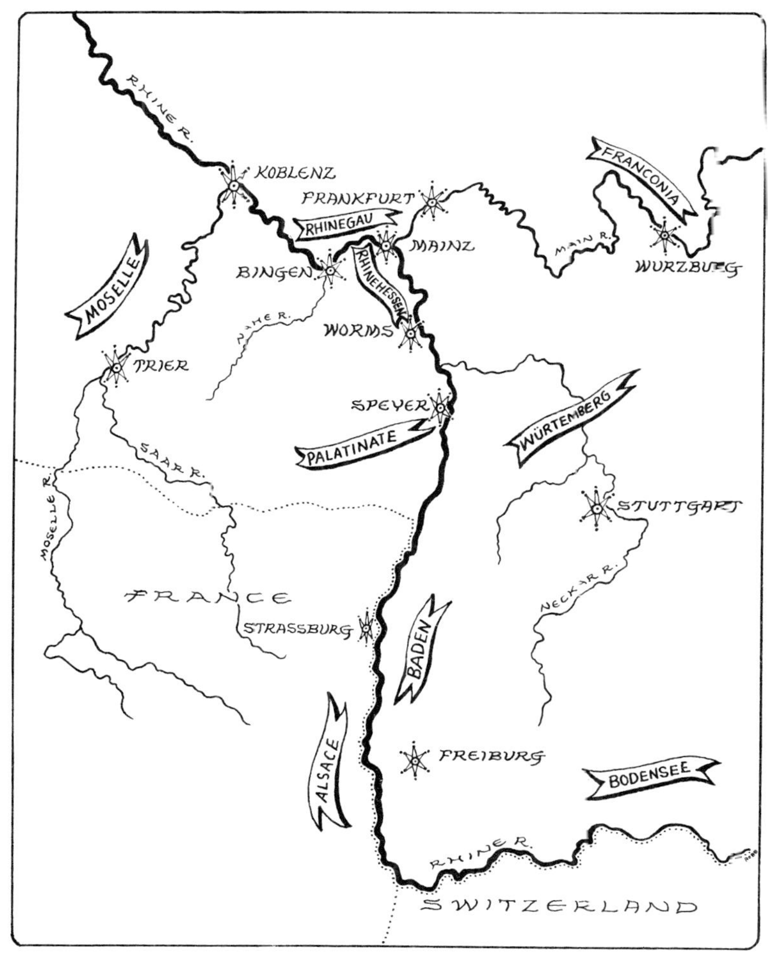

Fig. 31. Main wine districts of Germany.

223

Slightly to the north, in the Pfalz (Palatinate), many good wines and occasionally great wines are produced. In this district Sylvaner predominates, but some White Riesling is planted here also. Most of the vineyards face to the east.

Farther north, still on the Rhine, is the Rheinhessen, a district of many common wines, but occasionally a better quality of white wine is produced. Again, Sylvaner is the predominant variety, but some White Riesling is also planted here. From it in the best years and locations the finer wines are produced. Across the river from Pfalz and Rheinhessen, grapes are grown in Würtenberg, but they are hardly worth the detour, with a few local exceptions. At the northwestern corner of the Rheinhessen there is the small Nahe River wine district. Some of its wines are excellent.

The most famous and finest wine district of Germany, the Rheingau, extends from Wiesbaden directly west to Rudesheim. Here the vineyards are growing on the north bank of the river, facing south, where the exposure to the sun is most favorable. In contrast to the earlier districts, the White Riesling is the predominant variety. The wines of the Rheingau are by far the biggest and most powerful wines of Germany. They are usually the finest wines of Germany, particularly in certain years.

From Wiesbaden the Main River leads south and east, and near Würzburg is the important district of Franconia where fine wines are produced. Again, Sylvaner predominates, but the soil conditions are somewhat different here and the wines have a different flavor and a lower acidity than those of the other German districts. This may be owing to differences in soil. The wines are always bottled in stubby bottles called *Boxbeutel* (or *Bocksbeutel*) rather than in the tall and graceful brown and green bottles which predominate on the Rhine and the Moselle, respectively.

The last important wine district in Germany is along the Moselle River, and its tributaries the Ruwer and Saar. Vines

224

Fig. 32. Terraced vineyards on the Moselle. Source: Presse- und Informationsamt der Bundesregierung, Bonn.

are grown where they will get the best drainage, hence warmer soils, and the best exposure to the sun, Figures 32 and 33. The White Riesling is the predominant variety and in the opinion of many connoisseurs the wines of the Moselle at their best are equal to, and sometimes better than, those of the Rheingau. In general the wines of the Moselle are a little more tart and perhaps have a more definitely flowery aroma than those of the other German districts.

Since most of the musts of Germany need to be sugared, it is important that we be able to recognize from the label whether a wine has been made from a sugared must. The word *Naturwein* (or *Natur, Rein, Naturrein,* etc.) on the label means that the wine is not made from a sugared must. Also, if it is labeled *Spätlese, Auslese, Beerenauslese, Trockenbeerenauslese, Original-Abfüllung, Cabinet* (or *Kabinett*), *Kellerabzug, Fass No.* (or *Fuder No.*), it will not have been sugared.

In general, German wines are sold with the village name and this will be followed by the vineyard name for the better wines. Wines which are labeled simply Moselle or Rhine are likely to be of lower quality. There are several exceptions to the village-vineyard type of naming. For Schloss Johannisberg, the name of the Schloss is considered sufficient to identify the wine. *Schloss* is the German equivalent of the French château. Schloss Vollrads and Steinberg are other examples. Liebfraumilch at one time meant a wine of the Rheinhessen, but now means almost any white wine from Germany and has no quality standards whatever. Most of the wines of Germany would be dry if they were not fermented at low temperatures and if no sugar were added. The *Auslese* series of wines are always sweet because they are made from botrytised grapes. (See p. 63.)

If the grapes are simply picked late, they may be labeled *Spätlese.* In most wines some botrytised grapes are included and the wine will usually be slightly sweet. *Auslese* (to pick

FIG. 33. Terraced vineyard on the Moselle. Source: Presse-
und Informationsamt der Bundesregierung, Bonn.

out) wines, on the other hand, are made from selected clusters or parts of clusters that have become botrytised. They are
always sweet. *Beerenauslese* (to pick out berries) wines are
produced only in the most favorable years. Parts of the clusters of well-botrytised grapes are harvested. The wines are very
sweet and have an intense concentration of aroma. *Trockenbeerenauslese* (to pick out dry berries) wines are seldom produced. Only botrytised berries which have shriveled are used.
The wines are even more concentrated than those of the *Beerenauslese* and are even more expensive—up to $20 or more per
bottle. The sweeter German wines are best used with desserts.
Botrytis infection is generally most effective in the warm years:
1959 was an exception possibly because of the excessive heat.

German technology has made it possible to filter these wines

227

through germproof filters so that they need not be too high in sulfur dioxide. However, some German wines are still often excessively high in sulfur dioxide and this reduces their quality. Owing to the high standards of enological technology the wines are often clarified and bottled within six months of the vintage. Except for the sweeter types they are best within five years.

A few red wines are produced in Germany, chiefly from Pinot noir grapes, but their quality is only moderate. A good deal of sparkling wine, called *Sekt*, is produced, both by the tank and bottle process. It is well made and reasonable in price but not notable in quality. The best dry German wines for everyday drinking are those with the name of the village and the vineyard, made from unsugared musts and made and bottled by the producer of the wine. Shippers' wines are commonly sold with regional or proprietary labels. They are often inexpensive and are usually of ordinary quality.

Germany again illustrates the importance of variety, soil temperature, and exposure. It also indicates how modern technology can be applied to an old industry without reduction in quality.

The best bargains in German wines are usually not the shippers' wines but those of individual growers, particularly those made without sugaring. Often the lesser-known wines of the Nahe or Pfalz are of comparable quality and more reasonably priced than the better-known Moselles and Rheingaus.

SWITZERLAND

It is surprising that wines are made at all in Switzerland, for the climate is unfavorable for grapes. Most of the vineyards are planted around lakes where the drainage, exposure, and moderating influence of the lake help to ripen the grapes. Even so, to get reasonably ripe grapes it is necessary to use very early ripening varieties: in western Switzerland, where most of the wine is made, the table grape variety, Chasselas doré, is used for wine making. This is not a very satisfactory grape because it is too neutral in flavor for a good wine grape. However, it does ripen sufficiently to reduce the acidity to manageable levels in most years. Nevertheless, its musts usually have to be sweetened. In the very best years it makes a pleasant enough wine which is sometimes bottled with a little carbon dioxide to freshen up its flavor. In eastern Switzerland the Pinot noir is used. The prevalence of fungus diseases causes early harvesting and adds color-destroying enzymes to the must. In spite of all these problems the wines of Switzerland are well made and technically are above reproach. Switzerland illustrates the limitation in quality which a cool climate can impose and the success which technology can make possible.

CZECHOSLOVAKIA

The wines of Czechoslovakia are mainly white and are made of a number of western European varieties such as White Riesling, Sylvaner, Traminer, and others. They tend to be rather light in character, and not high in alcohol, which is what we would expect from the cool climate. It is a small industry, however, and exports little wine.

AUSTRIA

The wines of Austria are primarily white wines, although a few red wines are produced. The most important vineyards are along the Danube, but vines are found in several other parts of Austria as well. The wines are most frequently sold with the name of the grape variety: Traminer, Rotgipfler, Veltliner, etc. Many are sold directly from the barrel as soon as they become brilliantly clear. There is a small export market of Austrian wines. These are reasonable in price, but are often rather neutral in character, lacking the crisp, tart, and flavorful characteristics of German wines.

Because of Austria's cool climate, the major possibilities for the future appear to be in white wines. The varieties are not so standardized as in Germany nor are the regions so highly

229

classified. Therefore one seldom finds a poor Austrian wine and even less often a truly great wine. They are everyday drinking wines. Technically they are well handled, with cooled fermentations and proper clarification.

HUNGARY

The wines of Hungary are of very ancient renown and Tokay (or more correctly, Tokaj) was considered one of the great wines of Europe before the First World War. There are as many acres of vineyard in Hungary as in the United States, about 500,000. Both red and white table wines are produced in Hungary, and the present government has sponsored the expansion of the industry particularly on the sandy soils where lesser quality wines are frequently produced. The government has also officially classified the districts.

In the traditional wine district producing Tokay one revealing grape is the Furmint. Both dry and sweet Tokays were produced, but the most famous were those which retained a certain degree of sugar. Two factors account for the high sugar content: the natural drying of the grapes, which are allowed to hang on the vines until late October; and, in some years, a considerable amount of *Botrytis* infection, which helps to raise the sugar concentration.

In the very finest years the best crushed grapes were piled up and the free-run juice produced by the weight of the berries on each other was kept separate and used to make Tokay *Essenz*. This very sweet wine of low alcohol content was very expensive, fully comparable in price to that of the best *Trockenbeerenauslese* wines of Germany. Little, if any, *Essenz* has been produced since the Second World War.

The less sweet Tokays have more or less of this very sweet juice added to the regular pressed must to raise the sugar content. These were sold as two, four, or six *puttonyos*, the *puttonyo* being a bucketful of the sweet juice added to regular must. These were usually sold under the appellation Aszu

230

Tokay. The drier type is called Szamorodni. They are bottled in a graceful long-necked bottle holding about 500 milliliters (compared to the usual bottle of 700–750 milliliters).

Since the Second World War most of the Tokays on the markets in Western Europe have been found to contain a high amount of hydroxymethylfurfural. This obviously means that grape concentrate has been used to sweeten the must. A further indication of the use of concentrate has been the amber color of the wines. They have therefore not been traditional high-quality Tokays. The Tokays before the Second World War were usually yellow to light gold in color.

In the other districts a wide variety of Western European and local varieties are planted. Ezerjo is a well-known local white variety and Kadarka a local red. The climate varies markedly from season to season and tends to be cool. The white wines are thus usually better than the reds. The best districts are Morer, Badacsony, Debro, Villany-Pecser, Eger, and Somlyöi. Few Hungarian red or white wines reach the American market. They sell at reasonable prices and make an interesting comparison with similar types from other countries. Some of the reds would improve with additional aging.

RUMANIA

The various wine types produced in Rumania have never achieved much fame outside the country. One of the basic problems is that table grape production is important in this country and some of the table grapes inevitably find their way to the crusher and are used for the production of wines. Table grapes are low in acidity and rather high in sugar content and thus are not suited for the production of table wines. This and the use of direct-producing varieties tends to reduce the quality of the wines of this area.

However, there is a good technological background for both viticulture and enology, and marked improvements can be expected. Many fine Western European varieties are grown.

231

All types of wine are produced under both varietal and regional names. The best are said to be the whites, which may indicate rather cool growing conditions. Recently we have tasted some well-made white table and dessert wines from Rumania.

BULGARIA

This is primarily a table grape producing region, but many table and dessert wines are made for local consumption. Local varieties are employed for the most part. The dessert wines are often only 16 to 18 per cent alcohol but with 10 to 18 per cent sugar. The use of table grapes for producing table wine is, again, a negative quality factor, but some wine is produced from fine wine grape varieties.

RUSSIA

The vineyards of Russia are increasing very rapidly in acreage and by 1970 it is estimated that there will be nearly 3,000,000 acres of grapes. Production is only moderate since the vines in many areas must be covered during the winter to prevent winterkilling. This practice weakens the vines and reduces production.

The main districts where grapes are grown are Moldavia, a small district next to Rumania; the Ukraine, which includes the Crimea; the Federal Republic in the region of Krasnodar and Rostov; Georgia, in the Caucasus; Armenia, to the south of the Caucasus; Azerbaidzhan, east of Georgia along the Caspian Sea; and Uzbekistan to the east of the Caspian. A small amount of grapes are grown in other of the Asiatic republics, but they are not very important as yet. Some raisins are made in Uzbekistan and table grapes are important in several areas of the Soviet Union.

All types of wines are produced in Russia, but the best are the dessert wines: wines of very moderate alcohol content, usually from 14 to 16 per cent, but of very high sugar content, from 20 to 24 per cent. This means that the musts are fortified

232

very soon after pressing and have undergone very little alcoholic fermentation. The high sugar content gives the wines some protection against yeast and bacterial contamination and they tend to remain stable. Some have a rather distinct raisin odor, indicating that they have been made from very ripe grapes. The muscats made from Muscat blanc are very interesting wines and of excellent quality. A number of red sweet wines are also made, and many baked wines, which are called "madera." They are also beginning to produce film-yeast sherries. The table wines include a large number of European varieties such as Aligoté, White Riesling, Sylvaner, and Cabernet Sauvignon. There are also a number of native varieties such as Rkatsiteli and Saperavi. While many of the table wines are pleasant, they are not as distinctive or of as high quality as the dessert wines. The appearance (clarity) of some of their wines could be improved.

The Russians have always had a keen interest in sparkling wines. At present they are increasing their production at a very rapid rate. The tank process is used, but it is being modified for continuous operation. The wines are of moderate quality, but have a very good clarity. As would be expected from the taste of Russian consumers for sweet wines, most of them are distinctly on the sweet side. The Russians are increasing their brandy production. The best brandies are said to come from Georgia and Armenia; however, brandies are produced in other districts as well. They are generally aged in the wood, although new processes of treatment of brandies are being introduced.

Summary.—In all the countries discussed in this chapter the white wines are far more important than the reds, primarily because of the difficulty of producing high-quality red wines in regions of high humidity and low temperatures. The exceptions may be some of the red wines of Hungary, Rumania, Bulgaria, and of the Soviet Union.

233

The limitation of climate also restricts the whites to varieties ripening early or in mid-season, well-drained and south-facing slopes, and areas near lakes. Nevertheless, by taking advantage of the action of *Botrytis cinerea* a number of sweet wines are produced. In the Soviet Union and Rumania fortified sweets are also made.

Technology is being increasingly applied to wine-production problems in all these countries.

There's none of these demure boys come to any proof; for thin drink doth so overcool their blood . . . that they fall into a kind of male greensickness; and then when they marry, they get wenches. . . . If I had a thousand sons, the first human principle I would teach them should be, to forswear thin potations and addict themselves to sack.—WILLIAM SHAKESPEARE (Falstaff)

Chapter 15

THE WINES OF SOUTHERN EUROPE

Portugal, Spain, Italy, Yugoslavia, Greece, Cyprus, and Israel * produce wines of distinctly different types from those of the northern countries. Some of the wines of southern Russia, Rumania, and Bulgaria could have been considered here rather than in the preceding chapter.

PORTUGAL

Portugal is one of the most important wine-producing regions of Europe, with an annual production of over 225 million gallons. Most of this is table wine produced in the Estremadura region. It is consumed with meals by the working people of Portugal. Only a few of the table wines of Portugal are above standard quality. One of these, from the Dão region in north-central Portugal, is a soft red wine which responds well to aging. The red wine from the Colares district on the Atlantic coast near Lisbon has some reputation but production is rather low. The wine, however, is interesting because of its high salt content (from ocean breezes). Individual producers produce good wines in a number of other regions, including sparkling, sweet table and dessert types.

---

* Included here for convenience even though not in Europe.

Owing to the intelligent activity of the semigovernmental Junta Nacional do Vinho, table-wine production has been improved greatly. If even higher standards of wine quality could be established, the varietal complement of the vineyards could be changed, and standards developed for different types of wines.

The wines of the Minho region north of Oporto are well known in Portugal. These unique wines are called *vinhos verdes*, literally green wines, from their highly acidic taste. Grapevines are grown on trees in this region. They are thus difficult to prune properly and tend to overproduce. The result is that the grapes do not ripen and are very high in total acidity and low in sugar. During and after the alcoholic fermentation a malo-lactic fermentation occurs and the acidity is somewhat reduced. The wines are bottled, however, at a very high total acidity and the malo-lactic fermentation continues in the bottled wine so that the wines are very gassy when opened. They are thus naturally sparkling red and white wines, but the sparkle has been produced from the malo-lactic rather than from an alcoholic fermentation. The alcoholic content is usually below 10 per cent. Though interesting, they are not high-quality wines in the classical sense—being too low in body, alcohol, and varietal character and some have unusual flavors of bacterial origin.

But the production of two fine dessert wines makes Portugal especially important enologically. Red sweet wines are produced in the valley of the Douro River, which runs in an easterly direction from Oporto into Spain. Here the grapes are planted on steeply terraced slopes in a limited geological area starting about forty miles inland. A wide variety of grapes are grown here; among the most important are Touriga, Tinta Francisca, Bastardo, and Souzão. The reason for the mixture of varieties is that climatic conditions vary rather widely from one year to the next, and it is desirable to have grapes which have high color in the warmer years to blend with grapes which have

236

lesser amounts of color. It is doubtful, however, whether the ideal variety or varieties have yet been determined for this region.

The grapes are crushed, primarily by treading in rather shallow concrete *lagares*. The reason for the treading is more for economy than for quality, since labor has been cheap in this region. As the cost of labor increases the introduction of mechanical equipment for crushing can be expected. The treading continues intermittently for several days and has the effect of keeping the cap submerged a good part of the time. It also seems to cause some disintegration of the skins. Both result in a better extraction of color. During the fermentation, when the sugar content is reduced from 22–25 per cent to about 12–14 per cent, the juice is drawn off and fortified with brandy. The fortification is made to about 18 or 19 per cent alcohol. Later in the year the wines are shipped from the Douro to Oporto for aging. More brandy is added when needed, particularly to the best wines. The typical Douro cask is the port pipe which holds about 138 gallons.

Three different types of wines are produced in the Douro. The very best wines of the best years, which generally means in the cooler years, are shipped to London in casks and are declared a "vintage" port. There they remain for two years and are then bottled. These wines are high in flavor and color and are fortified up to about 21 per cent of alcohol. They age very slowly in the bottle, but after ten to twenty years achieve a distinctive bottle bouquet, the tannin content decreases, and the wines acquire a remarkably soft character. Vintage ports are the epitome of port quality and are always expensive because of the long aging required and the limited quantities available. Dated ports which have been aged in the cask for many years before bottling never have the quality of those which are aged in the classical way in bottles.

Standard red wines are aged in the cask for three or four years before bottling. They have a full red color and are sold as ruby ports. These are the standard drinking wines which are used as a before- or after-meal drink in the English pubs or after dinner in middle-class homes.

A considerable amount of wine with a tawny red color is produced in the Douro. The tawny red color results from the use of the lesser-colored varieties, such as the Bastardo, and also from longer aging of normal red wines. These tawny wines are often lower in sugar than the ruby port wines and have been used as an apéritif wine. However, they are usually served after the meal. Some people prefer the tawny to the ruby ports. A very small amount of white port is produced in the Douro, but it has not achieved great popularity. Some of the drier white ports have also been used as an appetizer, but they are still much too sweet for a proper apéritif.

Port is a "manufactured" wine in the sense that a variety of different styles and qualities of ruby and tawny port are produced by the shipping firms. Large stocks of young and old wines are stored by the shippers in their lodges (storage rooms) at Vila Nova da Gaia (opposite Oporto). The original wines coming down from the Douro are often blended from one *quinta* (the Portuguese equivalent of the French château) to another to achieve the standard types that are necessary. From these different basic types, blends are made to achieve exactly the style and quality of wine which a given consumer might wish. Thus wines differing slightly in color, sugar content, flavor, age, and, of course, price and quality are produced.

Port is one of the great classical types of wines. Soil, climate, and varietal components are undoubtedly important. However, the classification of the wines according to type and quality and the careful blending to produce distinctive types seem equally important. The treading is apparently not a unique factor. The demands of the English market have been paramount in the production of port. The English have obviously developed the type concept and have maintained high standards of quality. Production of port has declined, however, owing mainly to decreased consumption in Great Britain. This is related not to any change in port quality but to changes in English drinking habits. The decrease may be due to the more general use of central heating in the home and hence to a reduction in after-dinner drinking. Health (particularly in relation to obesity) may also be a factor.

Another dessert wine produced by the Portuguese is Madeira, from the main island of the Madeiras on which Funchal is located. This region, 600 miles off the coast of North Africa, has a semitropical climate. Because of the high humidity it is difficult to grow grapes without fungus infection. Before these fungus diseases were introduced in the mid-nineteenth century, from America, grape growing was apparently less difficult. A considerable amount of Jacquez grapes, a variety of American origin, is grown. This variety is believed by the shippers to account, in part, for the moderate quality of some of the modern Madeiras. However, some of the old *Vitis vinifera* varieties such as Boal (Bual in Portuguese) and Verdelho are grown also. However, little Sercial is grown, although some Sercial wine is sold. The musts are generally fermented fairly dry and are then baked in concrete tanks at about 140° F. for three or four months. The wines are then sweetened with fortified grape juice, called *vinho surdo*, and fortified to about 18 per cent (if this is not done earlier) with alcohol (from sugar cane molasses). The driest wines are sold as Sercial; the medium sweet wines, as Boal; and the sweetest wines, as Malmsey. Originally, these referred to the varieties of grapes from which they were produced, but for the standard Madeiras that are shipped today, these refer more to the sugar content than to their varietal complement, although more or less of the variety named may have been used. All these wines have an amber color and a slight caramel flavor from the baking. Again, blending is very important as wines of different ages and different characteristics are blended to make different styles and qualities of Madeira.

239

Occasionally, very old Madeiras reach the market. These are wines which have been kept in a single barrel for a long time and finally bottled, or have been bottled for many years. When they are authentic they can be of high quality, but some of them seem to be overpriced. One of the common negative quality factors to look for in Madeiras is the tendency of the wines to have rather high volatile acidity, an indication of poor wine-making practices. This is an undesirable characteristic and the taster should recognize volatile acidity and avoid it.

Madeiras were much appreciated in the colonies and in the late eighteenth and early nineteenth century in the United States. Their rather high alcohol content, 19 to 20 per cent, recommended them to the colonists; also the fact that they could be bought rather cheaply from the ships which were trading with Madeira; and finally they could be and were aged for long periods of time. A number of American and English firms imported large quantities of Madeiras and gave their own names to these wines. However, it is no longer possible to obtain high-quality Madeiras which have been aged and bottled in this country. The demand for Madeira has been decreasing and probably one of the reasons has been a decline in quality. The baneful influence of the Jacquez variety should also be recognized. The early development of fungus diseases forces early harvesting and prevents the development of the ripe-grape aroma. As better methods of fungus control are developed, this may lead to abandonment of Jacquez and the planting of better-flavored varieties.

SPAIN

Vineyards were probably planted in Spain by the Phoenicians, or at least by the early Greek colonists. A large wine industry was in existence there at the time of the Roman occupation. A number of table grape varieties were imported into Spain during the Moorish domination, but many of the original wine grape varieties were still planted. Today Spain has nearly four million acres in grapes, but production per acre is low. About half a billion gallons of wine are produced annually—mainly table wine—far less than in France or Italy.

The best table wine areas are those of the Rioja, where Grenache and Tempranilla are the leading varieties. This region was developed to its present high standards mainly through the French colonists who settled here when phylloxera invaded the vineyards of France. This is another example of the tremendous economic effects which phylloxera had in that country. The Rioja wines are mainly reds which are usually aged in the Bordeaux fashion, that is, in 50-gallon containers. Some fractional blending (p. 243) was formerly done here and the date on the label simply reflected the vintage of the oldest wine. Nowadays the date on the wine bottle (particularly since 1960) at least usually reflects its actual vintage.

Many red and white table wines are made in the regions around Barcelona, near Valencia, and especially in La Mancha. The latter is the largest and most concentrated vineyard area of Spain. It is planted primarily to white grapes. These wines are rather low in alcohol—11 to 12 per cent—and are not high in acidity. They are the usual bar drink in Spain. They frequently are not very well standardized or stabilized, but they sell at a very low price, only a few cents per glass in the ordinary bars. The increasing standard of living and the quality of the beer and whiskey available, together with the lack of quality of many of these La Manchan whites, has sharply reduced wine consumption in Spain. The reds from Valencia are often high in alcohol. Good standard table and sparkling wines are produced near Barcelona plus a number of dessert wines. Of these the best are those of Sitges (white) and from the region called Priorato (*rancio* types)

Spain is important as a wine-producing country on the international market primarily because of two dessert wine types: the sherry and the sherry-like types of wines of Jerez de la Frontera and Montilla and the Málaga type of wines produced

241

in or near the town of Málaga. Tarragona and Priorato dessert wines were formerly exported and presumably could be again if they were standardized in quality and if a demand could be developed.

The wines of Jerez de la Frontera have been known in England for many centuries, and were mentioned by Shakespeare as "sack" or "sherris sack." Up until the middle of the nineteenth century they seem to have been white wines of 15 or 16 per cent alcohol, both dry and sweet, aged by rather normal processes in large *bodegas*. However, the process of developing a yeast film on the sherry seems to have achieved wide acceptance in the district in the early nineteenth century, and since that time many of the best-known wines of the sherry district have been produced by this interesting process.

A number of white varieties are grown, but the Palomino is the most important. It is planted mainly in highly calcareous soils. The importance of the soil is generally admitted, possibly owing to a higher sugar in grapes grown on these soils. To get the sugar content even higher the grapes are often left on trays for two or three days before crushing. The crushing is traditionally done by walking on the grapes and the pressing is done both in a primitive hydraulic presses and in modern continuous presses. Currently the crushing and pressing is being modernized—another reflection of the increasing cost of labor.

Palomino may not be the ideal grape for sherry production because of the moderate normal sugar content, the pulpy nature of the fruit, and the low total acidity of its musts. For this reason calcium sulfate is commonly added to increase the acidity. This is called "plastering." Tartaric acid has also been used to raise the acidity.

After fermentation the new wines are allowed to remain in the same containers in which the must fermented. At this time the containers are only about three-quarters full. A secondary stage of the wine yeast, which causes the alcoholic fermentation, in this case *Saccharomyces beticus*, or a closely

242

related species, forms a film (called *flor* in Spain) stage on the surface of the wine. This film stage utilizes alcohol and acetic acid as a carbon source and produces aldehydes as one of several important odorous products. The film process may continue for a number of years. The film is not present on the surface of the wine continuously throughout the year. Usually it forms on the surface during the spring and again during the fall. Thus a rather large deposit of yeast forms in the bottom of the container and the flavor of these *flor*-type sherries seems to be due to both the aldehyde and aldehyde by-products which are formed by the film itself and to autolysis products from the yeast deposit. The production of the cheaper *flor* sherries could probably be speeded up by keeping the casks at a constant temperature

The sweeter, darker, more tannic, and generally lower quality wines may be fortified to 18 or more per cent alcohol shortly after the vintage and thus never undergo a film stage. These wines become the *oloroso* type when blended and aged.

But the film process or the classification into *fino* and *oloroso* types does not explain the uniformity of quality and type of the different Spanish sherries. A system of fractional blending has been used for many years in the sherry district and this, the *solera* system, accounts for the uniformity in quality and in type characteristics of wines. In the *solera* system, casks containing wine of the same type, but of various ages are arranged on top of each other or at least near each other. Careful sensory examination to classify the wines into types is, of course, a necessary prelude to successful operation of the system. Anywhere from 5 to 30 per cent of the wine from the casks in the oldest tier may be removed. This is then replenished with wine drawn and blended from casks in the next oldest tier and so on up to the youngest. These *soleras* may be from four to as many as eight steps or stages in depth. The wine coming from the oldest barrel will, in the second year of operation, contain wine one year older than it was originally,

243

Fig. 34. Sherry butts in a Spanish bodega.

244

plus the younger wine from the next oldest tier used to replace it, which will also be one year older, Figure 34. Thus, as only a limited amount of wine is taken from the lower (older) stage each year, the average age of the wine from the lower barrel continues to rise until it reaches a constant value. If the *solera* is eight stages deep and if 25 per cent is removed each year, the composition of the wine coming from the oldest container will reach an average and constant age of about eight years after ten years of operation. Therefore, the first advantage of the *solera* system is that it produces wine of a constant average age after a period of operation, Figure 35.

Another advantage of the *solera* system is that if the wine of one particular year is of lesser quality it will not all reach the older stage at the same time and hence its lesser quality will tend to be blended out. Its lower quality will thus not have an abrupt adverse effect on the quality of the *solera*. One other advantage of the *solera* system is that, because of the periodical renewing of the wines, the alcohol content does not go up so rapidly and the *flor* yeast continues to grow on the surface. The reason for this is that under the very dry conditions of the

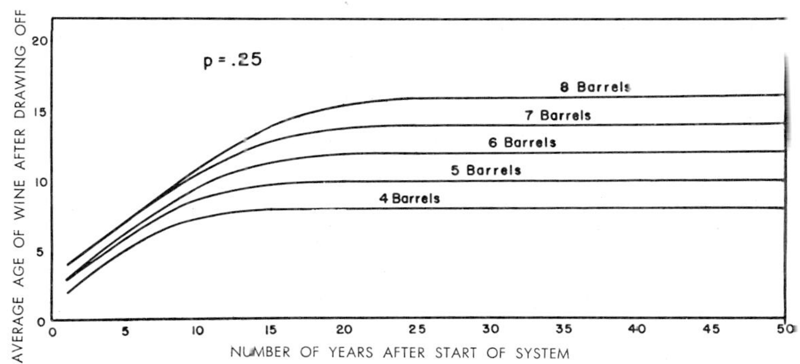

Fig. 35. Average age of the wine in the oldest container for 4-, 5-, 6-, 7-, and 8-barrel systems after operation for up to 50 years when 25 per cent of the wine is removed twice a year

245

sherry district the wines increase in alcohol, since moisture is lost from the surface of the containers faster than alcohol. The *flor* yeast will not grow much above 15.5 or 16 per cent alcohol; so, unless a certain amount of renewal was taking place constantly, the alcohol in the oldest container would gradually go above 16 per cent and the *flor* yeast would no longer form. Even so, it is common for the lower (and older) stages to have little or no yeast growth on the surface.

Not all the *flor* sherries are of the same character; different *soleras* produce slightly different quality products, and a given firm may have two or three different dry (*fino*) types of *flor* sherries on the market at the same time. A great deal of blending of one type of wine with another takes place, which helps the winemakers to produce and maintain uniformity in different types of *fino* sherries. The older type of *finos* are called *amontillados*. The *finos* produced in the area of Sanlúcar de Barrameda are called *manzanillas*. At the time of export from Spain most of the *fino* wines are fortified to 18 or more per cent alcohol with brandy or industrial alcohol. However, in Spain *finos*, particularly the *manzanillas*, are sold at only 14 to 16 per cent alcohol.

Very different from the dry *fino*-type sherries which are now so important are the *oloroso* type, wines of moderate quality and with less favorable prospects for forming a good *fino* wine. At no time do they have a *flor* film on the surface (since they are fortified to about 18 per cent alcohol). They are aged, however, by the *solera* process in exactly the same kind of containers as the *flor* sherry wines. Many of the *oloroso soleras* are even older than those of the *flor*-type sherries. Obviously it does not make any difference whether their alcohol goes up or not, since there is no yeast-film growth to interfere with. Occasionally an *oloroso solera* reaches 21 or even 22 per cent of alcohol. Some blending sherry is made from boiled-down grape juice and fortified juice from very ripe grapes. These are also aged in *solera* systems and used for blending. Modern sherry is a highly blended product: it is blended not only in the *soleras* from year to year but between *soleras* in order to produce wines of distinctive and uniform types, and there are shipping *soleras* for the final aging of the blended wines.

The wines of the Montilla district south of Córdoba are quite similar to those of Jerez de la Frontera and are of great interest, though unfortunately they are less well known in this country. These wines are produced primarily from the Pedro Ximenes variety of grapes, but they are crushed much as the Palomino variety is in the Jerez de la Frontera district. Both *flor-* and *oloroso-*type wines are produced. They are usually very good buys, when one can obtain them, because they are less expensive than the traditional sherries.

The important quality factor of the drier sherries and *montillas* is that they have undergone a film stage. The careful classification of the wines and the aging and fractional blending are also important. The critical demands of the English market have had a highly important influence in raising and maintaining the quality standards for sherry.

The wines of Málaga are made from grapes which have been allowed to partially or almost completely dry (i.e., raisin) in the sun before they are crushed. The grapes are then crushed and pressed. They ferment very slowly. Some wines are fortified to about 16 per cent alcohol rather soon after fermentation begins. Therefore some Málagas contain as much or more sugar than alcohol They all have a very distinct raisin flavor and are usable only as dessert wines. Our grandparents' use of them in cooking was as rational as any other use. Surprisingly, they are rather cheap considering the expense of producing them. The variety of grape used is Muscat of Alexandria, and of course the raisins of Málaga have been well known in commerce for many years. Málaga, essentially, is a raisin-flavored wine. The strong and obvious raisin flavor and its low acidity and high sugar do not recommend it to many consumers. However, in Málaga one may taste some complex old aged wines of notable quality.

ITALY

The wines of Italy have been known since pre-Roman times. Modern Italian wines, except for Chianti, vermouth, and Marsala, have not achieved international consumer recognition. Nevertheless, Italy is often the largest producer of wine with over four million acres producing 1.5 billion gallons of wine. Per capita consumption is high, though not as high as in France.

Because of the overpopulation of Italy, the fertile plains are needed for the production of grains and vegetables. In most regions vines have been pushed onto the less fertile and often warmer slopes. The result is generally low yields and in the southern regions excessive sugar. This alone, however, would not be so objectionable were it not for the multicrop or promiscuous culture system which the small and overcrowded farms make necessary. Vines are grown on or between trees and in competition with potatoes, tomatoes, olives, and other crops in the fields. It is estimated that 70 per cent of the vineyards of Italy are of this type. Obviously vines on trees cannot be properly pruned or sprayed for disease control. When several crops are grown on the same plot there is always the problem of the timing of the proper care of each. None, therefore, can receive as much attention as when a single crop is planted.

The wine-making procedures are frequently rather primitive. The small size of the vineyards makes it difficult for the winemaker to receive proper training. There are more schools for training winemakers in Germany than in Italy. Many of the practices are outmoded. The *governo* process of Tuscany, for example, is admittedly poor, but continues to be used. In this process one variety of grapes, Colorino, is placed on trays to dry until December or January. It is then crushed and about

10 per cent by volume of the fermenting must is added to the regular new red wine. This adds color, tannin, and alcohol, but it also may result in undesirable or incomplete fermentations. In northern Italy many of the red wines are *frizzante* (gassy) from continuing malo-lactic fermentations. In Calabria table wines of 15 and 16 per cent alcohol are common. Many of the white wines are too amber in color or too low in acidity.

This lack of attention to wine quality is not simply because the small untrained winemakers use outmoded processes and grapes of poor quality. It is a result also of a fundamental difference in attitude toward wine of the Italian as compared to the French. Wine is as necessary as bread or oil to the Italian. He drinks it much as we eat bread, without thought or critical evaluation. Consequently, the small wine producers of Italy are able to sell wines which in other countries would not be acceptable. The average wine found in many of the stores and restaurants, particularly in the rural districts, is simply not up to commercial standards of other countries.

The Italian industry has other handicaps. The main one is that Italy was not a national entity until the middle of the nineteenth century. Thus, while there was a great deal of local pride there was little interest in the wines of one district as compared to those of another district. Hence wines received very little critical attention from connoisseurs of other parts of Italy. The wines of Naples were virtually unknown in the north of Italy, and likewise the wines of Verona were (and are) seldom found on wine lists in Rome or in southern Italy. This robbed local wine producers of an export market and of the critical attention to quality which the export market would have brought to them. It emphasizes again the great value of the English and Belgian markets in improving the quality of the wines of France, and the English influence on port and sherry. Italian wines lacked distribution throughout Italy, and until the twentieth century had very little export trade with other countries. The main exceptions, even today, are vermouth, Marsala, and to a lesser extent the wines of Tuscany and Piedmont. Recently, many Italian wine districts have been delimited, which is to be applauded.

Thus, in summary, the wines of Italy are made from small vineyard holdings in mountainous areas in promiscuous culture, and the many untrained winemakers use rather primitive techniques. The wines do not enjoy sufficient distribution among critical consumers either inside or outside Italy to force an improvement in the quality. The average Italian consumer is not critical of the quality of his wines.

The best-known wine districts of Italy are those of Piedmont, the Brenner Pass region near Bolzano, Lombardy, the region north of Venice, Tuscany, the hills near Rome (Castelli Romani), Naples, eastern Sicily near Etna, and western Sicily near Marsala. Wines are, of course, made in many other parts of Italy.

The wines of Piedmont are usually sold with varietal labels. Some of them are gassy from malo-lactic fermentation, but when properly aged they can be among the best red table wines of Italy. Typical varietal names are Barbera, Fresia, Grignolino, and Nebbiolo. Barolo is a district wine produced from the Nebbiolo grape. A small amount of sparkling muscat is produced from Muscat blanc. The wines of Piedmont are generally of better quality because mixed planting is comparatively rare here. Also, several large and modern wineries have raised the standards.

The highest standard of quality of Italian wines is in the Brenner Pass region, where varieties such as Merlot, Riesling, Traminer, and Pinot noir are widely grown and made into very acceptable wines. If the district were not so small it might develop a considerable export trade. It is significant that it is a German-speaking district, which belonged to Austria before the First World War, and the labels and wineries all reflect German influence. They are seldom of exceptional quality, but are well-made wines.

250

Just to the south near Verona are the wines of Lombardy, many of which are very palatable if not exceptionally high-quality dry table wines. Among the best known are Valpolicella and Bardolino, both of which are red, and Soave, which is white. Although these are not classical wines of high quality, they are among the most pleasant drinking wines of northern Italy. A great variety of wines of similar character and quality are produced in the region to the north and west of Venice.

Tuscany is perhaps the best-known wine district in Italy because of the Chianti wines which are sold in the typical raffia-covered *fiaschi*. Both red and white wines are made in Tuscany, but the reds are by far the best known and the best in quality. The varieties used are Sangioveto and Colorino. In many cases when only the Sangioveto is planted the *governo* process is not used. The wines are normally aged for two or three years and then bottled. The *fiasco* is not a very good bottle for aging, and some Bordeaux type bottles are used, particularly for the wines from Montepulciano. Of white Chiantis and Orvietos which are made from Saint-Émilion (here called Trebbiano) and Malvasia bianca, the less said the better. They are usually slightly oxidized and almost always too low in acid. Many of the Orvietos are made *abboccato*, which means they are sweet. A well-aged red Chianti can be very good.

The wines of Castelli Romani are of only moderate quality. Often they are carbonated for the tourist trade of Rome and sold at exorbitant prices. The wines of Naples and of Vesuvius are likely to be of ordinary quality, also. Even the famed Lacrima Christi, produced from vines grown on the slopes of Vesuvius, will not be found memorable. These are often made into sparkling wine by bottle- or tank-fermentation processes. The wines are of very moderate quality and are usually sweetened to cover up their normal defects. The wines of Capri and Ischia, which are well known to the tourist, perhaps should stay on the islands and be left for the tourist as they certainly are not worthy of export. The wines of the Etna

251

district, in spite of their southern origin, can be quite pleasant, especially some of the red wines. They are seldom exported.

The wines of the Marsala district are the most interesting of the Sicilian wines. This district was consciously developed by English wine merchants at the end of the eighteenth century and throughout the nineteenth century as the source of a substitute for sherry. The raw products which the wine merchants had to deal with were very unpromising: dry white wine (usually oxidized), grape juice, boiled-down grape juice, and alcohol. Later, when the production of concentrate became possible, grape concentrate was used. The dry white wines were blended with the grape juice, with a certain amount of the boiled-down grape juice to give it color and a burnt flavor, and fortified with alcohol up to 18 or 19 per cent. These were made more or less sweet and rather highly colored and were aged for some years in oak casks. The different types of Marsala were blended in a sort of fractional blending system so that wines of a fairly constant age and type were being produced.

The English influence began to diminish after the First World War and was completely eliminated during the Second World War. There is a feeling in the trade that the quality of the Marsalas has not been as high after the Second World War as it was earlier. Certainly the postwar export trade of Marsala has been limited. Marsala has such a strong flavor that it takes time to acquire a taste for it. In Italy the drier and less alcoholic types are used as apéritifs, but in this country they may be too strong in flavor for the purpose. They are probably best used in cooking and occasionally the sweeter types are served with certain kinds of cake. Marsala is another example of how careful attention to blending and classification of wines produces distinctive wines of uniform type and quality which have gained consumer acceptance.

Vermouths are produced primarily in the district near Turin in northern Italy. These are direct descendants of the flavored wines of the Greeks, but in the eighteenth and nineteenth centuries they were much improved. About fifty or sixty different herbs are used in the production of the Italian type of vermouth. The raw material is sweet muscat wine originally from the Piedmont district. The herbs are macerated in the wine for shorter or longer periods of time, then are separated from the wines, and the product is aged. In the more modern process the flavors of the herbs are extracted with alcohol solutions. These extracts are clarified and aged, and various amounts are then blended directly into the wines. Sweet vermouth is always slightly amber in color owing to the use of caramel syrup and is quite sweet—usually about 15 or 16 per cent sugar—and contains only about 17 per cent of alcohol. It is used without blending as a sweet dessert wine in Italy, but in this country is used mainly in manhattan cocktails. Dry vermouths are also produced in Italy—nowadays usually of very light color for the American market. Also some half and half blends of the two are produced. The best vermouths should not have any dominating characteristic of a single herb but a well-blended herb flavor. The presence of too much vanilla odor in sweet vermouths definitely lowers their quality.

YUGOSLAVIA

Many of the vineyards of Yugoslavia are subject to a Mediterranean climate, but some have a typical continental climate. Grapes and wines are produced in all of the six republics: about 50 per cent of the production is in Serbia, 35 per cent in Croatia, 9 per cent in Slovenia, 4 per cent in Macedonia, 2 per cent in Bosnia-Herzegovina, and a negligible amount in Montenegro.

Serbia produces mainly red types which are usually named for the regions where they are produced: Zupa, Krajina, Vlasotinci (rosés), Smederevo (white), etc. Croatia produces mainly white table wines. In the Danube basin the wines are usually made from Walschriesling which may be a native variety. In Dalmatia (a part of Croatia) the reds are more important. The

253

best Dalmatian wines are made from a native variety, Mali Plavac. These are often high in alcohol and tannin and are much in demand as blending wines. In Slovenia many superior white table wines are made from western and northern European varieties such as Traminer, Sylvaner, or Sémillon. Merlot is widely used for reds. Yugoslavia has built many new wineries in recent years and the quality standards are being improved.

The Yugoslavian wines are now being standardized and are finding a place in the world market; 15 to 20 per cent are exported—mainly to central European countries. They have one labeling feature which is almost unique and is clearly desirable: the sugar content, as well as the alcohol content, is sometimes stated on the label. (Some wine labels in the Soviet Union also indicate the sugar content.) The white table wines on the American market seem more interesting than the reds.

GREECE

The wines of Greece go back to Homeric times, and were an important item of commerce in the pre-Roman and Roman period. Under Turkish domination the wine industry suffered, and it was not until Greece became a kingdom in the nineteenth century that wine making began again to become important. There was considerable German influence in the wine-making industry and many of the cellars reflect this. The wines, however, still show the influence of ancient practices in that one-third of the wines of Greece are resinated. These resinated wines, which contain 1 to 3 per cent of dry resin, have a very strong turpentine-like odor and are called *retsina*. The vineyard area of Greece covers over half a million acres and the wine industry produces over 100 million gallons per year. A limited amount of sweet muscat wine from the island of Samos is shipped to central Europe for blending purposes. The amber-red, slightly muscat-flavored wine called Mavrodaphne is a smooth tawny port type of wine made near Patras in Peloponnesus. Other than these, there are some pleasant but not outstanding white and red table wines.

Although phylloxera has not infested many of the vineyards of Greece, and especially those of the southern part, phylloxera in France had an important influence on the grape industry of Greece. When there was a great shortage of grapes in the 1880's and early 1890's in France, importation of raisins was encouraged. The raisin industry of Greece was then greatly expanded and very heavy plantings of grapes for making raisins were made, particularly in Peloponnesus. These grapes became surplus when the French vineyards were replanted and have remained so to this day. The overproduction of grapes still constitutes one of the largest single agricultural economic problems in Greece. Many of the surplus raisins have been converted to wine and distilled for industrial alcohol.

CYPRUS

The wines of Cyprus are very ancient. There was certainly a Greek colony on Cyprus in the pre-Roman period. However, the vineyards are highly subdivided and the quality of the grapes and of the wines is rather poor. A considerable amount of the musts are converted into concentrate for exportation to England for the making of "British wines." Only one dessert wine of importance is produced, called Commanderia: a tawny dessert wine, which has a slight raisin flavor. It was originated by the Knights Templars when they made their headquarters on the island of Cyprus. The Cyprus government is trying to improve the quality standards of the Cyprus industry, but it remains to be seen how much they will be able to do.

ISRAEL

The wines of Israel are, of course, very ancient, but during the Turkish domination the wineries were almost entirely eliminated and it was not until the late nineteenth century that one

255

of the Rothschilds encouraged the planting of grapes in what became Palestine. Several wineries were established and the grape acreage continued to expand, especially after Israel became a state in the 1940's. The Israeli wines are of both table and dessert types, but the latter are the more pleasant. This is because Israel has very warm climatic conditions, closely resembling Region V in California, and its grape varieties are more adaptable for the making of dessert wines.

Recently, Israel has agreed to abide by the Madrid agreements on appellations of origin; so they are no longer using "burgundy," "chablis," and other European-type names on their labels. This is an important step forward on the part of the Israeli government.

Israel enjoys a large export trade for their wines because of religious use. Wine is a part of Hebrew culture and is a necessary part of the religious ceremonies at the Passover and on other feast days. It is natural that the Orthodox Jewish family should prefer to use wines made in Israel on these occasions.

OTHER COUNTRIES

Syria has a large grape industry, over 170,000 acres, but being largely Moslem produces only half a million gallons of wine. Lebanon, with more Christians, produces a million gallons per year from its 60,000 acres. Turkey has nearly 1.9 million acres of grapes and produces about 12 million gallons of wine. Wine production was formerly under French direction and some fair red and white table wines were produced. Little or none has been exported. Malta has only 3,000 acres of grapes and produces about 1 million gallons. Some use of sugar occurs and little of the wine is exported. Japan has a small grape and wine industry.

Summary.—The Mediterranean countries have climatic problems, but from too much heat rather than too little. The production of dessert wines is thus favored, though some areas may

256

be too warm to produce the highest quality of dessert wine. In the Douro, for example, the best port is often produced in the coolest years!

Technologically, except for Israel and some small areas and individual wineries, the wine-making practices of these countries could be improved. The very small subdivisions of vineyards and primitive wine-making procedures in such warm countries—Italy and Cyprus, for example—do not lead to the production of high-quality wine.

Legal assistance is needed to define the wine types and to set up means of improving or protecting their quality. Wines which vary greatly in type and quality can hardly hope to achieve an export market. The great contribution of the English wine merchant (for port, sherry, and Marsala) was to emphasize the necessity of uniformity of types and quality standards.

The varietal complement of many vineyards is still too varied for production of wines of the highest quality. The planting of grapes and other crops together, as in Italy, does not lead to fine wines. Nevertheless, localized regions, as the Brenner Pass area, individual companies and growers, and careful wine merchants can combine to produce and export wines of quality. They have the added merit of being inexpensive. A spirit of adventure may yield pleasant results.

257

Chapter 16

WINES OF AFRICA, AUSTRALIA, AND CENTRAL AND SOUTH AMERICA

NORTHERN AFRICA

In northern Africa grapes are grown and wine is produced in Tunisia, Algeria, Egypt, and Morocco. Tunisian wines are exported mostly to France, since the Moslem religion forbids the consumption of alcohol by the orthodox. The wines are largely table wines, with 13 to 14 per cent alcohol. Most of them are exported for blending with the low-alcohol wines of the south of France.

The Algerian wine industry was developed by the French, particularly during the phylloxera period, to complement the low-alcohol wines of the south of France. They also helped to make up the deficit for the wines that could not be produced because of the ravages of phylloxera. Many of the vineyards were very large. They are planted to common varieties, such as Carignane, Alicante Bouschet, and Clairette blanche. Owing to the change in political status of Algeria, the future of the industry is uncertain. Some vineyards appear to have been abandoned but production is presently increasing. Even if the Algerian industry were promptly brought back to its pre-1960 condition, it is questionable whether France will want to accept large quantities of Algerian wines. The internal policies of the Common Market alone may make such large-scale importations impossible.

Most of the wineries were large and many of them were coöperatively owned. The wines are stored in large concrete containers much as they would be in California. The most popular wines are those of 13 and 14 per cent alcohol, which were shipped in tank ships or in barrels to France.

Since there are both cool and warm regions in Algeria, higher-quality wines could be produced if the demand should develop. However, this is very unlikely, since less than a million French people have remained in Algeria, and the amount of wine they will drink cannot be large. There seem to be no other export markets to replace France for large quantities of ordinary wine.

Morocco is likewise a Moslem country and, although it has a fair-sized resident French population, it can only consume a small part of the wine produced there. Hence the future of the Moroccan wine industry is likewise problematical. The grapes are grown mainly in a long valley running east from Rabat, which in many respects resembles Region IV in California. The wines produced are of the 12 to 14 per cent red and white table wine type, and most of them eventually find their way into blending tanks in France.

SOUTH AFRICA

The first vines were planted in South Africa some three hundred years ago by the first Dutch settlers. A commercial wine industry developed there during the seventeenth and eighteenth centuries. A red muscatel wine, called Constantia, became famous in Europe in the early nineteenth century. This seems to have been a tawny red muscatel, made from a red Muscat variety of grapes. Its disappearance has never been satisfactorily explained. The most probable reason is that the red muscat are rather low in acid, and their high pH wines are readily subject to *Lactobacillus* spoilage. If all of the wineries of the region became infected with *Lactobacilli*, eventually the wines may have become so mousy that they lost their export market. It is the only wine of South Africa that has ever achieved international reputation, and the industry is now bringing it back into production. Under the British from the 1890's onward the wine industry was again developed and expanded for the shipment of table grapes to the home market and for the production of port and red sweet wines, likewise for shipment to the English market. These were quite successful ventures and eventually the vineyards were overplanted. Therefore the South African government in the 1920's had to organize some control over prices to forestall a disastrous economic depression for the growers and the small wineries. This was done by organizing the KWV (Afrikaans initials for the coöperative winegrower's organization), a semigovernmental agency which controls the price of grapes, of fortifying alcohol, and of new wine. It also directly or indirectly controls the quality and price of wines and brandies which are exported from South Africa. The KWV provides technical assistance to its own wineries as well as to others, and in general has had a salutary effect on the South African industry. It has been instrumental in developing two important types of products. A *flor* sherry is produced by the Spanish process of growing it on the surface of wines in barrels. This is possible in South Africa because of the low cost of Bantu labor. The quality of South African brandies has been improved, also, by improving the distilling procedures and by tasting and standardization of the blends.

However, South Africa is dependent upon the English market for the disposal of many of its dessert wines, especially port, and likewise red table wines. The English market has tended to demand rather sweet and cheap ports and rather alcoholic and inexpensive table wines from Australia as well as South Africa. Consequently, the South African wines have not had

260

the best reception among wine connoisseurs in England. This is an example of how wine merchants can sometimes prevent the best wines from reaching potential consumers by demanding only low-quality and cheap wines from new wine-producing countries. In the cooler districts of South Africa some creditable white table wines are produced, but perhaps the best of the South African table wines are those of the Petite Sirah type—rather slowly aging red table wines.

Because of climatic conditions, it is unlikely that a wine industry will develop in the southern part of the continent except in the Republic of South Africa. Some areas in Rhodesia might be suitable for grapes, but with the decreasing European population it is unlikely that a stable wine industry will develop there. Africa seems to be the only continent where the grape acreage is not increasing at the present time.

AUSTRALIA

The Australian and the Californian wine industries started about the same time in the late eighteenth century. Many European varieties were imported. As in California, dessert wines form the bulk of the wine trade. Almost from the start wines were exported to England. The industry is still somewhat dependent on this export market (just as the California industry is on shipments to eastern United States).

About 130,000 acres of grapes have been planted, mainly in South Australia, New South Wales, and Victoria. Table and raisin grapes are important. A strict quarantine has been imposed to keep phylloxera out of South Australia. Unfortunately, this also prevents rapid introduction of new and better varieties. Wine production is about 40 million gallons, but some of it is distilling material, and about 25 million gallons of finished wine are produced. Climate does not seem to be a limiting factor, although it is rather humid in the Hunter River district and irrigation is required in some districts.

A wide variety of types of wine are produced: red and white

261

table, *flor* sherry, sweet sherry, red dessert, muscatel, sparkling, and so on. There is a lively interest in improving Australian wines and many special bottlings and well-aged wines are available for special tastings. The wineries are modern and have good technological control.

One interesting feature of the Australian industry is the number of family-owned firms which have been in existence for more than a hundred years. These take great pride in the quality of their product and have certainly been a positive factor in improving Australian wines.

As in California, the use of appellations of European origin is common, and no doubt has a baneful effect on quality improvement and the development of unique local types. The demand of the English market for cheap and very sweet dessert wines and for inexpensive and alcoholic red table wines has also not been the best influence. The difficulty of getting new varieties into South Australia has been mentioned. The large beer consumption is a factor which may repress wine drinking.

New Zealand imports wine from Australia, although it has a small grape and wine industry of its own. The climate is cool, but with the proper varieties and techniques quality table wines may be produced if excessive use of sugar can be prevented.

CENTRAL AND SOUTH AMERICA

The discovery of America was followed rather soon by the conquest of Mexico and this, in turn, by the settling of Spanish colonists in the New World. Simultaneously, large numbers of missionaries came to the New World to Christianize the natives. The Catholic religion required wine for its ceremonies, and consequently one of the important items of export from Spain was wine during the colonial period. Moreover, life was not easy on the frontier and wine was welcome to the civilian and military personnel.

Mexico.—It is not known whether vines or seeds were first

brought to Mexico, but it is certain that a small grape industry was started north of Mexico City in the sixteenth century. The variety of grape which they began to develop, either from cuttings from Spain or seeds brought from Spain, was eventually called Criolla in the Spanish-speaking countries. It was taken farther north in Mexico and eventually was imported into the new missions which were developing in Baja California. The cuttings were brought from Baja California into California proper some time after the establishment of the San Diego Mission in 1769. The Criolla, then, is closely related to the variety we call Mission in California.

The Mexican industry developed slowly because of the very warm climate in the interior of Mexico and in Baja California. However, just before and after the First World War a number of new plantings were made in the Aguascalientes area and near Ensenada in Baja California. These plantings were expanded during the 1920's and 1930's, and at the present time Mexico has about 25,000 acres. The best wines produced in Mexico have been of the dessert type and we have tasted excellent muscatels from a winery at Ensenada. The disadvantage of the Mexican industry has been the difficulty of preventing the sophistication of the wines with alcohol and sugar. These alcohol-sugar wines can be sold at a very cheap price and tend to prevent the development of a quality wine industry. Recently this practice seems to have been stopped.

Peru.—Grapes were taken from Mexico to Peru soon after the downfall of the Inca empire. A small grape industry developed there, based upon the Mexican Criolla type of grape. Again, climatic conditions were too hot and, in Peru, far too dry for the development of a quality wine industry. It is no wonder that in the nineteenth century much of the wine was distilled and made into a colorless brandy called *pisco*. Many a miner's thirst in California during the gold rush days was slaked with *pisco* brandy from Peru. There was an expansion of the vineyards and some attempt to improve wine quality in the

263

early twentieth century, but the industry today is still rather primitive. None of the wines are of exportable quality and most of them are sold to the lower classes as a week-end beverage.

Chile.—In contrast to the climatic conditions of Peru, those of Chile range from Region II to Region IV conditions, and there is adequate moisture in most of the vineyard areas except those in the northern part of Chile. Furthermore, the background of the Chilean grape industry is entirely different. Because of the large migrations of Englishmen and Frenchmen into Chile, particularly at the time of phylloxera, the Chilean industry has developed on the French model rather than on the Spanish or Italian. The two most important varieties, Sémillon and Merlot, are both from France. The aging procedures in the making of the white and red wines resemble those used in France.

The white wines, however, tend to be aged in the wood too long. They thus acquire a woody taste and are too dark or amber in color. They have not been very successful on the international market. Attempts have been made to import them into the United States in various kinds of fancy bottles, but so far none of these attempts have been permanently successful.

On the other hand, many of the red wines are well aged and have a good barrel and bottle bouquet. Many are fully worthy of exportation. Again, some may be aged too long, but the better-quality red wines of Chile could easily compete on the international market.

A small amount of red sweet dessert wine and some *pisco* brandy are produced in Chile. It is sad that Chile is one of the few countries where wine constitutes the principal source of alcoholism. This is a part of life on the large haciendas, where the workers are often allowed as much cheap wine as they can drink on week-ends. The result is that alcoholism from wine is a serious Chilean social problem.

Argentina.—The Criolla grapes which originated in Mexico

were exported to Peru, later to Chile, and were brought across the Andes to Argentina, certainly by the beginning of the seventeenth century. They are still planted there, but a large number of other varieties, both French and Italian, have also been planted. Argentina is the largest producing region in the Western Hemisphere, with 550,000 acres of grapes and about 370 million gallons of wine. The average annual consumption of wine in Argentina, per capita, is also greater than that of other Western Hemisphere countries. The predominant influence on the Argentine wine industry has been that of the Italian immigrant, who demands wine daily but is not particularly interested in quality. The vineyards are extensive, often 1,000 to 2,000 or more acres, and the wineries themselves are frequently very large. The wines are generally of moderate quality. The red and white table wines are shipped and sold in bulk to the lower and middle-class workmen in Buenos Aires and other large cities. Some moderate quality sparkling wine is produced.

The most important area for the growing of grapes in Argentina is in Mendoza. Here some palatable red wines from Merlot are produced, but the emphasis is generally on high production and quick turnover. With few exceptions the wines do not reach the international standard that are found in the red wines of Chile.

Brazil.—The grape regions of Brazil are too warm and humid for the best growth of *Vitis vinifera* grapes. It is therefore no surprise to find many American varieties and direct producers growing in Brazil. The Isabella is a well-known grape in this country. In some regions *Vitis vinifera* grapes can be grown, but these areas are small. A number of different ethnic influences have been brought to bear on the Brazilian wine industry: Portuguese, Italian, Spanish, French, German, and Japanese. It is no wonder, then, that the quality standards of the Brazilian wine industry fluctuate very widely. The exportation of a Brazilian Riesling to the New York market has met with only moderate success because it is not of exceptionally high quality. Wines meet great competition from other alcoholic beverages in Brazil. This competition, along with the climatic handicap, makes it unlikely that a large wine industry will develop in that country. However, some good experimental work is being done and the amount of wine with a high volatile acidity seems to be decreasing in Brazil.

Others.—Uruguay has a very small wine industry, and some fairly good wines have been made in that country. Likewise, there are small plantings of grapes in Paraguay and Ecuador, but these are not likely to become important grape regions because of poor climatic conditions. In Venezuela, where there is a large Italian population, a considerable amount of wine is being produced from imported grape concentrate to satisfy the demand of recent migrants for some sort of table beverage.

Summary.—The future of wines in northern Africa seems doubtful unless the European markets can be maintained. So far they have seldom been of high quality. South Africa, on the other hand, has developed several quality products, particularly sherry and brandy, which could hold their own on the world markets. Australia also has a flourishing export trade and many good wines.

European grapes were first grown in Mexico from where they were carried to California and to Peru, Chile, and Argentina. The original vines produced well but the quality of the wine was poor. Later, better vines were imported from Europe. The hot climate is the biggest handicap of Mexico, Peru, and Brazil. The largest vineyards are in Argentina and Chile. The aged red wines of the latter are especially praiseworthy. Some of the cultural factors influencing the types of wines produced in these countries are discussed.

Chapter 17

THE WINES OF THE EASTERN UNITED STATES AND CANADA

One of the world's richest floras of the genus *Vitis* is found in the Mississippi Valley, in the eastern United States, and in parts of Canada. Although many native species of vines were growing in the eastern United States, and elsewhere east of the Rocky Mountains, none of these appeared very useful to the early settlers for eating or wine making. One reason for this was that most of the vines were growing in trees. The clusters and berries were very small. The grapes had low sugar, high acidity, and a distinctive and strange new flavor, which eventually became known as "foxy." It is not surprising, therefore, that many varieties of grapes were brought from Europe to the New World by the early settlers. All these early ventures into the growing of *Vitis vinifera* varieties in the Western Hemisphere failed. There were, and still are, several reasons for their failure to do well in the eastern United States. The most important was probably the extremely low winter temperatures in certain years. Another reason was the extremely high humidity of the summer months, which led to the infection of the vines with mildew, oïdium, black rot, and other fungus diseases and insect pests. Moreover, the root-infesting insect phylloxera was present in this country but not in Europe. It was not immediately recognized that phylloxera was one of the causes of the early failure of V. *vinifera* in the United States, for the causal organism was not identified until the middle of the nineteenth century.

Probably virus diseases were a problem for varieties of V. *vinifera* under the warm humid summer conditions of the eastern United States. The attempts to bring in V. *vinifera* continued in spite of the failures. There are even reports of importations of soil from Europe! A large number of European grape growers and winemakers came to this country with the idea of establishing a wine industry based on use of varieties of V. *vinifera*. These attempts succeeded for a few years and a fair quantity of wine was made. But finally the vineyard succumbed to one or another of the causes listed above, and the experiments failed.

The colonists turned to three different methods of acquiring an alcoholic beverage. One was the importation of wines from Europe, especially from the Madeira Islands. Madeiras became the most important wines in colonial America, and the most appreciated. However, many French and German wines were also imported.

Second, large amounts of hard cider were made from apple juice, and eventually applejack, or distilled cider. This became one of the most important alcoholic beverages of the New World. Apples were grown in the New England states and farther south, and there were numerous apple distilleries, particularly in Massachusetts. Wines were made also from peaches and distilled into peach brandy and New England imported molasses from the West Indies and made rum.

The third type of endeavor to supply alcoholic beverages was the development of the whiskey industry. This is related to the American frontier and its peculiar demands for easily transportable alcoholic beverages. Whiskey supplied this need better than any other alcoholic beverage except brandy and rum, and it became the most used alcoholic beverage on the American frontier.

Because the attempts to establish V. *vinifera* failed, interest in grapes of the native species gradually increased. Between 1800 and 1852 many attempts were made to domesticate varieties from the native species, such as V. *labrusca* and V. *rotundifolia*. It was found that there was a rich supply of native grapes of different colors, ripening at different periods, and with a sugar content somewhat better than that of varieties which the colonists had first used.

Among the varieties which came from this period were Isabella, Ives Seedling, Delaware, Niagara, Catawba, and the well-known Concord. The Isabella was a red variety with a very strong foxy flavor but of very attractive appearance. Catawba had a tawny red color, again with a rather strong foxy flavor, but not too high a total acidity. Ives Seedling is a red variety, one of the most important for the production of red wines before Prohibition. Delaware is perhaps the least foxy of the group. It has a pink color and is the main eastern variety which can be made into wine without the use of sugar.

However, the Concord finally dominated, and still dominates plantings in viticultural regions of the eastern United States. The Concord is a vigorous grower with good production. Although it is not high in sugar, usually about 16 per cent, and has a rather high foxy flavor, it appealed to the grower because of its regularity of production and its freedom from fungus and other diseases.

Whether all these varieties are pure American species or represent accidental hybrids with V. *vinifera* is not known. A large number of grape breeders and nurserymen were at work in the eastern United States. Some of the new varieties developed during the nineteenth century may have been chance hybrids between V. *vinifera* varieties growing in the nursery and the new varieties of American species growing near them.

269

Use of seeds for developing new varieties was still common at this time and makes this more probable. Especially for the Delaware there seems to be evidence that some V. *vinifera* may be present.

The new varieties were not the same as those to which the original immigrants had been accustomed in Europe. However, several generations had been born in this country and had forgotten much of their taste for European wines. The nineteenth century saw the development of a native American wine industry throughout the eastern United States. Wineries were established in almost every state except the northernmost New England states. Even the Niagara Peninsula in Canada became an important viticultural region. The wineries were small and sold their wines to a local clientele, but there were a large number of wineries and they produced a very wide range of wines from American varieties of grapes. Some of these new varieties have unique flavors and their future on the American market does not seem to have been adequately tested.

From the time of the introduction of the Concord, interest in native varieties gradually slackened. The areas devoted to growing grapes in the eastern United States began to decline about the turn of the century. The Prohibition period eventually caused restrictions in grape planting in the eastern United States, although transitory increases occurred after Repeal. Grape plantings in the eastern United States are now mainly confined to five areas and have less acreage than before Prohibition.

The most important vineyards for wine grape production in the eastern states are in the Finger Lakes district of New York state. Here the narrow and deep lakes ameliorate the winter as well as the spring and summer temperatures. Large areas are planted to vineyards on the lower slopes around the lakes. A few vineyards survive in the Hudson River area, but are not important. The Finger Lakes region is important not only because it is the center of an important grape-producing industry but also because it is the center of the eastern wine industry.

Eastern United States and Canada

Virtually all the sparkling wines made in the eastern United States come from this region. The sparkling wines made from eastern grapes have achieved a recognition which their non-sparkling counterparts lack. Apparently the foxy flavor in a sparkling wine is not as objectionable or as strange as it would be in a table wine. This region has developed a process for treating fortified foxy wines with oxygen to remove the foxy flavor. This old French treatment, which was originally proposed for table wines, leads to aldehyde formation, darkening of the color in white table wines (or browning in red table wines), and reduction of the foxy flavor. However, it is very well adapted to the production of sherry, since the formation of aldehyde is a desirable part of the process of producing sherry.

In Ohio, Nicholas Longworth was one of the first to plant vines and was their greatest protagonist. He was especially fond of the Catawba variety which had been introduced into Ohio about 1826. It is preferred for producing sparkling wines.

In western Pennsylvania and along the shores of Lake Erie in Ohio a large Concord grape industry has grown up, primarily for the production of grapes for juice purposes. Some of the grapes are used in the local markets as table grapes. The Concord grapes do not need to become very sweet for the production of grape juice and a stable industry has developed in this region.

Along the Lake Erie shore near Sandusky a wine-producing area was formerly very important. A number of islands just off the coast by Sandusky were planted to wine grapes and there were several wineries in this area. Only a few of these remain today and the region is now of much less consequence than it was. The significant factor was the moderating effect of the lake climate on the growing of grapes. This had to do with less winterkilling, as well as warmer conditions during the autumn ripening season. It is not impossible that a quality wine-producing industry could develop in these areas of moderate winter temperatures if the proper varieties were planted.

Also, because of the ameliorating effect of the Great Lakes,

271

a vineyard area in southern Michigan produces a number of wines from Concord and related varieties, but none seems to have achieved any recognition for quality.

In Canada, on the Niagara Peninsula, there are several large wineries and an extensive area is planted to grapes. Not only Concord but a number of other eastern varieties, direct producers, and a few V. *vinifera* varieties are grown.

French hybridizers attempted to develop a direct producer which would incorporate the resistance to phylloxera, winter cold, and fungus of American species with the flavor qualities of varieties of V. *vinifera*. This attempt was carried to great extremes in France and many thousands of hybrids were produced. Many are still planted in France and a few have achieved recognition for production of quality wines.

The resistance to phylloxera has been lost in many of the hybrids, but some seem to be good producers with a fair degree of cold- and mildew-resistance. Unfortunately, few of them have entirely lost their foxy flavor.

There is a small vineyard area near Baltimore, Maryland, where direct producers are grown. One winery in this region converts them into very palatable wines. It would be a grave error to assume that direct producers capable of producing high-quality wines cannot be developed.

The wines of Canada as well as those of all the eastern United States enjoy the privilege of diluting the must with as much as 35 per cent by volume of a sugar-water mixture. This dilution reduces the acid content and also dilutes the foxy flavor. It gives these winemakers an economic advantage which California producers do not enjoy.

Formerly there was a rather large grape and wine industry, based on grapes of *Vitis rotundifolia* in Virginia and North and South Carolina. These grapes look more like cherries than grapes. They have a very distinctive flavor, somewhat different from that of the Concord type of grape. There are still a number of small wineries in this region, but the quality of the wines is

272

ordinary at best, and the industry does not seem to have much permanence unless the wines can be improved and standardized.

There are only small plantings of wine grapes in Illinois, Missouri, and Arkansas.

The long series of experiments in the eastern states to acclimate V. *vinifera* to the Western Hemisphere has generally been a failure. Recent experiments in New York state appear a hazardous undertaking. The contention that use of cold-resistant rootstocks would permit growing V. *vinifera* scions without winterkilling is not clearly established. The most recent experience during the cold 1962–63 winter seems to be that the experiment is still not a success. The wines produced, however, are very good and one can still hope that V. *vinifera* grapes will be permanently and successfully grown east of the Rockies.

Hence the future of the wine industry in the eastern states seems to be: (1) to produce wine with more or less of the foxy flavor of the V. *labrusca* type of grapes or with the strong flavor of the V. *rotundifolia* type of grapes; (2) to produce blends of foxy-flavored eastern wines and California wines; (3) to produce wines from direct-producers; and (4) possibly to make wines from V. *vinifera* varieties. Plant breeders may eventually develop a variety with all the good flavor qualities of V *vinifera* and the desirable cold- and mildew-resistance of the native species of *Vitis*. This is certainly still in the future.

In the meantime, California wine is shipped to eastern states for blending with native varieties, primarily to dilute their foxy flavor. California wines are less expensive than wines produced in the east and consequently there is an economic advantage in blending of this kind. One can always determine whether the wine is 75 per cent or more from New York state or Ohio because that is the minimum amount of native wine which is required before it can be labeled with the geographical appellation. Wines bottled in the eastern states which are labeled "American" wines almost certainly contain more than 25 per cent Cali-

273

fornia wine. Otherwise they would have a geographical appellation of New York, Ohio, and so on.

Summary.—Canada and the eastern United States generally have cool climatic conditions for growing grapes. Most areas are unsuitable for varieties of *Vitis vinifera* because of winterkilling, high humidity, lack of fungus resistance, and susceptibility to virus diseases. European grapes cannot be grown unless grafted on phylloxera-resistant stocks. The strong foxy (methyl anthranilate) odor of many eastern wines, particularly those made from Concord varieties, makes them unacceptable to wine tasters who have a taste for wines made from European grapes.

However, the possibility of acclimating V. *vinifera* varieties to conditions in the eastern United States and in Canada is still under active study.

Chapter 18

THE WINES OF CALIFORNIA

The first missionaries from Baja California arrived at San Diego
in 1769 and within one or two years vines had been transferred
from the missions of Baja California to San Diego. Almost certainly the variety which they brought with them was one of the
Criolla type which had originated in Mexico. It was finally called
the Mission variety in California. The missions had an abundance
of very cheap labor and needed wine not only for sacramental
purposes but also for the use of the monks at meals and as
an article of commerce. The largest vineyards in southern California seem to have been planted at Mission San Gabriel
Archangel, but all the missions in the southern and central
coast counties developed vineyards. The first vineyard failures
were at Santa Cruz and San Francisco and later at Santa Clara.
So far as we know, no vines were ever grown to production at
these missions and the reason is now obvious—the Mission
grape would not ripen properly in these very cool localities.

At San Gabriel wine was produced and a number of brandy
stills were introduced in the early nineteenth century. The
brandy was used as an article of exchange for ships visiting the
Los Angeles harbor as well as for sale to local settlers. This
mission also apparently began the development of a new type

of wine, containing three parts of grape juice and one part of brandy, which we now believe to be the origin of the type known as angelica. The most important contribution of the Mission period, however, was to show that vines could be grown in many regions of the state and that the Mission variety was well adapted to the warmer regions. The development of the angelica type is also a notable achievement. However, the Mission vine proved to be a late ripener, to have inadequate color for the production of red wines, and insufficient acidity for the production of table wines. It is probable that the angelica type was developed because table wine types made from Mission grapes often spoiled because of their low acidity.

The secularization of the missions occurred during the Mexican period in 1833 and thereafter their vineyards gradually deteriorated. Some of the vines at San Gabriel were preserved for a longer period of time, but the Mission period contributed little directly to the future of the grape industry except for the Mission variety of grapes and the angelica type of wine. However, the Mission period was important because it introduced grape growing to the state and showed how widespread was the area suitable for grapes. The idea of producing brandy may also be attributed to this era.

Prior to the Gold Rush in 1848 a number of settlers from Europe and the eastern United States settled in the Los Angeles area. One of them, Jean Louis Vignes, a Frenchman, imported *Vitis vinifera* directly from France in the early 1830's. This is probably the first direct importation of V. *vinifera* into California from Europe. Although we are not certain of any varieties still growing which he introduced, it began a long series of importation of varieties directly from Europe, a practice which still continues. Vignes was the first large-scale commercial wine producer. The vineyards around and near Los Angeles were used not only for the production of wine but also for table grapes. Even before the Gold Rush, grapes, wines, and brandy were shipped from Los Angeles to San Francisco. A

Kentuckian, William Wolfskill, was Vignes' chief competitor in wine production in Los Angeles in the 1840's.

The most important man in the 1850's was Colonel Agoston Haraszthy, who settled at San Diego in 1849. Haraszthy, a Hungarian, had apparently had some experience with grapes in Europe. At any rate, he was an enthusiastic grape grower. He began to develop a vineyard near San Diego and imported vines from Europe in 1851. Before he had progressed very far he moved to northern California. There he established a vineyard in the region near Crystal Springs, not far from San Mateo. In 1857 he established the Buena Vista vineyard in Sonoma County, one of the largest, if not the largest, of the vineyards established in the state in the late 1850's. His most important contribution, however, was a pamphlet in 1858 on grape growing and wine making which led directly to his appointment to a committee to study grape production. As a member of this committee he convinced Governor Downey that a trip to Europe to collect grape cuttings was necessary. The importation in 1862 by Haraszthy of about 200,000 cuttings, as well as his earlier importations of European varieties, was undoubtedly of prime importance for the future industry. Unfortunately, the political temper of the legislature had changed on his return and when Haraszthy presented the bill for his trip to Europe he was on the wrong side of the political fence. He was never paid for the cuttings. Many were sold on the market and obviously helped improve the varietal complement of California vineyards. There is evidence that the Zinfandel variety was here before Haraszthy's 1862 importation. He wrote a book about his trip to Europe in which he gave advice on the growing of grapes and the making of wine. He had one of his sons trained in France in the production of sparkling wines. The development of sparkling wines at Buena Vista, while not the earliest in California history, was one of the most important.

The vineyard area increased rapidly in all parts of the state in the period 1860 to 1900. Among the early vineyardists were

General Vallejo, near the present town of Sonoma; Sutter, of Sutter's Fort fame, who was of Swiss origin; Drummond, in the Valley of the Moon, of English origin; Wilson, at Los Angeles, from Ireland. The Wentes in Livermore Valley came from Germany, as did Krug in the Napa Valley, and Kohler the pioneer wine merchant of San Francisco. Captain Gustave Niebaum, who developed Inglenook, was a Finn. The huge German colony at Anaheim, started in 1857, planted one of the largest vineyards in the state. It was destroyed by a virus disease in 1888.

Some of the best white varieties of the Livermore Valley were imported directly from Bordeaux and some of the original Sauvignon blanc vines survived until after the Second World War. The immigrants brought with them European methods of growing grapes, making wines, and labeling them according to European nomenclature. The use of European appellations for American wines has plagued the industry since the 1860's.

During the period 1860 to 1900 grape growing expanded rapidly in all parts of the state—from Escondido near San Diego to Vina, Senator Stanford's huge vineyard in the northern Sacramento Valley. Heavy plantings were made in Sonoma and Napa counties, near Livermore, and in Fresno County. The Zinfandel was especially popular and became the most widely planted red wine variety by 1900.

However, the industry soon suffered from overproduction and a period of reduced prices. This up-and-down economic fact has been the picture of the California industry from about 1870 to the present. The early industry suffered from planting the wrong varieties, from failure to harvest early enough, and from poor control of fermentation, particularly of the temperature. The predominance of the Mission variety was partially responsible for the poor wines. In 1862 the California Wine Growers' Association was founded to deal with these problems. It was particularly concerned with reducing the tax on California wines and increasing the tax on imported wines. These have been consistent objectives of the California wine industry since that date. Haraszthy made two trips to Washington to lobby for the industry, with some success.

Still, from time to time overplanting inevitably occurred. The quality was often poor, not only because of the Mission variety but because of the inexperience of the new winemakers. The first depression lasted from 1876 to 1878. Wine sold at 10 to 15 cents a gallon and many vineyards were abandoned.

In 1880 two progressive steps were taken. The California legislature provided funds for research in viticulture and enology at the University of California and established a Board of State Viticultural Commissioners.

The University's research was under the direction of Eugene Waldemar Hilgard. Professor Hilgard recognized at once two of the critical problems: the adaptation of varieties to the different climatic regions of the state and the much warmer conditions in California compared to Europe. It was these warm climatic conditions which led to the harvesting of grapes after full maturity. Musts of the high-sugar, low-acid grapes would not ferment completely dry. These slightly sweet, flat wines spoiled easily and rapidly. As late as 1900 salicylic acid was widely used to prevent spoilage, and the practice ceased only after the passage of the Pure Food and Drug Act of 1906.

Between 1880 and 1892 Hilgard attacked the varietal problem in a masterful study of the composition and quality of the musts and their wines of the major varieties of grapes growing in different regions. These studies established the importance of grape variety to the quality of the wine produced, and no doubt had a salutary effect on the generally high quality of the grape varieties in the vineyards of the state before Prohibition. Hilgard was also known as a determined protagonist of high-quality wines and of better wine-making practices. He was, accordingly, not popular with some of the commercially oriented wineries.

The Board of State Viticultural Commissioners began at

once to try to change the public attitude toward California wines. They carried on educational activities, sponsored conventions, published translations of important European enological treatises, and wrote reports on industry statistics and problems. Although the legislature abolished the Board in 1894, its work was important. The present Wine Institute and Wine Advisory Board perform some of the services of the original Board.

This Board also was responsible for the fight on phylloxera which had appeared in Sonoma vineyards in the 1870's. The legislature specifically delegated the Board to establish quarantines to prevent spread of the pest. The present California plant quarantine regulations date from this legislation. The second depression in wine prices occurred in 1886 and lasted until 1892. This too was partially due to the sale of poor quality wine.

The depression of the 1890's led to the formation of the California Wine Association, financed by San Francisco businessmen. A very large and modern aging and bottling plant was constructed at Richmond, California. They purchased wine from wineries throughout the state, often at prices of their own choosing, and sold them under their own label throughout the United States. It has been said that the California Wine Association never sold a bad bottle of wine or a great bottle of wine. However, they certainly had the highest standards of any of the bulk distributors of wine. In Henry Lachman they had one of the finest tasters of wine which the California wine industry has produced. Mr. Lachman's legendary abilities were supposed to include infallibility in identifying wines of different varieties and from different districts. The California Wine Association had one of the first chemical laboratories, and analyzed the sugar content of the new wines. Charles Ash, as the chief chemist of the Association, became a recognized authority in the industry. Since residual sugar was one of the most important causes of spoilage of wines in the state, work on this problem was a great help in preventing spoilage and improving quality. The Association was supposedly ruthless in controlling the market and did not favor competition. They established a winery in the Fresno area for the production of dessert wines.

Two other large wineries were established around the turn of the century. One in northern California, north of Santa Rosa at a town called Asti, was established by San Francisco philanthropists for Italian-Swiss colonists who were unable to find work in the San Francisco area. They planted vineyards and built a large winery. Both the vineyards and the winery prospered. They became well known, especially for their Tipo chianti, in the pre-Prohibition period. Later, apparently at the suggestion of the Italian government, this became simply Tipo red and Tipo white. Immediately after Repeal it was probably the best-known American wine.

In southern California a very large vineyard and winery under Italian philanthropists was developed near Ontario. This Italian Vineyard Company at one time had about 4,000 acres of grapes. Because of sandy soil and lack of water the vineyards were not high in yield. The company planted a large number of good varieties of grapes and made a variety of different types of wines.

Many small wineries with high standards made and bottled wines which were widely distributed in the immediate pre-Prohibition era. In fact, the demand for California wines seems to have been good between 1895 and 1918. Some of this demand was probably due to the 6,000,000 wine-drinking southern European immigrants who entered the United States between 1901 and 1915.

However, with the approach of Prohibition these wineries began to go out of business and during Prohibition only a few were still in existence. Most of the wineries were dismantled, although some kept their cooperage. A few, perhaps four or five, continued in limited business for the production of wines for sacramental and medicinal purposes. In this category were wineries in the San Joaquin Valley, Livermore Valley, and Napa Valley.

Prohibition did not have the effect which had been predicted. Instead of the price of grapes dropping, it went up. The reason for this increase was the unexpected and very large demand for California grapes on the eastern markets. These grapes were intended for the production of wines at home, which was legal at that time. Unfortunately, most of the thin-skin red wine grape varieties were unsuited for shipment to the eastern seaboard and there was a rapid change-over in varietal plantings to meet the demand for red wine grapes in the eastern United States. The most sought-after variety was the Alicante Bouschet, which had a skin thick enough to stand shipment and an intense color so that, after the juice was drawn off, sugar and water could be added and a second wine could be made which would still be red. It is estimated that some eastern winemakers were able to make as much as 600 and even 700 gallons of "wine" from a ton of grapes by this method. This had an unfortunate effect on the industry, however, in that it rapidly reduced the acreage of the finer wine grape varieties, especially of the better whites as they were grafted over to red varieties.

Prohibition had other influences; there was a gradual decrease in drinking of wines with meals at home and, of course, no wine was served in restaurants. The winemakers, having lost their profession, gradually moved into other fields; so, at the time of Repeal, although it was only thirteen years after Prohibition, there was a very serious shortage of trained winemakers. The distribution system of wines had completely broken down. When Prohibition was repealed, a new type of distributor appeared in the wholesale business in many areas, the converted bootlegger. And bathtub gin had reduced the taste of Americans for wines. Consequently, at the time of Repeal in 1933, the industry found itself with vineyards planted to varieties of grapes which would produce only ordinary qualities of wine, without an adequate amount of cooperage in which to ferment the wine, without enough well-trained winemakers to make the wine, without a distributing system in the hands of trained personnel, without retail stores and wine waiters in hotels and restaurants to sell and serve the wine, and, most important, without a clientele who were familiar with California wines.

Repeal, therefore, did not bring the expected boom to the California wine industry. During the great flurry of wine making in 1933 and 1934, nearly 800 wineries were established in California, many by men with little experience in producing wines and few with experience in producing wines which could be aged. The standards of the new industry were frankly low, partly dictated by the poor quality of the available grapes, but mostly because of the poor methods used to produce the wine. Some of this wine was rushed on the market and naturally the consumers found it to be unpalatable. Then the price of wines fell and the price of grapes was very low: the new industry was suddenly in the throes of another economic crisis.

To solve these problems, the industry established the Wine Institute, a nonprofit organization composed of most of the wineries of California. The Wine Institute continues to exist to this day with its main office in San Francisco. Its first and most important activity was to deal with the multitudinous problems which the Twenty-first Amendment to the United States Constitution had brought to the alcoholic beverage industry. Under this Amendment the control of alcoholic beverages is reserved to the states. Each state set up a little trade kingdom of its own and established new and often difficult rules for the importation of wines and other alcoholic beverages into the state. Many of these rules had to do with the percentage of alcohol, putting a special tax stamp on the bottle, and irrational and excessive taxes on wines. To protect the supposedly important local grape and wine industries a number of states, especially Washington and Michigan, established rather high import duties on wines from other states. The Wine Institute's legal department was active throughout this period in trying to reduce these inequalities. They also set up a wide program for the improvement of standards in California wineries. They now have a technical staff to deal with problems of sanitation and the development of new methods and equipment for California wineries. The Wine Institute was also responsible for the advertising of California wines and its public relations program. They have done much educational work and have published many pamphlets on the use of wine. The WAB correspondence course on wine and wine appreciation has been especially successful.

The California Department of Public Health, through its Food and Drug Inspection Division, was also active during this period. It established standards for California wines which were aimed primarily at preventing dilution of wines with water and the sale of wines of high volatile acidity or vinegary character. The enforcement of this was fairly strict, but as the wineries improved their practices enforcement gradually became unnecessary.

The University of California, primarily through its Department (then Division) of Fruit Products at Berkeley, instituted a wide range of training programs and conferences for raising the standards of the California wine industry. Professor W. V. Cruess and his staff organized classes for potential winemakers. These had a salutary influence, but many small wineries remained outside the scope of the program and continued to produce poor wines. In trying to improve the quality of California grapes the Department (then Division) of Viticulture at Davis was active in the same conferences, and instituted a long-range program of research aimed at showing the growers the importance of planting better varieties of grapes for making high-quality wines. These activities continue. Most of the research and training in this field are now in the Department of

Viticulture and Enology, which is part of the College of Agriculture at the University of California, Davis.

The enological and viticultural research at the University now covers a wide range of fundamental and applied projects and serves as the major American source of technical information in these fields. Enological experiments on grape pigments and aroma-producing compounds, factors influencing color extraction and stability, controlled fermentation and aging, submerged culture of *flor* sherry, use of *Botrytis* mold for sweet table wine production, fractional blending, malo-lactic fermentation, variety evaluation, new antiseptics and clarification agents, brandy production, waste disposal, use of concentrate, automation of winery operations and sensory examination of wines have been or are under way. Viticultural research on acid formation, effect of mold attack, maturity evaluation, development of new varieties, influence of rootstocks, fertilizers, irrigation, pruning, and other practices on grape maturity and wine quality and on automation of vineyard operations is in progress.

When the surplus of grapes was most acute in 1938 the Bank of America and the federal government organized a prorate program which was aimed at distilling wine and removing it from the market. This program was pursued energetically during 1938, and millions of gallons of wine were converted into brandy. Had it not been for this program many wineries could not have operated during the 1938 season, so tenuous was the financial position of the industry at that time. In the normal course of events this prorate brandy would not have been easy to dispose of, since surpluses each year would have had to be converted into brandy. However, the Second World War created a market for almost any alcoholic beverage, and all the prorate brandy was gradually moved into the channels of trade and disposed of before the end of the war.

The men of the industry felt at this time that they were not getting adequate advertising. Under a state law which

285

permitted a small tax on all California wines which have been prepared for market, for the purpose of advertising these products, the Wine Advisory Board was established under the Director of Agriculture of the State of California. He in turn appoints an advisory board to advise him on the spending of the funds collected from the tax. Over two million dollars of tax per year has been collected in this program, most of which is used for trade promotion, public relations, and advertising. However, under the terms of the State Marketing Act some of the funds can be used for research to improve the quality of California wines, and the Wine Advisory Board has had and still has an important research program for this purpose. Much of this research has been done on the medical aspects of wine —some of it to counter the attacks on the wine industry by those who claim that wines cause disease, and the rest on constructive research on the beneficial effects of wine in certain kinds of medication. (See also pp. 321–328.)

The prosperity which the Second World War brought to the California wine industry ended abruptly in 1947 when the price of wine dropped very rapidly throughout the state. The activities of the Wine Advisory Board continued throughout the nation, but the industry was far from prosperous from 1947 to 1960. However, the consumption of wine increased slightly, and there were no extreme years of very low or very high prices. By 1960 surpluses of grapes were again developing and the federal government established the so-called set-aside program of 1961, which was continued into the 1962 season. This program called for setting aside a certain percentage of the wines or brandy or concentrate from the San Joaquin Valley, the main surplus area of grapes, and later disposing of these products into other channels of trade. So far most of the surplus has been disposed of in the form of alcohol for industrial purposes. It is not certain what the future of this type of program will be, but the likelihood of developing methods of removing this surplus to channels of trade outside the wine industry does not seem very favorable.

The most important tendency of the California wine industry since the Second World War has been the trend toward centralization. A few wineries have gradually absorbed the middle-size wineries so that five or six companies now control 65 to 75 per cent of the total production of California wine. The centralization trend for ordinary wines has definite economic advantages. Larger equipment can be used and the cost per gallon can be markedly reduced. This gives the larger winery an economic advantage over the smaller winery, and gradually the latter finds it impossible to continue in business.

The logical development, then, is for the smaller winery to turn its attention to the production of high-quality wines which are unsuited to the processes used by the larger wineries, and this seems to be what is happening in the industry at the present time. There are perhaps thirty to forty wineries producing wines on a rather large scale; another twenty-five to fifty wineries produce high-quality wines primarily for bottling and selling at good prices. A number of small family wineries and wineries for local trade, Figures 36 and 37, still continue, and will probably survive on local-pride basis for some time, but the future of the industry seems to lie with a few highly industrialized wineries producing wines at competitive prices and several more wineries specializing in high-quality wines.

The California wine industry today includes a number of large firms with national distribution and advertising which distribute bottled wines of sound character at less than $1 per bottle. These are usually labeled with generic names: claret, sauterne, sherry, or port, and provide a good value for the money.

Several wineries with national distribution market wines which sell in the $1 to $1.50 range. They market both generic and varietal wines, but seldom with a vintage date. These

287

Fig. 36. Vineyard in the Santa Cruz Mountains. Source: The Wine Institute.

wines are considerably better values than most of the imported wines in the same price range.

Many small wineries in the state may sell a special wine locally and sell the rest of their produce in gallon containers. Occasionally these special wines are high-quality products. We remember a Zinfandel of a small winery which was as fruity and characteristic as one could wish. Many of these wineries sell most of their wine in bulk to larger wineries and sell only a small amount locally under their own label.

There are two or three dozen California wineries whose main efforts are directed toward the production of the finest quality of varietal wines, often with a vintage date. These may be priced at $2 to $4 per bottle. They may also simultaneously market generic and nonvintage wines of lesser quality in the $1 to $1.50 range. We do not mean to imply that every $2

FIG. 37. Barrels and oak ovals for aging table wines in an underground cellar. Mold growths on the stone ceiling are normal. Source: The Wine Institute.

vintage wine is great and every $1.50 nonvintage wine less fine. In individual cases the opposite may be true, but, in general, one gets about what one pays for.

Because of the favorable climatic conditions for growing grapes to produce high quality table wines, the best California wines are produced in the cooler coast counties: Mendocino, Sonoma, Napa, Alameda, Santa Clara, San Benito, and Santa Cruz. Recently large plantings have been made in Monterey County. The best California table wines, for reasons already outlined in Chapter 3, are labeled with the variety from which they are produced. Contrariwise, the best dessert wines are produced from grapes grown in the warmer districts.

Summary.—The California wine industry was established during the Mission period. The variety planted, the Mission, was a poor one for table wine production, but was suited to the production of angelica, a fortified dessert wine.

Many European vines were imported between 1830 and 1862. Haraszthy was an important figure in popularizing the new varieties.

The center of the first commercial industry was Los Angeles, but this gradually shifted to northern California in the 1860's. Vineyards were planted throughout the state at an increased rate between 1850 and 1880.

The industry suffered a severe depression in 1876 and again in 1886, because of overplanting and wines of poor quality. However, through the efforts of the Board of State Viticultural Commissioners and the University of California's College of Agriculture, the quality gradually improved.

The early winemakers brought European wine-making practices and nomenclature with them. Use of foreign names for California wines still plagues the California industry.

Prohibition had a severe effect on the industry because the vineyards of fine varieties were gradually grafted to varieties which could ship to distant markets without spoilage. It also drove trained winemakers into other professions, allowed the cooperage to deteriorate, disrupted distribution channels, and interrupted the consumers' acquaintance with California wines.

Repeal, however, showed the industry to have much resilience. A severe depression in prices in 1937–38 required federal assistance. The Wine Institute and Wine Advisory Board have had an important influence in solving the industry's legal, economic, technical, and public-relations problems. The University of California's College of Agriculture has supplied scientific information and trained personnel.

Recently the industry has become more centralized. A few wineries now produce and distribute most of the standard competitive wines, and several smaller wineries produce the higher-quality, more expensive, wines. Many of these wines have gained a world-wide reputation for quality. Both types of wineries produce wines which represent some of the best buys for the American wine consumer.

Chapter 19

WINE APPRECIATION, EVALUATION, AND SERVICE

The most important requirement of any wine is that it give pleasure. However, appreciation of wines is a two-way street. It involves not only the composition of wine itself but also the attitude and experience of the consumer. Those who drink wines or other alcohol beverages to excess can have little or no real appreciation of quality. It is also true that the newly initiated wine taster has a very limited range of appreciation; he may like only one or two wines, or may change his evaluations from one tasting to another.

In the appreciation of quality in wines, as in the appreciation of any aesthetic creation, a learning curve is involved. At first we like products which are easily recognized and understood. Later, with more experience, we demand greater complexity in foods, music, or art for aesthetic appreciation.

Just so with wines: at first the simple, white (low tannin), slightly sweet, low-alcohol, American sauterne-type of wine seems to be the easiest for the new consumer to appreciate. This is probably one reason why the German Liebfraumilch has been so popular in this country; it is low in alcohol and rather highly sugared. Of all the German wines it is the least complex. With time, however, the drier, more flowery, and more distinctive varietal California wines or those of the Saar, Moselle, and Rhine are preferred. And from whites there seems to be a progression in the learning curve to reds and specifically to older reds. The consumer who has never tasted a red wine which has been aged in the bottle for ten or fifteen years can have very little concept of the additional quality gained by such aging. But to the connoisseur an old bottle of California Cabernet wine, one that has been in the bottle for fifteen years, has an incredibly richer and more complex aroma and has assumed a very different character from that of the wine when it was younger. With such complex wines repeated tasting does not bring satiation but reveals new aspects of quality.

To summarize, then, quality in wines is associated with complexity, and this is not easily achieved without special techniques, as in the production of the *Auslese* wines of Germany or the Sauternes of France or the use of very great varieties such as the Chardonnay for the white Burgundies, or the use of great varieties and aging as in the red Burgundies and red Bordeaux or in a California Pinot noir or Cabernet Sauvignon.

But it would be foolish to say that quality was altogether in the wine. The appreciation of quality is in the consumer and his experience with wines will determine his appreciation of them. Some people appreciate one type of wine more than another. Many people in England do not care for the richer, more alcoholic wines of Burgundy; and many people in the Burgundy region or in Belgium do not care for the harder, drier, more acid, and more tannic wines of Bordeaux. These differences are due primarily to differences in experience, but some of them seem to depend also on differences in individual temperament.

The eclectic taster, however, is one who has had experience with many wines and has learned to appreciate different types. The claim of some Europeans that the wines of California or of South Africa are not of high quality is based largely on the fact that they have had very limited experience in tasting these wines, and particularly the better wines. It would be the same if an American went to France and formed his opinion of all French wines on the basis of a single tasting of an ordinary red in some small restaurant in Cette or Bezier in the wine district of the Midi, the *vin ordinaire* district.

Wine appreciation demands quality in the wine and critical experience and evaluation from the consumer.

The problem of wine classification is simple compared to the problems of wine appreciation and evaluation. Man receives impressions from the world about him through his senses. As far as wines are concerned our impressions are based upon visual, olfactory, gustatory, and feel sensations. From our mental synthesis of these sensations comes appreciation. The visual appreciation of wines is one of the important aspects of wine evaluation. Not only is there an aesthetic appreciation when the wine is an appropriate and beautiful color, but our future evaluation of quality will be based partly upon what we see. Visually, we are aware of two aspects of wines: appearance, that is, freedom from suspended material, and color. The appearance of wine is frequently a good indication of its condition.

Wines should be brilliant when served. Most commercial wines are now filtered before shipment and normally reach the consumer in brilliant condition. Occasionally a white wine becomes cloudy, particularly slightly sweet wines such as Graves. This is usually due to growth of yeasts in the wine. If it is pronounced enough to give the wine a yeasty odor or to make the wine gassy, it is a negative quality factor.

Wines may have a slight haze if they were not stored under cool enough conditions to remove the excess cream of tartar which young wines contain. In some wines tartrate crystals may be found in the bottom of the bottle. Such wines may be decanted and served free of the crystals. Even though the tartrate crystals have no harmful effect on the flavor, they are aesthetically unappealing.

Red wines after some years in the bottle will develop a precipitate of coloring matter. This is unavoidable and is almost a guarantee of the age of the wine. In old wines it is thus not a negative quality factor. However, if the deposit is disturbed and clouds the wine it detracts from the appreciation of the wine. By proper decanting it is usually possible to secure a brilliant wine.

Color is one of the most attractive aesthetic features of wines. Wines come in many different colors and the different types of wines have their appropriate color range. An acceptable California rosé is neither too light nor too dark a red. If it is on the light side and has a brown tint we can be sure that it has become somewhat oxidized or been aged too long. And if it is on the purple side, that is, too dark, it is probably rather bitter for a rosé (owing to having been left on the skins too long). One learns only by experience the appropriate color for each type, but in general the white table wines should be free of brown color, since browning usually indicates excess oxidation and the development of vapid or aldehyde-like odors. The young red table wines should certainly have a full red color, but a slight browning (shift toward orange) of the color is expected in old red wines.

Dessert wines come in an even wider range of colors, all the way from the very light yellows of a young *fino* sherry to the almost amber dark colors of some Marsalas. Among the reds are wines with a very slight amber red, as in the California tokay, to the very deep purple-red of a young vintage port. In the older red wines a certain amount of browning of the color is permissible.

The accompanying tabulation indicates the desirable ranges in color and preferred usage of different types of wines.

295

	Preferred color	*Preferred usage*
WHITE TABLE		
White Riesling	greenish yellow to yellow	apéritif, with fish and entrée, with meats
Chablis	light yellow	apéritif, with fish and entrée, with meats
Chardonnay	yellow to light gold	apéritif, with fish and entrée, with meats
Sauvignon blanc	yellow to light gold	apéritif, with fish and entrée, with meats
SWEET TABLE		
Auslese	light gold to gold	with cheeses, fruits, desserts
Sauternes	light gold to gold	with cheeses, fruits, desserts
Tokay (Hungarian)	light gold to gold (no amber)	with fruits, desserts
Rosé	pink (no amber or purple)	apéritif, with fish and entrée, with meats
RED TABLE		
Pinot noir	low to medium red	with meats and cheese
Cabernet Sauvignon	medium red	with meats and cheese
Zinfandel	medium red	with meats and cheese
SHERRY		
Fino (flor)	light amber yellow	apéritif
Oloroso	brownish gold to amber	with desserts or after meals

	Preferred color	*Preferred usage*
Dry baked	light amber	apéritif
Sweet baked	medium amber	with desserts or after meals
RED DESSERT		
Tawny port	amber-red	with cheese, fruits, desserts or after meals
Ruby port	ruby red	with cheese, fruits, desserts or after meals
WHITE DESSERT		
Muscatel	light amber-gold to gold	with fruits, desserts or after meals
Tokay (California)	pink-amber	with fruits, desserts or after meals
White port or angelica	medium yellow	with fruits, desserts or after meals
Málaga	dark amber	with desserts or after meals
VERMOUTH		
Dry	light yellow	apéritif or in cocktails
Sweet	medium to dark amber	with desserts or in cocktails
CHAMPAGNE		
Red	red	with meats, cheese
Rosé	pink	apéritif, with fish and entrée, with meats and cheese, fruits, desserts
White	light yellow	apéritif, with fish and entrée, with meats and cheese, fruits, desserts

There are many acceptable variations which such a list cannot show. Old reds, Cabernet Sauvignons, for example, have a definite amber tint. The rule is that the tint must be appropriate not only to the type but to the age of the wine. Within the sweet baked sherry group are wines almost pure gold in color and others very amber.

The "made" wine types, such as Marsala, *flor* sherry, Madeira, and baked sherry, thus may have a color appropriate to the standards of the producer. Even within a single type the winemaker may produce a variety of subtypes each with a distinctive color.

As beautiful and appropriate as color is, it is an external matter. The most important quality factor is the odor—more important than taste because of the infinite variety of delicate, subtle differences which are possible. Odor consists of inappropriate or undesirable odors and natural and appropriate odors. The olfactory sense can distinguish around 4,000 or even more different odors! Connoisseurs who have studied the wines of a given district for many years are able to detect differences in odors between wines of different vintages and wines from different vineyards. The amateur, even the educated amateur, who does not study the wines of a given district thoroughly and carefully rarely acquires such an appreciation of the differences between vintages and vineyards. Although a good deal can be learned about the differences among wines from their color, certainly among different types but also between wines of the same type, difference in odor is the critical factor in evaluating or differentiating wines. Since the sensitivity to odor of the amateur is generally as good as that of the professional, there is no reason why the interested wine drinker cannot learn to identify a wide variety of vinous odors if he acquires sufficient experience.

The good or desirable odors of wines come from the variety of grape from which they are produced, from the by-products of alcoholic fermentation, and from treatments given during aging or by the aging process itself. The odors originating in the grape we call aromas, those from processing or aging, bouquet. The varietal aromas which we expect are particularly important in wines which are named after the variety of grape from which they are produced. Thus we expect muscatels to have a muscat aroma, Cabernets to have a Cabernet aroma, Rieslings to have a Riesling aroma, and so on. In a number of the regions of the world all the wine of the region is made from a single variety of grape and thus, even though the wine does not have a varietal label, we expect it to have a varietal aroma. This is true, for example, of the Burgundy region of France, where Pinot noir is the predominant variety planted: we expect the red wines of Burgundy to have a Pinot noir aroma. The same thing is true of the wines of the Bordeaux district, where the variety designation is often omitted. However, a Cabernet aroma is to be expected, since Cabernet-type varieties of grapes predominate in that region.

Fermentation odors are the background odors that we find in all wines. They are apparently due to ethyl alcohol, higher alcohols, and small amounts of a large number (about 150 odorous, volatile compounds have been identified from wines) of compounds, particularly esters. These compounds give the wine its grapy and winy character and further reactions among them give the aging changes.

The odors which are due to treatments given during aging or to the aging process itself are often of great importance. Among such odors are those due to baking of Madeiras or California sherries, the odors resulting from the addition of boiled-down grape juice, as in the Marsalas, and the odors arising from the activities of a *flor* yeast, as in Spanish sherries and *montillas* and California, South African, or Australian *flor*-type wines. For odors due to aging, we have the gradual disappearance of fermentation odors during short periods of aging. The characteristic odors of red table and dessert wines develop during long aging. One effect of aging seems to be due to the dissolving of a slight amount of the flavors from the wood, in red table and dessert wines and in brandies. There also seem to be special odor constituents, possibly from amino acids and esterification, which are slowly formed during aging. Wine in the bottle develops special odors called bottle bouquet. These odors are much desired, particularly in old red table wines and vintage ports, and they are also to be looked for in fine white Burgundies, California Chardonnay, most Sauternes, and the sweeter German wines.

The most common off-odors found in wines are fermentation or yeast off-odors which appear to involve hydrogen sulfide and mercaptans. These usually disappear owing to oxidation and aeration during the early aging of the wine. Occasionally, however, a wine retains more than a threshold amount of the fermentation off-odors. We sometimes object to too much higher alcohol in fortified wines; however, a recognizable amount seems to be favored by producers of Portuguese ports. This emphasizes the difference in standards. The consumer who is willing to appreciate a variety of wines obviously will find more wines to enjoy.

Off-odors resulting from excessively warm fermentations, called pomace odors, are usually found only in red table wines. Off-odors can arise from the use of moldy grapes. The most common off-odors are due to excessive oxidation in table wines or to the use of too much sulfur dioxide as an antiseptic agent. Many German, most Graves, and some other white wines, particularly of the cheaper competitive domestic types, contain excessive sulfur dioxide. A new antiseptic agent, sorbic acid, has an undesirable odor when used in excessive amounts. Formerly a good deal of acetic acid was present in table wines, but since Pasteur, particularly since 1900, it is rather rare to find a bottled wine which has an acescent or vinegary smell. However, in countries where wine is distributed in bulk, particularly in Italy, some wines may have a vinegary odor. Actually the smell is due more to excessive ethyl acetate than to acetic acid, but it is easily recognized as being a vinegary type of odor.

At present few wine disorders are permitted to develop to the stage where an off-odor develops. Yeastiness has been mentioned as one possible odor if excessive yeast growth occurs (or if wines are bottled very soon after fermentation). Off-odors from lactic acid bacteria are occasionally found in wines from Burgundy and from Italy. There seems to be, however, some desirable odorous by-products from a properly conducted malolactic fermentation.

If the grapes are not picked soon enough in California and in regions of similar climate, a raisin-like odor may occur. Also, very late-harvested grapes of low total acidity and high pH have an undesirable (rubber-boot) odor.

Occasionally, particularly in red table wines that have been bottled for a number of years, the cork may communicate an off-odor to the wine. Corkiness is a very undesirable odor, reminiscent of moldiness, and when unmistakably present is sufficient excuse for refusing the wine in a restaurant.

Excessive aeration of table wines, particularly of white table wines, leads to an oxidized or aerated odor. While this may be desirable in some dessert wines it is not in table wines. With whites it is often accompanied by a slight brownish tint.

Table wines seldom have excessive woodiness from overaging in small cooperage. A slight woodiness is desirable in some red table wines, in brandies, and in many dessert wines, but not in white table wines.

In contrast to the multiple nuances of odor which we are able to distinguish, we seem to be limited to four taste characteristics: sour or acid, sweet, bitter, and salty. Wines rarely have a salty taste, although occasional wines from the Colares district, on the Atlantic seaboard near Lisbon, seem to have a salty taste. It has been reported in certain wines from the south of France, from Italy, and in highly plastered wines. (See p. 165.)

The sour or acid taste, in contrast to the opinion of the amateur, is a very necessary and desirable part of the taste of the wine. The amateur's negative reaction is less likely to occur if the wine is consumed with food. Without acidity the wines would be exceedingly flat, would be subject to bacterial spoilage, would not ferment as well, and would not have the lovely yellow and red colors which give so much pleasure. However, the acidity must be appropriate for the type. In some wines we expect more acidity than we do in other types of wines. Rieslings taste fresher and fruitier if they have a rather high total acidity. All dry white table wines require a degree of acidity to give them interest. In red table wines we wish a moderate acidity, but they should not be too tart, since their tannin may accentuate tartness. Excessively high acidity in sweet table wines or in dessert wines is not desired, since a very intense sweet-sour taste tends to be unpleasant. However, some individual variation in reaction to the sweet-sour taste does occur. Furthermore, the sweetness is usually sufficient to add a dominant note of interest to the wine. Where the sugar content is low, as in dry sherries or dry vermouths, the processing and herb flavors provide a focus of interest. This does not mean, however, that sweet table wines and dessert wines should not have reasonable acidity. Many dessert wines are too low in acidity, some Málagas and California tokays, for example, and thus taste flat and uninteresting.

The sweet taste in wines is due primarily to the presence of two sugars: glucose and fructose, as well as to the alcohol glycerol. Fructose is considerably sweeter than glucose, but in most sweet wines they are present in about equal proportions. The sugar threshold for the sweet taste in wines is somewhere between 0.75 and 1.5 per cent, depending on the sensitivity of the individual. Wines with less than 1 per cent sugar are usually noted by the wine judge as being without sweetness. This sweet taste is partially masked by acids, and vice versa.

The sugar content of different wines should be appropriate for the type. It is customary for most ports to have 10 to 14 per cent sugar. The Russians, however, produce a number of dessert wines with over 20 per cent sugar and the wines of

Málaga are often equally sweet. The wines of Sauternes may range from 5 per cent to as much as 15 per cent sugar In sparkling wines, the driest kinds have only about 1 per cent sugar and are labeled *brut*. The *sec* (or dry) types may have as much as 3 per cent sugar and some even sweeter types of sparkling wines are occasionally produced. The driest sherries are actually somewhat sweet, usually with 1 to 2 per cent sugar. The same is true of most of the dry vermouths, which may have as much as 4 per cent sugar.

Wine connoisseurs tend to "look down their noses" at sweet wines. It is true that defects in wine are easily masked by raising the sugar content, particularly in sparkling wines. Thus the connoisseur has the assurance that when the wine is dry and very good it is also very honest. This is not entirely a fair comparison, however, because sweetness is a desirable taste and it is not out of place in certain kinds of wines. Sugar is inappropriate in wines which are intended to be drunk with foods. Here the presence of sugar tends to appease the appetite and thus reduce the enjoyment of food. Certainly with our meals we need wines which are quite dry just as we normally eat foods which are not sweet. A number of California red wines contain 1.5 per cent of sugar. This low amount of sugar probably does not have a major effect on appetite. However, unfortunately, the tendency seems to be to sugar contents of over 1.5 per cent in table wines, as in many German and other European white table wines and in California rosés.

The bitter taste is not normally appreciated by new wine drinkers, but with experience consumers do develop an appreciation for a moderately bitter taste. The bitter taste in wines is due to some tannins, flavonoids, and probably other compounds. Since white wines have a very low tannin content they are also generally nearly free of a bitter taste. Even in rosé wines the tannin content is low and the wines have only a slightly bitter taste. Only in red wines, particularly young red wines, is the tannin content high enough to be noticeable to

303

the taste. Modern technology can reduce the tannin content of young wines so that it will not be objectionably high. However, the tannins act as antioxidants in the wine and guarantee it against overoxidation during aging in the bottle. In addition, the side products of the oxidation of tannins may lead to the development of desirable flavors in red wines after they have been bottled. However, even a well-aged red wine retains a slightly bitter taste which is not objectionable to the connoisseur. A related but apparently separate sensory response is that to astringency, which relates to the "feel" of the wine more than to the bitter taste. A "smooth" wine is one lacking in astringency and a "rough"one is too high in this character.

A great deal has been written about the "body" of wines. Often this seems to have been based on the feel or texture of the wine. It is difficult semantically to define body. We prefer to think of body as a measure of the alcoholicity of the wine which is expressed in the degree of "wateriness" or the viscosity of the wine. A wine of low alcohol would then be said to have a low body or have a "thin" feel. Wines of higher alcohol content would not be thin. It is almost impossible to react to this alcoholicity, within limits, if the wines are very sweet. High sweetness makes it difficult for the palate to distinguish the alcoholicity (or body) of the wine. Nevertheless, the term "body" is useful if it is restricted to the meaning we have indicated. Certainly its use as a measure of the glycerol content is not correct. The amount of glycerol in wines is only slightly above the glycerol threshold, and in the presence of high amounts of sugar the sweetness of the glycerol is completely covered. The total nonsugar solids may be related to the body, since this is generally higher the greater the alcohol content.

The trigeminal or free nerve endings in the nose may be stimulated by excess sulfur dioxide, causing sneezing. Some other constituents of special wines may stimulate the pain receptors, especially in wines of high aldehyde content.

Theoretically, if wine tasting has been properly done the visual, olfactory, gustatory, and feel impressions should comprise all the sensory characteristics of a wine. However, flavor is a useful term for a synthesis of taste and odor. A number of odorous characteristics do not come to the attention of the wine taster until they have been received in the mouth. Among the most important is the fruitiness of the wine. While this is measured somewhat by the degree of acid taste, it may be related also to the presence of a small amount of leaf aldehyde or other fruity kinds of aromatic constituents.

When we say that a wine has a hot taste, this may refer to a flavor characteristic of aldehydes or other similar compounds. The earthy character of wine is rarely perceived until the wine has been in the mouth several seconds. While this is apparently an odor it is usually perceived along with other mixed sensations and can properly be spoken of as a flavor. The earthy flavor is found in wines made from grapes grown on certain types of soil. Wines which have been left on the yeast too long (so that there has been excessive yeast autolysis) will sometimes get a rotten type of flavor which is perceived with difficulty when present at threshold concentrations. The "corked" characteristic of many wines should be noted early in the tasting under the "off-odors," but sometimes it is not perceived until the wine has been tasted. This is true also of the moldy taste of wines which have been made from moldy grapes.

If the tasting has been properly done, all the sensory impressions should summate to give the quality of the wine. However, this does not seem to be true, for when score cards are used the wine does not seem to be quite the sum of the individual sensory impressions. This implies that there is a sensory summation which may be called "general quality." This has also been demonstrated by a mathematical technique known as factor analysis; hence the characteristic known as general quality, although not precise, does seem to have some justification. The after-taste or finish of the wine is also important,

305

although we do not know its precise parameters. Lack of extreme bitterness is the most obvious. As a first approximation, "general quality" can be thought of as the sum of the "after-taste" and the "over-all" impression of the wine.

The amateur wine taster will not wish to bother with the elaborate score cards used in the sensory examination of foods. However, he may wish to use a simple score card when attending wine tastings, visiting wineries, or for comparative home tastings. Score cards have another advantage in that they force the taster to examine the wine systematically and not to forget any of its characteristics. We suggest a simple score card with twenty points. This has the advantage in that many of the European wine score cards also have twenty points.

The visual aspects, appearance and color, are rated at two points, or 10 per cent each, for a total of 20 per cent. The visual aspects are more important to some tasters, and especially with some white wines may be worth more than 20 per cent. The olfactory characteristics of aroma and bouquet and the vinegary smell add up to six points, or 30 per cent of the total. The two points for flavor and the two points for general quality are partially based on olfactory sensations; so, of the total score, at least 40 to 50 per cent is probably due to olfactory sensations. The gustatory characteristics are rated under acidity, sweetness, and bitterness for five points, or 25 per cent of the total. Again, a certain amount of the flavor and general quality is based on gustatory sensation; hence taste is approximately 30 per cent of the total. The texture or feel sensations get only one point, or 5 per cent of the total.

SCORE CARD FOR WINE

APPEARANCE   2
   Cloudy 0, clear 1, brilliant 2
COLOR   2
   Distinctly off 0, slightly off 1, correct 2

AROMA AND BOUQUET	4
Vinous 1, distinct but not varietal 2, varietal 3	
Subtract 1 or 2 for off-odors, add 1 for bottle bouquet	
VINEGARY	2
Obvious 0, slight 1, none 2	
TOTAL ACIDITY	2
Distinctly low or high 0, slightly high or low 1, normal 2	
SWEETNESS	1
Too high or low 0, normal 1	
BODY	1
Too high or low 0, normal 1	
FLAVOR	2
Distinctly abnormal 0, slightly abnormal 1, normal 2	
BITTERNESS	2
Distinctly high 0, slightly high 1, normal 2	
GENERAL QUALITY	2
Lacking 0, slight 1, impressive 2	

As a guide to the consumer we suggest that wines of outstanding characteristics should score between seventeen and twenty points. Sound commercial wines with no outstanding defect or merit will normally score between thirteen and sixteen points. It is not likely that many commercial wines will have less than thirteen points; however, wines of nine to twelve points are of commercial acceptability but with a noticeable defect. Obviously the effective scoring range for most commercial wines can be graded within a score card of no more than ten points. This is probably about the maximum quality range which can be distinguished.

Sometimes the consumer (and often the producer) will wish to know whether there is a really noticeable difference between two specific wines. Since the odds are 50 per cent that one or the other wine may be correctly identified in a single blind trial by guessing, it is necessary to repeat the test in order to make sure that there is a statistically significant difference between them. In a test with two wines where each wine is presented simultaneously, the wine must be correctly identified in nine out of ten tests to be significant at the 5 per cent level. Significance at the 5 per cent level means that only once in twenty times would such a result be due to chance. Other methods of determining differences between two samples to standardize blends, et cetera, are outlined in the publication by Amerine *et al.* (1959).

If more than two wines of the same type are to be judged on a single occasion, it may be desired to rank them in the order of their quality. The difficulty in a ranking procedure is that not all the judges may have the same quality standard for all the wines. If one judge considers the appearance and color to be exceedingly important aspects of the quality, he may rank the wines on the basis of their freedom from sediment and their conformity to the proper color. Another judge may feel that appearance and color are of minor importance and may judge the wines primarily on odor or on taste. It is unlikely that the rankings of the two judges will conform well. The averaging of their ranks will certainly not give a good measure of the relative merits of the wines. The judge who ranks mainly on visual aspects may rank the wines BCDAE, while the judge who ranks on odor or flavor may rank the wines EADCB. The average rank is then the same for all the wines! Therefore, all the judges should clearly understand the basis of the ranking.

Even after the ranking has been done, however, we have no information on how much difference there is between the wines. For example, there might be two very good wines and one exceedingly bad wine. In the rankings these would rank "one," "two," and "three" and we would think that the difference between rank two and rank three was the same as the difference between rank one and rank two but of course it is not.

Evaluation of wine quality is not an easily acquired art. A good deal of practice and comparisons of various wines are necessary for the taster to gain confidence in his opinions. The best way to acquire this experience is in the company of an experienced person who knows the difference between the qualities of different wines and can explain the reasons for his evaluations. This can sometimes be obtained from the personnel at wineries. However, since winery tastings are an adjunct of the winery's public relations program, the relative quality of the wines is rarely explained. In some wineries, both foreign and domestic, all the wines of the particular winery are said to be of the highest quality, which may be patently untrue.

There are occasional reliable evaluations of wine quality in the literature. However, many of these are out of date almost before they have been published, since the wines are now too old. Also, the evaluations of wines in the popular journals are frequently written, or ghost written at least, by writers who are working for one or another part of the industry and might be somewhat biased.

When the wine judgings at fairs have been made on a true quality basis and not on a ranking basis they are sometimes a good indication of quality. Many wine judgings lack validity, for they are not made by experts and the representation of wines of a district or country is far from complete. The methodology used at the California State Fair is probably the best now in use. The professional judgings in Australia, Hungary, Yugoslavia and South Africa also seem to be well done.

However, in the final analysis, quality is an individual matter and must be determined by each consumer. Thus, some consumers may like the Pinot noir better than Cabernet Sauvignon. Others may prefer well-aged tawny ports to the more fruity ruby ports; some may find the more flowery German wines better than the French white wines. Actually, an appreciation of the differences among wines is worth while since it increases one's range of enjoyment. To refuse to taste Pinot noir because one prefers Cabernet Sauvignon deprives one of the very real merits of Pinot noir.

The finest wines, especially well-aged red wines, are often spoiled between the cellar and the table. The reason for this is that the wines gradually throw a small deposit as they are aged in the bottle and if care is not taken the deposit will be stirred up in moving the wine from the cellar to the table. The wine then appears on the table in a cloudy condition. The other aspect of bad wine service is the fact that wines are often served too cold or too hot.

Bottles of wine with no sediment can be stood on end and brought directly to the table. They do not need a wine basket to be poured from, but are better poured directly from the bottle. The small sponge rubber rings that fit around the neck of the bottle are useful to prevent the wine from running down the side of the bottle onto the tablecloth. Wine coasters in which the bottle can sit are also desirable to prevent staining of the table linen.

But for wine that has any sediment at all, special care must be taken in bringing it to the table. In white wines the amount of sediment is usually small; it is usually crystalline and very heavy, and if the bottle is placed on end a couple of hours before opening the sediment usually drops to the bottom. Only the last glass will get a few tartrate crystals. It is red wines that we have to worry about with respect to service. The types of deposit in red wines are of many kinds. They may be fairly granular or adhere well to the sides of the bottle. Or the deposits may be very light, finely divided, and easily disturbed; these require very special care. An old bottle should be lifted up and held over a candle or a small electric bulb (preferably unfrosted and with filaments) to inspect any deposit present. If there is deposit, the bottle should be laid on a table without having been turned to the right or left from its original position. It can be placed in a basket, but usually this does not help, for the bottle has to be tipped up to get it into the basket and this disturbs the sediment. Generally it is best to simply lay the bottle on a table and put an object on each side to prevent it from turning. The bottle should then be raised about an inch from the horizontal so that a slight air space develops under the cork. The cork should be removed carefully without turning or shaking the bottle.

Some of the many different types of corkscrews are illustrated in Figures 38 and 39. We personally prefer those which have a secondary-lever action, but it is most important that the screw on the corkscrew be fairly wide and that the screw be long enough to reach entirely through the cork. This is particularly important with some of the Bordeaux wines, where the corks are 2 to 2¼ inches long. The open spiral corkscrew without a center rod is also usually more satisfactory. Recently a simple apparatus, Figure 39, lower left, using carbon dioxide has been developed. A hollow needle is inserted through the cork and carbon dioxide is released. Because of the danger of the bottle exploding we prefer corkscrews.

With bottle held firmly, the screw is carefully inserted and the cork withdrawn. The bottle is then raised and a candle or small electric light bulb (again not frosted and with naked filaments) is placed under the neck. The wine is then slowly decanted into a clean dry decanter or bottle. As soon as the sediment reaches the neck of the bottle the decanting is stopped.

Decanting is always necessary with old wines which contain sediment. The decanting should not be done more than one hour before the wine is to be served. Very old wines should be decanted immediately before serving, as the wine rapidly loses its bouquet.

Some wines—such as many young whites, rosés, Beaujolais, and red Italian—profit by decanting, particularly if they are gassy or contain a slight residual fermentation odor. The advantage of decanting is that they lose the gassiness and fermentation odor.

White table wines should be chilled to about 55° F. Sparkling wines are best served at about 50° F. Rosé wines and most

311

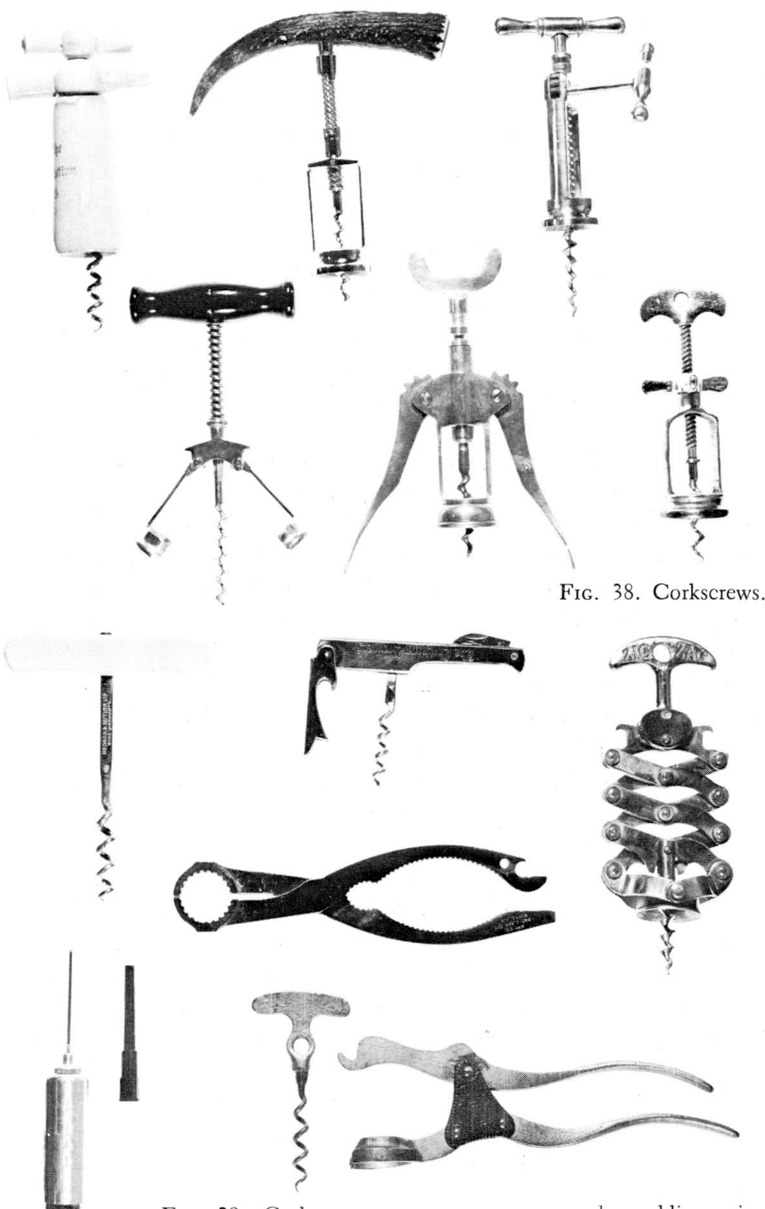

Fig. 38. Corkscrews.

Fig. 39. Corkscrews, pressure opener, and sparkling wine cork opener.

dessert wines require only a slight chilling to about 60° F. Red table and old port wines should be served at a cool room temperature, 65° to 68°.

Wine glasses are made in many shapes and colors. The more common types are shown in Figures 40 and 41. For everyday use a clear tulip-shaped glass holding six to eight ounces is satisfactory for all wines. For more formal occasions when several types are served a variety of glasses may be used. For dessert wines four-ounce glasses, such as Figure 40, left, may be used; for white table wines, four- to six-ounce glasses, Figure 41, left pair; for red table wines, eight- to ten-ounce glasses, Figure 41, right pair; for champagne, tulip shaped or hollow stem glasses, Figure 40, center. The brandy snifter, Figure 40, right, is useful for critical evaluation of wines or brandies, but the all-purpose glass is better for drinking. Colored glasses should never be used, for they prevent proper appreciation of the wine's color.

Wine glasses should be washed with detergent in hot water, thoroughly rinsed in soft hot water, and wiped after draining dry. The wiping cloth should be lint-free and thoroughly rinsed and dried. No water stains should remain on the glass.

Most of our best red wines, particularly California Cabernets, Bordeaux, Burgundies, and Rhones are being consumed too soon. They would greatly appreciate in value by longer aging. White table wines, on the contrary, are often kept too long. We prefer to err on the side of drinking white wines too young rather than too old. By this we mean within one to five years of bottling; heavier-bodied and sweeter types may profit by even longer aging.

Cellars for wine storage should have an even temperature throughout the year, preferably 55° to 60° F. The bottles should be laid on the side with no air bubble next to the cork.

The climatic conditions under which the grapes are grown influence the composition of the grape and hence the quality of the wine. Under the cool conditions of northern Europe this is particularly important. In the cooler years the grapes fail to

FIG. 40. Bottles and glasses for dessert wines, sparkling wines, and brandies. (From left to right: dessert wine fifth, sparkling wine fifth with crown cap finish, brandy fifth.)

ripen, have excess acidity, and are deficient in flavor. Hence the warm years produce the best wines. For Germany the last great years were 1959 and 1964. However, very good wines were produced in 1962, 1961, 1960, 1958, and 1957. The last poor years were 1965, 1963, and 1956. For France in Bordeaux, Burgundy, and Champagne the best recent vintages were 1964, 1962, 1961, 1959, and 1955. Good wines were produced in 1958 and 1957 (except in Champagne, where the wines were poor); the vintages of 1960, 1956, and 1954 were generally poor, some good red Burgundy was made in 1960. For the Rhone the same holds true: 1964, 1962, 1959, 1958, 1955, and 1953 were best; 1965, 1963, 1961, and 1960, good; 1957 was less satisfactory. While differences in table wines produced in different years occur in Spain, Italy, Switzerland, Portugal, Austria, and other countries, these are not so well documented and the buyer must establish the quality by tasting. Blended wines, such as

314

Fig. 41. Bottles and glasses for different types of wines. (From left to right: rhine fifth, Bordeaux tenth, fifth, and magnum, burgundy fifth.)

sherry, Madeira, Málaga, and Marsala, cannot be vintaged. Vintage port is, however, important. Generally the best ports are from the cooler years. For example, 1959 was a failure in the Douro, but very good elsewhere in Europe. The best recent vintage port years were 1965, 1963, 1960, 1955, 1950, and 1948. Good wines were produced in 1962, 1958, 1957, 1954, and 1953. Even in the best years not all the wines are superior, and in the poorest years some fine wine may be produced. No one should be a slave to vintage labeling, but one can get some guidance from the above list of vintage years.

In California there has been an unfortunate tendency to abandon vintage labeling. The producers say that restaurants do not understand why a vintage wine cannot be kept in stock. Also, changing the vintage means that the wine list must be reprinted. Salesmen and wholesalers object because they must carry more wines in stock. The producers claim that the legal

315

restrictions in labeling vintage wines are a nuisance and not worth the trouble (records, etc.).

However, the vintage is very important from the consumer's point of view, and we believe there should be more use of the vintage on the better California wines, particularly on varietal wines from the cooler climates. The vintage date is a guarantee of the age of a wine. It also enables the consumer to reorder and get the same wine. It is therefore important in building brand loyalty.

It is true that spectacular differences do not occur between years in California. However, 1948 and 1962 seem generally to have been less satisfactory. Also, wineries differ in their success with a given vintage. One winemaker may pick too early and produce a less satisfactory wine than his neighbor who waited; or, vice versa, the winemaker who waited to harvest may have been caught by prolonged rains and his wines may be poor. Thus even in years when most wines were fine, as, for example, 1959 in Europe and 1958 in the Napa Valley, poor wines were produced. Even in poor years some are more successful than others. We remember, for example, a 1948 Cabernet Sauvignon of Napa Valley which was excellent.

Summary.—The factors influencing wine appreciation are outlined, particularly the importance of experience. The actual evaluation depends on color, appearance, olfactory properties, taste, and other sensations.

The use of simple score cards and difference tests and ranking are recommended. For the best utilization they require training.

Simple rules for the service of wines are presented, particularly with respect to decanting, temperature of serving, and storage. Although a summary of the quality of recent vintages has been given this is not to be taken too seriously. The proof of the quality of a wine is in the contents, not on the label.

Chapter 20

WINE AS ALCOHOL

Physiological and social ills are associated with the excessive consumption of alcoholic beverages. The problems are complex and informed opinions differ as to their nature and solution. A short discussion seems necessary. Too few persons who might be described as "permissivists" have dared to speak over the clamor of the restrictionists and prohibitionists. Products do not survive in commerce unless consumers consider them useful and desirable. The long-continued and wide sale of alcoholic beverages in spite of all manner of prohibitions, exorbitant taxes, and other restrictions indicates that they are valued by a large segment of the adult population. Part of this value attaches to their flavor and attractiveness as beverages and part to their content of alcohol. In this chapter we are concerned primarily with the latter.

Alcohol produces physiological and behavioral effects in normal individuals. This has been known since beverages containing alcohol were discovered. The term "spirits" and the German term "Weingeist" (brandy) hark back to the ancient belief that the spirit, ghost, or "soul" in wine enabled the consumer to communicate with the nether and/or heavenly worlds. Even in recent times, primitive cultures—some not so primitive

—often reserved alcoholic beverages for priests. If they were available to the populace, their consumption was often reserved for infrequent special occasions, usually a communal "religious" orgy in which drunkenness prevailed.

Alcohol acts as an irregularly descending depressant of the central nervous system. The higher levels of cortical control are inhibited first. This helps to account for the fact that a physiological depressant has been considered a stimulant. Alcohol is often a social stimulant because inhibitions may be suppressed. Something one wishes to do, but ordinarily would repress, may be done more easily after consumption of a certain amount of alcohol. Imagine the stimulation of the social climate if, at a cocktail party, one's wife loses her inhibitions to the point of speaking frankly about the hat worn by the wife of one's boss. In a more serious vein, this effect may be used deliberately or unconsciously by criminals to allow them to commit acts that they would otherwise be afraid to do. If so, at least most jurists believe, the legal intent to commit the act was there and the man, not the alcohol, should be blamed.

In moderate doses repeated at reasonable intervals the effects of alcohol appear to be completely reversible with no evident residual effect. The symptoms of the influence of alcohol on the human system and of intoxication depend upon the amount, kind, timing, and rate of alcoholic beverage consumption. The common symptoms of intoxication are an alcoholic breath, flushed face, dilated pupils, gross changes in gait, gross abnormality in speech, and a significant level of alcohol in the blood. If the level of alcohol in the blood is less than 0.10 per cent the person is unlikely to be intoxicated. At 0.20 per cent he is unlikely to be sober. Blood levels of 0.30 per cent generally correspond to a reeling stupor, 0.40 per cent to coma, and 0.45 per cent or more is likely to produce death. Individuals differ in their response to the same level of alcohol in the blood and the same individual may react differently at different times. Although 0.15 g./100 ml. (%) is considered the limit for

318

reasonably normal behavior and is the legal test for drunkenness in several states, about 10 per cent of a large group of people behave as if drunk before reaching this level. Impairment with respect to some activities can be demonstrated at lower blood levels (0.03 to 0.10 per cent). Some cases have been reported of clinical sobriety at 0.4 per cent in the blood and survival after blood levels in excess of 0.5 per cent. Heavy drinkers *may* develop some tolerance, but nervousness, head injuries, and general debility often lead to lower tolerance to alcohol. The performance of some tasks (such as timed solving of arithmetic) may be improved by small amounts of alcohol. Probably this is due to decreased tension and nervousness, and increased confidence.

The consumption of sufficient alcohol to produce a blood level of 0.15 per cent in the average man approximates 6 ounces of 100-proof whiskey within two hours on an empty stomach. It would seem that such consumption would not be accidental. Alcohol is absorbed very quickly and efficiently. About 20 per cent of the dose may be absorbed from the stomach, which is an unusually high percentage compared to other foods. The remainder of the alcohol consumed is absorbed in the small intestine with none appearing in the feces. The entire dose consumed is ordinarily in the blood stream within about two hours. It is rapidly distributed in all body liquids. The smaller individual will reach a higher blood level with the same consumption than will a larger person. Body fluids total about 30 liters, or nearly 8 gallons per 100 pounds of body weight, and this estimate will enable one to predict the blood level and effect of given doses of alcohol.

The form and manner of consumption of alcohol affect its absorption. Presence of food in the stomach delays absorption. Alcohol in the range of 10–35 per cent solutions is more rapidly absorbed. Lower concentrations delay absorption, owing to dilution; higher concentrations produce pylorospasm and prevent passage from the stomach. If consumption is continued,

319

regurgitation results. Carbonated mixtures are more rapidly absorbed because the pylorus is relaxed by carbon dioxide solutions and rapid passage into the intestine hastens absorption. Such nostrums as cream before drinking to increase safe capacity have little value except as they serve as diluents or affect the pylorus. Solid foods and fats are retained in the stomach longer than watery fluids. Maximum delay in complete absorption and therefore lowest peak blood levels of alcohol are obtained by a combination of solid foods plus a reasonable volume of diluents, that is, a meal.

The alcohol in the blood is only 2–10 per cent excreted via the lungs and kidneys. The remaining 90–98 per cent is completely metabolized to yield 7 kilocalories of useful energy (per gram of alcohol), carbon dioxide, and water. A 3-ounce serving of table wine or champagne supplies about 80 calories, of sherry and dessert wines about 120–170 calories, and one ounce of brandy about 80 calories. In contrast, a 6-ounce serving of cola beverage contributes about 85 calories, a 1.5-ounce jigger of whiskey about 120 calories, mixed drinks about 110–320 calories per serving, and a 12-ounce bottle of beer about 170 calories. A convenient rule of thumb is that 1° proof or 0.5 per cent of alcohol yields about 1 kilocalorie per one ounce serving.

The liver contains the enzyme alcohol dehydrogenase which produces acetaldehyde from alcohol. This product can be noticed in the odor of the breath of intoxicated persons (ketosis). The acetaldehyde is converted enzymatically to acetyl co-enzyme A. This substance is also a major product in the catabolism of fat, sugars, and some other dietary constituents, and enters into the normal metabolism of the body. The first step in the liver is the limiting one in clearing the alcohol from the system. The maximum rate of this reaction is roughly 15 milliliters of alcohol per hour. Coffee and most other "sobering up" treatments help little or none. This maximum rate is approximately equivalent to one-fifth of a gallon of whiskey in 24 hours. This amount of alcohol supplies about 2,000 kilocalories

320

—near the normal dietary need for energy. It is no coincidence that the terminal alcoholic often consumes about one bottle (⅕ gallon) of strong spirits per day and eats little food.

Alcoholic beverages and wines in particular have a long and honorable history of usefulness in both lay and formal medical therapy. With the development of the modern more specific and more potent drugs, the use of alcohol in medicine has declined but not disappeared. Alcohol has been said to be the most thoroughly studied, most valuable, and safest tranquilizer known. It helps reduce pain, anxiety, and tension. In a palatable form such as wine it can serve as a tonic. Use of wine, especially for the aged or convalescent, can lend interest and flavor to the diet. The appetite and feeling of well-being can be stimulated. Dry wine can be a source of nonsugar calories as well as dietary variety for diabetics and others on restricted diets. Wine is normally low in sodium and high in potassium (unless stabilized by sodium ion-exchange). This and alcohol's effect in dilation of peripheral blood vessels make wine worthy of consideration for persons with arteriosclerosis and hypertensive vascular conditions. Alcoholic beverages, moderately used, may help induce sleep, stimulate gastric secretion, and produce mild diuresis. Properly handled and with consideration for contraindications (e.g., stimulation of gastric secretion is highly undesirable in the gastric ulcer patient) wine and other alcoholic beverages have medical utility.

Alcoholism is a very serious problem. Reliable statistics are few, but it has been estimated that there are 60 million fairly regular consumers of alcoholic beverages in the United States. Of these, from 2 million to 6 million are considered excessive drinkers and about 600,000 are definitely alcoholics. The costs of alcoholism, including public support of dependents of alcoholics, clinics, and prisons, have been estimated at $350,000,-000, and the wages lost are another $400,000,000 per year. Alcoholism is not easy to define, but it implies a compulsion to drink alcoholic beverages that is so strong and so frequent that

321

it leads to serious and continuing undesirable personal and social consequences.

There is good reason to believe that many of the people who become alcoholics are compulsive—needing escape or gratification—before they take a drop. The feelings of well-being, the apparently diminished pressure of circumstances, and perhaps the complete oblivion eventually achieved during drinking episodes seem to afford means of escape from themselves. The pain and shame of returning to normal may add to their need for escape and reinforce the pattern. In the incipient stages, the origin of alcoholism seems to lie in the realm of personality defects. However, if alcohol becomes the major part of the caloric intake, as it often does, nutritional deficiencies contribute to metabolic breakdown and further psychological or neurological lesions. They may also contribute in the form of "cravings" misinterpreted by the afflicted person and driving him to further drunkenness instead of the needed food.

Cirrhosis of the liver has been thought to be the result of alcohol consumption, but in one statistical study only 3 per cent of chronic alcoholics were found to have cirrhosis at autopsy. Even where liver damage is associated with alcoholism, it may be the result of the associated vitamin deficiencies rather than primarily a result of the alcohol. Delirium tremens and the so-called withdrawal symptoms of alcoholism are best treated with thiamine and other B vitamins and sleep. Thiamine deficiency produces nerve involvement, polyneuritis, and again the consumption of alcohol may be only an indirect cause.

What conditions predispose or oppose an individual's becoming an alcoholic? There are some suggestive clues. Italians as a group consume a considerable amount of alcohol in the form of wine. They have about the same incidence of general neuroses as Americans and yet have a much lower incidence of alcoholism. This apparent advantage is progressively lost in the families of Italians who have immigrated to the United States. It therefore seems cultural, and probably lies in the differing attitudes toward the use of alcohol in the two countries. Studies comparing these factors not only between the United States and Italy but also in France, England, and other cultural and ethnic groups have produced a general picture of conditions favoring and opposing alcoholism.

In the typical case the child who avoids alcoholism contacts alcohol early in life. It is a part of the daily diet and the child may receive diluted wine along with the adults. He sees it in a family environment as a part of meals and no particular importance, positive or negative, is attached to it. By the time the child reaches adolescence he probably has been drunk. This might happen when the family has left the table and the child proceeds to consume the remainder of the wine. The obvious results follow—sickness and remorse. The father takes the recuperated child aside and tells him that any food can be consumed to the point of illness and he has learned a lesson. Overindulgence and drunkenness are childish and as he becomes an adult he will learn not to do these foolish things. The father also impresses upon him that he must not drink to excess or he will disgrace the family. Similar patterns of early contact in the family circle, close family ties, drinking of beverages of lower alcohol content, and self-respect being antagonistic to drunkenness seem to be common to groups such as the Italians, Chinese, and Jews, who have a low incidence of alcoholism and yet consume alcohol.

Conditions favoring alcoholism seem to include first experience with alcohol later in life and viewing ability to "handle" large amounts of it as proof of manhood or virility. Parental attitude strongly against or strongly in favor of alcohol seem to favor alcoholism in the children. Drinking of strong spirits rather than wine or beer definitely favors alcoholism.

Wine has an undeservedly bad name as being the culprit for the lowest form of American alcoholic, the "wino." It has been determined that the "wino" drinks wine because it is the least expensive beverage for the amount of alcohol. In countries where other forms of alcohol are cheaper, the drunk who is limited in cash does not turn to wine but to their cheapest form of alcohol. When the price is not limiting, that is, at the beginning of drinking bouts or drinking by relatively well-to-do alcoholics, stronger spirits are desired by the excessive, compulsive drinker.

Wine, and particularly table wine, seems to be much less likely to produce alcoholism than are most other alcoholic beverages. Table wines are a rather dilute source of alcohol. Alcoholism has been defined as the daily consumption of a minimum of 135 milliliters of alcohol. Based upon this modest and perhaps questionable definition, an alcoholic would have to consume about a dozen 12-ounce cans of American beer every day. This would seem to be a rather uncomfortable and time-consuming method of maintaining status as an alcoholic. On the same basis, 135 milliliters of alcohol per day, the consumption of two bottles of table wine and one bottle of dessert wine every day would be required as compared to half a pint of 100-proof spirits. Of course, the ethyl alcohol consumption of many heavy drinkers and alcoholics may be much higher than this minimum figure.

Most wines are properly consumed in association with a meal. The presence of other foods in the stomach delays absorption and lowers the level of alcohol in the blood attained with a given amount of alcohol. The alcohol in wine is absorbed more slowly than alcohol in water alone at the same concentration.

The connoisseur's approach to wine is a strong deterrent to alcoholism. Fine wine provides a truly aesthetic experience to the connoisseur. He samples, evaluates, and enjoys the color, the odor, and the flavor. He savors it and does not gulp it down just for the alcoholic effect. He values it as an adjunct to pleasant, sophisticated, adult dining and entertaining. He enjoys its flavors and searches for the best quality, not the most alcoholic. A simple well-made wine may please him, but a harsh, coarse one will not, regardless of their respective alcohol contents.

Summary.—Alcohol produces an inevitable sequence of effects as its level increases in the blood stream. As with any physiologically active agent, the size and condition of the individual and the manner of administration of the dose affect the height and duration of the alcohol level in the blood. The effects of alcohol can be medically useful, and wine is often an especially advantageous form for such use.

Serious individual and social problems can result from excessive, compulsive, or addictive drinking of alcoholic beverages. The low alcohol content of beer and table wine tends to act against development of drunkenness or alcoholism. The consumption of wine along with food in family settings helps to explain why population groups with high levels of wine consumption tend to have a lower incidence of alcoholism than those who consume primarily other alcoholic beverages.

A quote from Julian Street's book *Wines* expresses our attitude: "Never let a drunkard choose your wine. You may be sure that he knows nothing about it. It is only sober people who know how to drink." And, from Fitzgerald's Rubaiyat of Omar Khayyam:

> Why, be this Juice the growth of God,
>   Who dare
> Blaspheme the twisted tendril as a
>   Snare?
> A blessing, we should use it should
>   We not?
> And if a curse—why, then, Who set
>   It there?

SUPPLEMENTARY READING

Chapters particularly supplemented are listed after each citation. This list has been selected from books in print so far as possible. Inclusion of a book does not indicate the authors' approval of its contents.

For current information in English see the following journals: *American Journal of Enology and Viticulture* (Davis, California), *Australian Wine, Brewing and Spirit Review* (Kensington, Victoria), *Harpers Wine and Spirit Gazette* (London), *Vintage* (Bristol, England), *Wine & Food* (London), *Wine Institute Bulletin* (San Francisco), *Wine Magazine* (London), *Wines & Vines* (San Francisco), and *Wine, Spirit & Malt* (Stellenbosch, South Africa).

Adams, L. D.
>   1958. The commonsense book of wine. New York: David McKay Co., Inc. 178 pp.   Chapters 18 and 19.
>   1960. The commonsense book of drinking. New York: David McKay Co., Inc. xv + 210 pp.   Chapters 19 and 20.
Allen, H. W.
>   1932. The romance of wine. New York: E. P. Dutton and Co. 264 pp.   Chapters 1, 11, 13.
>   1951. Natural red wines. London: Constable and Co. viii + 320 pp.   Chapter 13.
>   1952a. Sherry and port. London: Constable and Co. 214 pp.   Chapters 10 and 11.

1952*b*. White wines and cognac. London: Constable and Co. 278 pp.
Chapters 11 and 13.
1957. Good wine from Portugal. London: Sylvan Press 59 + 4 pp.
Chapter 15.
1961. A history of wine. London: Faber and Faber. 304 pp.
Chapters 1, 13, 15.
1964. The wines of Portugal. New York: McGraw-Hill Book Co.,
Inc. 192 pp.   Chapter 15.

AMBROSI, H.
1959. Die Weine Südafrikas. Deut. Wein-Ztg. 95:482, 484, 498, 500,
502.   Chapter 16.

AMERINE, M. A.
1948. An application of "triangular" taste testing to wines. The Wine
Review 16(5):10–12.   Chapter 19.
1954. Composition of wines. I. Organic constituents. New York: Aca-
demic Press, Inc. Advances in Food Research 5:353–510.
Chapter 7.
1955. The well-tempered wine bibber. 1955 Vintage Tour of the Los
Angeles and San Francisco Branches of the Wine and Food
Society. San Francisco: The Grabhorn Press. Pp. 5–19.
Chapter 19.
1958. Composition of wines. II. Inorganic constituents. New York:
Academic Press, Inc. Advances in Food Research 8:133–224.
Chapter 7.
1959*a*. Chemists and the California wine industry. Am. J. Enol. and
Viticult. 10:124–159.   Chapter 18.
1959*b*. The romance of Pan-American wines. Pan-American Medical
Association, San Francisco Chapter, Annual Bulletin 1958:24–27.
Chapter 16.
1960. Laboratory procedures for enology. Davis: University of Cali-
fornia, Department of Viticulture and Enology.
(Rev. ed., 1965. 100 pp.)   Chapter 7.
1962. Hilgard and California viticulture. Hilgardia 33(1):1–23.
Chapter 18.
1964*a*. Der Weinbau in Japan. Die Wein-Wissenschaft 19(5):225–231.
1964*b*. Wine. Scientific American 211(2):46–56.   Chapters 7 and 19.
Chapter 16.

AMERINE, M. A., H. W. BERG, AND W. V. CRUESS
1967. The technology of wine making. 2d ed. Westport, Connecticut:
The Avi Publishing Co., 784 pp.   Chapters 6–19.

AMERINE, M. A., AND M. A. JOSLYN
1951. Table wines: The technology of their production in California.
Berkeley and Los Angeles: University of California Press. 397
pp.   Chapters 6, 8, 9, 18.

AMERINE, M. A., AND G. L. MARSH
1962. Wine making at home. San Francisco: Wine Publications. 31 pp.
Chapter 7.

Supplementary Reading

AMERINE, M. A., AND E. B. ROESSLER
  1952. Techniques and problems in the organoleptic examination of wines. Proc. Am. Soc. Enol., 1952:97–115.   Chapter 19.
  1958. Field testing of grape maturity. Hilgardia 28(4):93–114.
          Chapter 3.
AMERINE, M. A., E. B. ROESSLER, AND F. FILIPELLO
  1959. Modern sensory methods of evaluating wine. Hilgardia 28:477–567.   Chapters 6, 18, 19.
AMERINE, M. A., AND A. J. WINKLER
  1938. Angelica. Wines & Vines 19(9):5, 24.   Chapter 18.
  1944. Composition and quality of musts and wines of California grapes. Hilgardia 15:493–673.   Chapters 3 and 18.
  1963a. California wine grapes: Composition and quality of their musts and wines. Calif. Agr. Exp. Sta. Bull. 794. 83 pp.
          Chapters 2 and 18.
  1963b. Grape varieties for wine production. Calif. Agr. Ext. Service Leaflet 154. 2 pp.   Chapter 18.
ANDRES, S. P.
  1960. Die grossen Weine Deutschlands. Berlin: Im Verlag Ullstein. 199 pp.   Chapter 14.
ANONYMOUS
  1947. Cognac et sa région, ses grandes eaux-de-vie. Bordeaux: Bordeaux et la Sud-Oeste. Editions Delmas. 101 pp.   Chapter 11.
  1950. Yugoslav wines. Belgrade: Chamber of Commerce of Yugoslavia. 46 pp.   Chapter 15.
  1958a. Grape and wine industry of Mexico. Am. J. Enol. 9:92–93.
          Chapter 16.
  1958b. Flavor research and food acceptance. New York: Reinhold Publishing Corp. 391 pp.   Chapter 19.
  1959. Produce better grapes for better wines. Calif. Agr. Ext. Service. 16 pp.   Chapter 3.
  1966. A survey of wine growing in South Africa 1965–66. Paarl: Public Relations Department of KWV. 56 pp.   Chapter 16.
ANTONIO DE VEGA L.
  1958. Guía vinícola de España. Madrid: Editora Nacional. 3 + 318 pp.
          Chapter 15.
ASH, C.
  1952. Reminiscences of pre-Prohibition days. Proc. Am. Soc. Enol. 1952:39–44.   Chapter 18.
BAILEY, L. H.
  1906. Sketch of the evolution of our native fruits. 2d ed. New York: The Macmillan Co. 472 pp.   Chapter 2.
BAKER, G. A.
  1954. Organoleptic ratings and analytical data for wines analyzed into orthogonal factors. Food Research 19:575–580.   Chapter 19.
BAKER, G. A., AND M. A. AMERINE
  1953. Organoleptic ratings of wines estimated from analytical data. Food Research 18:381–389.   Chapter 19.

329

Supplementary Reading

BAKER, G. A., M. A. AMERINE, AND E. B. ROESSLER
  1952. Theory and application of fractional blending systems. Hilgardia
  21:383–409.   Chapters 10, 15, 18.

BALZER, R. L.
  1964. The pleasures of wine. Indianapolis: The Bobbs-Merrill Co.,
  Inc. xiv + 319 pp.   Chapter 18.

BECK, FRED
  1964. The Fred Beck wine book. New York: Hill and Wang. xiii +
  242 pp.   Chapters 17 and 18.

BENSON, C. T.
  1959. The Canadian wine industry. Wines & Vines 40(9):23.
                                                                 Chapter 17.

BENVEGNIN, L., E. CAPT, AND G. PIGUET
  1951. Traité de vinification. Lausanne: Librairie Payot. 2d ed. 583 pp.
                                                                 Chapter 14.

BENWELL, W. S.
  1961. Journey to wine in Victoria. Melbourne: Sir Isaac Pitman and
  Sons. 120 pp.   Chapter 16.

BERG, H. W., F. FILIPELLO, E. HINREINER, AND A. D. WEBB
  1955. Evaluation of thresholds and minimum difference concentrations
  for various constituents of wines I. Water solutions of pure substances. II. Sweetness: The effect of ethyl alcohol, organic acids
  and tannin. Food Technol. 9:23–26, 138–140.   Chapter 19.

BERG, H. W., AND A. D. WEBB
  1955. Terms used in tasting. Wines & Vines 36(7):25–28.
                                                                 Chapter 6.

BERIDZE, G. I.
  1962. Vina gruzii. Tbilisi; Izd-vo "Sahchota Sakartvelo." 263 pp.
                                                                 Chapter 14.

BLAHA, J.
  1952. Československá ampelografia. Bratislava: "Oráč." 361 pp.
                                                                 Chapter 14.

BOBADILLA, G. F. DE
  1956. Viníferas jerezanas y de Andalucía Occidental. Madrid: Insti-
  tuto Nacional de Investigaciones Agronómicas. 272 pp.
                                                                 Chapter 15.

BODE, C.
  1956. Wines of Italy. New York: The McBride Co., Inc. 135 pp.
                                                                 Chapter 15.

BRUNET, R.
  1946. Dictionnaire d'oenologie et de viticulture. Paris: Editions M.
  Ponsot. 534 pp.   Chapters 13–19.

BUNKER, H. J.
  1961. Recent research on the yeasts. In D. J. D. Hockenhull (ed.),
  Progress in industrial microbiology, Vol. 3, pp. 1–41. New York:
  Interscience Publishers, Inc. 230 pp.   Chapter 4.

Supplementary Reading

Carosso, V. P.
1951. The California wine industry, 1830–1895: A study of the formative years Berkeley and Los Angeles: University of California Press. 241 pp. Chapter 18.

Chafetz, M. E., and H. W. Demone, Jr.
1962. Alcoholism and society. New York: Oxford University Press. 319 pp. Chapter 20.

Chaminade, R.
1930. La production et le commerce des eaux-de-vie de vin. Paris: Librarie J.-B. Ballière et Fils. 157 pp. Chapter 11.

Chappaz, G.
1951. Le vignoble et le vin de Champagne. Paris: Louis Larmat. xvii + 414 pp. Chapter 13.

Charley, V. L. S.
1949. Principles and practices of cider making. London: Leonard Hill. 367 pp. Chapter 12.

Chedeville, C.
1945. Manuel d'oenologie. Tunis: Bascone et Muscat. 137 pp. Chapter 16.

Church, R. E.
1963. The American guide to wines. Chicago: Quadrangle Books. 272 pp. Chapters 13–18.

Churchill, C.
1961. A notebook for the wines of France. New York: Alfred A. Knopf. xv + 387 + xxviii pp. Chapter 13.
1964. The world of wines. New York: The Macmillan Co. xii + 271 pp. Chapters 13–18.

Cocks, C., and E. Feret
1949. Bordeaux et ses vins, classés par ordre de mérite. 11th ed. Bordeaux: Féret et Fils. xi + 1135 pp. Chapter 13.

Conn, E. E., and P. K. Stumpf
1963. Outlines of biochemistry. New York: John Wiley and Sons. 391 pp. Chapter 5.

Constantinescu, G.
1958. Raionarea viticulturii. Bucharest: Academia Republicii Populare Romine. 153 pp. Chapter 14.

Cook, A. H.
1958. The chemistry and biology of yeast. New York: Academic Press, Inc. 763 pp. Chapter 4.

Cook, J. A.
1960. Vineyard fertilizers and cover crops. Calif. Agr. Ext. Service Leaflet 123. 2 pp. Chapter 3.

Cornelssen, P. A.
1954. Das Buch vom deutschen Wein. Mainz: Deutscher Weinverlag. 262 pp. Chapter 14.

Croft-Cooke, R.
1956. Sherry. New York: Alfred A. Knopf. 210 pp. Chapter 15.

331

Supplementary Reading

1957. Port. London: Putnam. 219 pp.   Chapter 15.
1961. Madeira. London: Putnam. 224 pp.   Chapter 15.

CRUESS, W. V.
1947. The principles and practices of wine making. 2d ed. New York: Avi Publishing Co. 476 pp.   Chapters 8, 9, 13, 18.

CSEPREGI, P.
1955. Szölöfajlárnk; ampelográfia. Budapest: Mezögazdasági Kiado. 386 pp.   Chapter 14.

DALMASSO, G., AND V. TYNDALO
1957. Viticoltura e ampelografia dell' U.R.S.S. Atti Accad. Ital. Vite e Vino 9:446–548.   Chapter 14.

DAVISON, A. E.
1963. Wine Institute sanitation guide for wineries. Rev. ed. San Francisco: Wine Institute. iv + 68 pp.   Chapter 6.

DE BOSDARI, C.
1955. Wines of the Cape. Cape Town, Amsterdam: A. A. Balkema. 95 pp.   Chapter 16.

DELAMAIN, R.
1935. Histoire de Cognac. Paris: Librairie Stock. 140 pp.   Chapter 11.

DETTORI, R. G.
1953. Italian wines and liqueurs. Rome: Federazione Italiana Produttori ed Esportatori di Vini, Liquori ed Affini. 158 pp.   Chapter 15.

DION, R.
1959. Histoire de la vigne et du vin en France. Paris. xii + 768 pp.   Chapters 1 and 13.

DUBOS, R. J.
1950. Louis Pasteur, free lance of science. Boston: Little, Brown and Co. 418 pp.   Chapters 1 and 5.
1960. Pasteur and modern science. Garden City, New York: Doubleday and Co., Inc. 195 pp.   Chapters 1 and 5.

FERRÉ, L.
1958. Traité d'oenologie bourguignonne. Paris: Institut National des Appellations d'Origine des Vins et Eaux-de-Vie. 303 pp.   Chapters 7, 8, 13.

FORNACHON, J. C. M.
1943. Bacterial spoilage of fortified wines. Adelaide: Australian Wine Board. 126 pp.   Chapter 4.

FREDERICKSEN, P.
1947. The authentic Haraszthy story. Wines & Vines 28(6):25–26, 42; (7):15–16, 30; (8):17–18, 37–38; (9):17–18, 34; (11):21–22, 41–42.   Chapter 18.

FROLOV-BAGREEV, A. M.
1946–62. Ampelografia S.S.S.R. Moscow: Gos. Pishchepromizdat. 7 vols.   Chapter 14.

FRUTON, J. S., AND S. SIMMONDS
1958. General biochemistry. 2d ed. New York: John Wiley and Sons. 1077 pp.   Chapter 5.

Supplementary Reading

GALHANO, A. B.
1951. A região dos vinhos verdes. Porto: Comissão de Viticultura da Região dos Vinhos Verdes. 37 pp. (Also published in French as Le vin "verde.") Chapter 15.

GALLAY, R., AND L. BENVEGNIN
1950. Les enseignements d'une dégustation. Rev. Romande d'Agric., Vitic. et Arbor. 6:38–39. Chapter 19.

GAUBERT, I.
1946. Armagnac, terre Gasconne. Paris: Edition Havas. 82 pp. Chapter 11.

GEORGIEV, IV.
1949. Vinarstvo. Sofia: Zemizdat. xvi + 456 pp. Chapters 7, 8, 13.

GOLDSCHMIDT, E.
1951. Deutschlands Weinbauorte und Weinbergslagen. 6 Aufl. Mainz: Verlag der Deutschen Wein-Zeitung. 263 pp. Chapter 14.

GONZALES GORDON, M. M.
1948 [1949] Jerez, Xerez, Sheris. Jerez de la Frontera: Jerez Industrial. 605 pp. Chapters 10 and 15.

GOT, N.
1953. La dégustation des vins. Beziers: Sodiep. 157 pp. Chapter 19.
1963. Le livre de l'amateur de vins. Perpignan: En Vente Chez l'Auteur. 357 pp. Chapters 14, 15, 19.

GROSSMAN, H. J.
1964. Grossman's guide to wines, spirits and beers. New York: Charles Scribner's. xvii + 508 pp. Chapters 11–18.

HALASZ, Z.
1962. Hungarian wine though the ages. Budapest: Corvina Press. 186 pp. Chapter 14.

HALLGARTEN, S. F.
1955. Rhineland, wineland: A journey through the wine districts of western Germany. 3d ed. London: P. Elek. 210 pp. Chapter 14.
1957. Alsace and its wine gardens. London: André Deutsch. 187 pp. Chapter 13.

HARASZTHY, A.
1862. Grape culture, wines, and wine-making, with notes upon horticulture. New York: Harper and Brothers. xxx + 420 pp. Chapter 18.

HARTMANN, G.
1955. Cognac, Armagnac, Weinbrand. Berlin: Carl Knoppke Grüner Verlag und Vertrieb. 124 pp. Chapter 11.

HEALY, M.
1949. Stay me with flagons. London: Michael Joseph, Ltd. 262 pp. (Another edition, 1963.) Chapter 13.

HEDRICK, U. P.
1908. The grapes of New York. Fifteenth annual report, Department of Agriculture, State of New York. Albany: State Printer J. B. Lyon. Part II. 564 pp. Chapters 2 and 17.

Supplementary Reading

1945. Grapes and wines from home vineyards. New York: Oxford University Press. 326 pp. Chapters 2, 3, 7, 12, 17.

HELIODORO VALLE, R.
1958. The history of wine in Mexico. Am. J. Enol. 9:146–154. Chapter 16.

HINREINER, E., F. FILIPELLO, H. W. BERG, AND A. D. WEBB
1955. Evaluation of thresholds and minimum difference concentrations for various constituents of wines. IV. Detectable differences in wines. Food Technol. 9:489–490. Chapter 19.

HINREINER, E., F. FILIPELLO, A. D. WEBB, AND H. W. BERG
1955. Evaluation of thresholds and minimum difference concentrations for various constituents of wines. III. Ethyl alcohol, glycerol and acidity in aqueous solution. *ibid*:351–353. Chapter 19.

INGRAM, M.
1955. An introduction to the biology of yeast. New York: Pitman Publishing Corp. 273 pp. Chapter 4.

ISNARD, H.
1951–1954. La vigne en Algérie. Gap: Ophrys. 2 vols. Chapter 16.

JACKSON, G. H.
1928. The medicinal value of French brandy. Montreal, Canada: Thérien Frères. 315 pp. Chapter 11.

JACOBY, O. F.
1948. Developing the vermouth formula. Wines & Vines 29(4): 73–75. Chapter 12.

JACQUELIN, L. AND R. POULAIN
1962. The wines and vineyards of France. New York: G. P. Putnam's Sons. 416 pp. Chapter 13.

JAMES, W.
1963. Wine in Australia; a handbook. Melbourne: Georgian House. 6 + 148 pp. Chapter 16.

JOSLYN, M. A., AND M. A. AMERINE
1941a. Commercial production of dessert wines. Calif. Agr. Exp. Sta. Bull. 651. 186 pp. Chapters 10, 12, 15, 18.
1941b. Commercial production of brandies. Calif. Agr. Exp. Sta. Bull. 652. 80 pp. Chapters 11 and 18.
1964. Dessert, appetizer and related flavored wines; the technology of their production. Berkeley: Division of Agricultural Sciences. 483 pp. Chapters 6, 7, 10, 12, 18, 19.

KASIMATIS, A. N., AND L. A. LIDER
1962. Grape rootstock varieties. Davis: Calif. Agr. Ext. Service AXT 47. 25 pp. Chapter 2.

KELLER, D. J.
1953. Pfalzwein Almanach. Neustadt a.d. Weinstrasse: Neustadter Druckerei. xvi + 448 pp. Chapter 14.

KITTEL, J. B., AND BREIDER, H.
1958. Das Buch vom Frankenweine. Würzburg: Universitätsdruckerei H. Stürz AG. 207 pp. Chapter 14.

Supplementary Reading

KLENK, E.
  1960. Die Weinbeurteilung nach Farbe, Klarheit, Geruch und Geschmack des Weines. Stuttgart: Eugen Ulmer. 95 pp.
  Chapter 19.

KRAEMER, A.
  1961. Im Lande des Bocksbeutels. 3. Aufl. Würzburg: Druck und Verlag Pius Halbig. 232 pp. Chapter 14.

LACHMAN, H.
  1903. A monograph on the manufacture of wines in California. U S. Dept. Agr. Bur. Chem. Bull. 72:25–40 Chapter 18.

LAFFER, H. E.
  1949. The wine industry of Australia. Adelaide: Australian Wine Board. 136 pp. Chapter 16.

LAFFORGUE, G.
  1947. Le vignoble Girondin. Paris: Louis Larmat. xi + 319 pp.
  Chapter 13.

LAFON, R., J. LAFON, AND P. COUILLAUD
  1964. Le Cognac: sa distillation. 4ᵉ édit. Paris: J.-B. Baillière et Fils. 276 pp. Chapter 11.

LANGENBACH, A.
  1962. German wines and vines. London: Vista Books. 190 pp.
  Chapter 14.

LARREA, R. A.
  1957. Arte y ciencia de los vinos españoles. Madrid: Siler. 135 pp.
  Chapter 15.

LAYTON, T. A.
  1959. Wines of Italy. London: Harper Trade Journals, Ltd. 221 pp.
  Chapter 15.

LEGGETT, H. B.
  1939. The early history of the wine industry in California. Master of Arts thesis, Berkeley: University of California. 124 pp.
  Chapter 18.

LEIPOLDT, C. L.
  1952. Three hundred years of Cape wine. Cape Town: Stewart. 330 pp. Chapter 16.

LEÓN, V. E.
  1947. Uvas y vinos de Chile. Santiago de Chile: Sindicato Nacional Vitivinícola. 340 pp. Chapter 16.

LEONHARDT, G.
  1954. Weinfachbuch. Leipzig: Fachbuchverlag. 374 pp. Chapter 14.

LICHINE, A.
  1963. The wines of France. 4th ed. New York: Alfred A. Knopf. ix + 382 + xvii pp. Chapter 13.

LIDER, L. A.
  1958. Phylloxera-resistant grape rootstocks for the coastal valleys of California. Hilgardia 27:287–318. Chapter 2.

335

1960. Vineyard trials in California with nematode-resistant grape rootstocks. Hilgardia 30:123–152. Chapter 2.

1963. Field budding and care of the budded grapevine. Calif. Agr. Ext. Service Leaflet 153. 2 pp. Chapter 3.

LODDER, J., AND N. J. W. KREGER-VAN RIJ
1952. The yeasts: A taxonomic study. New York: Interscience Publishers, Inc. 713 pp. Chapter 4.

LOLLI, G.
1960. Social drinking. Cleveland, Ohio: World Publishing Co. 317 pp. Chapter 20.

LOOMIS, N. H.
1963. Growing American bunch grapes. U. S. Dept. Agr. Farmers' Bull. 2123. 22 pp. Chapter 3.

LUCIA, S. P.
1954. Wine as food and medicine. New York: The Blakiston Co. 149 pp. Chapter 20.

1963a. Alcohol and civilization. New York: McGraw-Hill Book Co., Inc. 416 pp.

1963b. A history of wine as therapy. Philadelphia: J. B. Lippincott Co. 234 pp. Chapters 1 and 20.

McCARTHY, R. G.
1959. Drinking and intoxication: Selected readings in social attitudes and controls. New Haven, Conn.: Yale Center of Alcohol Studies. 455 pp. Chapter 20.

McCARTHY, R. G., AND E. M. DOUGLASS
1949. Alcohol and social responsibility: A new educational approach. New York: Thomas Y. Crowell Co. 304 pp. Chapter 20.

McCORD, W., AND J. McCORD
1960. Origins of alcoholism. Stanford, Calif.: Stanford University Press. 193 pp. Chapter 20.

MAGISTOCCHI, G.
1955. Tratado de enología adaptado a la República Argentina. Buenos Aires: Ed. El Ateneo. 765 pp. Chapter 16.

MARESCALCHI, A.
1949. La degustazione e l'apprezzamento dei vini. Casale Monferrato: Case Editrice Fratelli Marescalchi. vii + 153 pp. Chapter 19.

MARESCALCHI, C.
1967. Manuale dell'enologo. 13th ed. Casale Monferrato: Casa Editrice Fratelli Marescalchi. 700 pp. Chapters 8, 12, 15.

MARRISON, L. W.
1958. Wines and spirits. London: Penguin Books. 320 pp. Chapter 17.

MARTEAU, G.
1953. Recherche de la qualité par l'examen organoleptique des vins. Prog. Agr. et Vitic. 140:281–289, 310–313. Chapter 19.

MARVEL, T., ed.
1951. Frank Schoonmaker's dictionary of wines. New York: Hastings House. 120 pp. Chapters 6, 11, 13–19.

Supplementary Reading

MASSEE, W. E.
   1961a. Massee's wine handbook. New York: Doubleday and Co., Inc.
      217 pp.   Chapters 13–18.
   1961b. Wines and spirits: A complete buying guide. New York: Mc-
      Graw-Hill Book Co., Inc. 427 pp.   Chapters 11, 13–18.
MAVEROFF PIAGGIO, A.
   1949. Enología. Mendoza: J. Best. 511 pp.   Chapter 16.
MELVILLE, I.
   1960. Guide to California wines. 2d ed. San Carlos, Calif.: Nourse
      Publishing Co. xiv + 235 pp.   Chapter 18.
MENSIO, G.
   1957. Manuale sull'assaggio e l'apprezzamento dei vini. Asti: Ordine
      Nazionale degli Assaggiatori di Vino. 55 pp.   Chapter 19.
MUNSON, T. V.
   1909. Foundations of American grape culture. New York: Orange
      Judd. 252 pp.   Chapters 15 and 17.
NAVAS ROMANO, E.
   1950. La bodega moderna. 2d ed. Barcelona: Editorial Gustavo Gili,
      S.A. 399 pp.   Chapter 15.
NEILANDS, J. B., AND P. K. STUMPF
   1958. Outlines of enzyme chemistry. 2d ed. New York: John Wiley
      and Sons. 411 pp.   Chapter 5.
NELSON, K. E., AND M. A. AMERINE
   1957. The use of *Botrytis cinerea* Pers. in the production of sweet table
      wines. Hilgardia 26(12):521–63.   Chapters 3, 13, 15, 18.
OLMO, H.P.
   1948. Ruby Cabernet and Emerald Riesling, two new table-wine grape
      varieties. Calif. Agr. Exp. Sta. Bull. 704. 12 pp.
                                             Chapters 2 and 18.
OLMO, H. P., AND A. KOYAMA
   1962a. Niabell and Early Niabell, new tetraploid varieties of the
      Concord type. Calif. Agr. Exp. Sta. Bull. 790. 10 pp.
                                                     Chapter 2.
   1962b. Rubired and Royalty, new grape varieties for color, concen-
      trate, and port wine. Calif. Agr. Exp. Sta. Bull. 789. 13 pp.
                                             Chapters 2 and 18.
OUGH, C. S., AND M. A. AMERINE
   1963. Regional, varietal, and type influences on the degree Brix and
      alcohol relationship of grape musts and wines. Hilgardia 34(14):
      585–600.   Chapters 2 and 3.
PACOTTET, P., AND L. GUITTONNEAU
   1926. Eaux-de-vie et vinaigres. Paris: Librairie J.-B. Baillière et Fils.
      480 pp.   Chapter 11.
   1930. Vins de Champagne et vins mousseux. Paris: Librairie J. B. Bail-
      lière et Fils. 412 pp.   Chapters 9, 13, 18.
PENINOU, E., AND S. GREENLEAF
   1954a. Wine making in California. I. How wine is made. II. From

337

the Missions to 1894. San Francisco: The Peregrine Press.
35 pp. Chapter 18.

1954*b*. Wine making in California. III. The California Wine Association. San Francisco: The Porpoise Bookshop. 36 + 6 pp.
Chapter 18.

PESQUIDOUX, J. DE, E. JANNEAU, C. SAMARAN, L. MAZERET, J. LASCOUR-REGES, AND DE RAQUINE
1937. L'Armagnac. Condom, France: A Bosquet et Fils. 101 pp.
Chapter 11.

PESTEL, H.
1959. Les vins et eaux-de-vie à appellations d'origine contrôlées en France. Mâcon: Imprimerie Buguet-Comptour. 44 pp.
Chapter 11.

PEYER, E. AND W. EGGENBERGER
1965. Weinbuch. 5. Aufl. Zürich: Verlag Schweizerischer Wirteverin. 235 pp. Chapter 14.

PEYRONNET, F. R.
1950. Le vignoble nord-africain. Paris: J. Peyronnet. 357 pp.
Chapter 16.

PILONE, F. J.
1954. Production of vermouth. Am. J. Enol. 5:30–46. Chapter 12.

PITTMAN, D. J., AND C. R. SNYDER
1962. Society, culture and drinking patterns. New York: John Wiley and Sons. 616 pp. Chapter 20.

PRESCOTT, S. C., AND C. G. DUNN
1959. Industrial microbiology. New York: McGraw-Hill Book Co., Inc. 945 pp. Chapter 5.

PULS, E.
1939. Die Weinkostprobe. Prufung und Beurteilung von Wein. Neustadt a. d. Weinstrasse: D. Meininger. 24 pp. Chapter 19.

RAINBOW, C.
1961. The biochemistry of the Acetobacters. *In* D. J. D. Hockenhull (ed.) Progress in industrial microbiology, Vol. 3, pp. 45–70. New York: Interscience Publishers, Inc. 230 pp. Chapter 4.

RIBÉREAU-GAYON, J., AND E. PEYNAUD
1960–61. Traité de oenologie. Vol. I. Maturation du raisin, fermentation alcoolique, vinification. xl + 756 pp. Vol. II. Composition, transformations et traitements des vins. xxviii + 1065 pp. Paris: Librairie Polytechnique Ch. Béranger. Chapters 4, 7–9, 19.

RODIER, C.
1948. Le vin de Bourgogne. 3ᵉ édit. Dijon: Louis Damidot. xv + 350 pp. Chapter 13.

ROGER, J.-R.
1960. The wines of Bordeaux. New York: E. P. Dutton and Co., Inc. 166 pp. Chapter 13.

ROSE, A. H.
1961. Industrial microbiology. Washington, D. C.: Butterworth, Inc. 286 pp. Chapter 5.

Supplementary Reading

Rossi, R., Jr.
  1962. United Vintners expands its Madera premises. Wines & Vines 43
    (9): 24–25, 27.   Chapter 10
Roueche, B.
  1960. The neutral spirit: A portrait of alcohol. Boston: Little, Brown
    and Co. 151 pp.   Chapter 20.
Schellenberg, A., and E. Peyer
  1951. Weinbuch für die schweizer Wirte. 3. Aufl. Zürich: Schweizer-
    ischen Wirteverein. 204 pp.   Chapter 14.
Schoonmaker, F.
  1956. The wines of Germany. New York: Hastings House. 152 pp.
                                                                       Chapter 14.
  1964. Encyclopedia of wine. New York: Hastings House. 410 pp.
                                                                    Chapters 1–19.
Schoonmaker, F., and T. Marvel
  1941. American wines. New York: Duell, Sloan and Pearce. 312 pp.
                                                                Chapters 17 and 18.
Schultz, H. B., A. J. Winkler, and R. J. Weaver
  1962. Preventing spring frost damage in vineyards. Berkeley: Calif. Agr.
    Ext. Service Leaflet 139. 7 pp.   Chapter 3.
Seltman, C.
  1957. Wine in the ancient world. London: Routledge & Kegan Paul,
    Ltd. xvi + 196 pp.   Chapter 1.
Shand, P. M.
  1929. A book of other wines than French. New York: Alfred A. Knopf.
    162 pp.   Chapters 14–16.
  1960. A book of French wines. London: Jonathan Cape. 415 pp.
                                                                       Chapter 13.
Simon, A. L.
  1934. Champagne. London: Constable and Co. 140 pp.   Chapter 9.
  1957. The noble grapes and the great wines of France. New York:
    McGraw-Hill Book Co., Inc. xi + 180 pp.   Chapter 13.
  1958. A dictionary of wines, spirits and liqueurs. London: Herbert
    Jenkins. 167 pp.   Chapters 6, 11, 15–19.
  1961. Wines and spirits: the connoisseur's textbook. London: Charles
    Skilton, Ltd. 194 + 6 pp.   Chapters 7–10, 13–15.
  1962. Champagne. New York: McGraw-Hill Book Co., Inc. 224 pp.
                                                                       Chapter 13.
Simon, A. L., and S. F. Hallgarten
  1963. The great wines of Germany and its famed vineyards. New
    York: McGraw-Hill Book Co., Inc. 191 pp.   Chapter 14.
Singleton, V. L.
  1962. Aging of wines and other spiritous products: Acceleration by
    physical treatments. Hilgardia 32:319–392. Chapters 7 and 10.
Singleton, V. L., and D. E. Draper
  1961. Wood chips and wine treatment: The nature of aqueous alcohol
    extracts. Am. J. Enol. Viticult. 12:152–8.   Chapter 10.

Supplementary Reading

Smith, L. M., and E. M. Stafford
1955. Grape pests in California. Calif. Agr. Exp. Sta. Circular 445. 63 pp.   Chapter 3.

Sonneman, H. O.
1952. Ohio State wines: their history and production. Proc. Am. Soc. Enol. 1952:17–22.   Chapter 17.

Stillman, J. S.
1955. Fruit and berry wine production in California. Am. J. Enol. 6:32–5.   Chapter 12.

Storm, J.
1963. An invitation to wines. New York: Simon and Schuster. xii + 201 pp.   Chapters 13–18.

Street, J.
1961. Wines. 3d ed. New York: Alfred A. Knopf. 243 pp.
    Chapters 13–18, 20.

Theron, C. J., and Niehaus, C. J. G.
1948. Wine making. 3d ed. Union South Africa Dept. Agr. Bull. 191. 98 pp.   Chapter 16.

Thudicum., J. L. W., and A. Dupre
1872. A treatise on the origin, nature, and varieties of wine. London: Macmillan and Co. xvi + 760 pp.   Chapters 6, 13–15.

Troost, G.
1961. Die Technologie des Weines. 3. Aufl. Stuttgart: Eugen Ulmer. 702 pp.   Chapter 14.

Troost, G., and E. Wanner
1955. Weinprobe. Weinansprache. 3. Aufl. Frankfurt/Main: Verlag Sigurd Horn. 63 pp.   Chapter 19.

Underkofler, L. A., and R. J. Hicken
1954. Industrial fermentations. New York: Chemical Publishing Co. Vol. I, 565 pp.   Chapter 5.

United States Internal Revenue Service
1954. Rectification of spirits and wines. Part 235 of Title 26 (1954), Code of Federal Regulations. Washington, D. C.: U. S. Gov't Print. Office. IRS Publ. 167. 70 pp.   Chapter 11.
1955. Wine. Part 240 of Title 26 (1954), Code of Federal Regulations. Washington, D. C.: U. S. Gov't Print. Office. IRS Publ. 146. 59 pp.   Chapters 6–12.
1961. Regulations under the Federal Alcohol Administration Act. Title 27 (1954), Code of Federal Regulations. Washington, D. C.: U. S. Gov't Print. Office. IRS Publ. 449. 70 pp.
    Chapter 6.

Valaer, P.
1950. The wines of the world. New York: Abelard Press. 576 pp.
    Chapter 12.

Vaughn, R. H.
1955. Bacterial spoilage of wines with special reference to California

conditions. New York: Academic Press, Inc. Advances in Food Research 6:67–108. Chapter 4

WAGNER, P. M.
1937. Wine grapes: Their selection, cultivation, and enjoyment. New York: Harcourt, Brace and Co. 298 pp. Chapter 2
1965. A wine-grower's guide. Rev. ed. New York: Alfred A. Knopf. xii + 224 pp. Chapters 2, 3, 17.
1956. American wines and wine-making. New York: Alfred A. Knopf 246 pp. Chapters 7–9, 13, 17

WAIT, F. E.
1889. Wines and vines of California. San Francisco: The Bancroft Co. 215 pp. Chapters 1 and 18.

WASHBURNE, C.
1961. Primitive drinking. New York: College and University Press. 282 pp. Chapter 20.

WAUGH, A.
1959. In praise of wine and certain noble spirits. New York: William Sloane Associates. 304 pp. Chapters 11, 13–16, 19

WEAVER, R. J., AND S. B. MCCUNE
1961. Effect of gibberellin on vine behavior and crop production in seeded and seedless *Vitis vinifera*. Hilgardia 30(15):425–444. Chapter 3.

WEBB, A. D.
1959. The Australian wine industry. Wines & Vines 40(7):29–30. Chapter 16.

WILHELM, C. F.
1956. Im und Auslandsweine; ABC der internationalen Weinkarte Berlin: C. Knoppke Grüner Verlag. 188 pp. Chapters 13–15.

WILLIAMS, R. J.
1959. Alcoholism: The nutritional approach. Austin: University of Texas Press. 118 pp. Chapter 20.

WINKLER, A. J.
1959a. Pruning grapevines. Calif. Agr. Exp. Sta. Circular 477. 11 pp. Chapter 3.
1959b. Spacing and training grapevines. Calif. Agr. Ext. Service Leaflet 111. 2 pp. Chapter 3.
1962. General viticulture. Berkeley and Los Angeles: University of California Press. 633 pp. Chapters 2, 3, 18.

WINKLER, A. J., AND M. A. AMERINE
1937. What climate does. The Wine Review 5(6):9–11; (7):9–11, 16. Chapters 3 and 18.

WINKLER, A. J., AND A. N. KASIMATIS
1959. Supports for grapevines. Calif. Agr. Ext. Service Leaflet 119 2 pp. Chapter 3.

Supplementary Reading

YANG, H. Y.
    1953. Fruit wines. Requisites for successful fermentation. J. Agr. Food
        Chem. 1:331–333.   Chapter 12.
YOKOTSUKA, I.
    1955. The grape growing and wine industry of Japan. Am. J. Enol.
        6:16–22.   Chapter 16.

INDEX

Italic page numbers indicate main entry or entries.

beer, 8–10, 88, 262, 323, 324
Beerenauslese, 226–227
Belgium, 293
bentonite, *111*, 156, 161, 166, 193, 197
Beta, 32
biblical references, 9, 12–14
binning, 130
bisulfites. *See* sulfur dioxide
bitterness, 79, 190–192, 210, 301, *303–305*, 307
black rot, 267
blending, 114, 123, *137*, 150, 152, 156, *160–161*, 167, 168, 197, 220, 238, 239, 258, 259, 308; brandy, 182, 184, 260. *See also* fractional blending
blood levels of alcohol, *318–319*, 324, 325
bloom, 51–52
blue fining, 111
Boal (Bual), 86, 239
Board of State Viticultural Commissioners, 279–280, 290
bodega, 242, 244 (fig.)
body, 304, 307, 313; thin, 304
Bordeaux, 20, 22, 46, 49, 76, 128, 198, *211–217*, 293, 299, 311, 313; types, 81–82. *See also* France
Botrytis cinerea, 63–64, 83, 123, *215–217*, 226–227, 230, 285
bottle (bottling), 17, *114*, 224, 240, 251, 264; aging in, *122*, 123, 130, 131, 162, 237, 251, 293, 300; biblical, 13; brandy, 180–185, 314 (fig.); château bottling, 214; dessert wine, 156, 167, 314 (fig.); openers, 310–311, 312 (fig.); precipitates in, 294–295, 308, 309–311; sparkling wines, 139–141, 143, 146, 219–220, 314 (fig.); table wine, 122, 125, 130, 315 (fig.)
bouquet, 108, 306, 307, 311; bottle, 122, 237, 264; sparkling wine, 139, 220. *See also* aroma, odor

Bourgueil, 217
Boxbeutel (*Bochsbeutel*), 224
brandy: beverage, 149, *178–185*, 233, 260, 301; aging, 180; bottle, 314 (fig.); consumption, 7; peach, 268; snifter, 313; tasting, 185–186; tax, 8, 180, 185; types, 185–186. *See also* Cognac, wine spirits, and various countries
Brenner Pass, 250
Brix, 102, 120, 124, 125, 153, 155; definition, 93; determination, 93–94. *See also* concentrate, fermentation, fortification, hydrometry
browning, 95, 98, 99, 121, 122, 162, 166, 196, 301
brut, 79–80, 141, 220, 303
Buena Vista, 277
Bulgaria, 232, 235
bung, 105, 106 (fig.), 107, 128
Burger, 36, 120
burgundy, 28, 82, 201, 256; sparkling, 147
Burgundy, 18, 22, 49, 76, 81–82, 183, 198, 200, 203–208, 216, 293, 299–301, 313, 314
butts, 244 (fig.)
by-products, 187–189, 197
Byrrh, 77, 193

Cabernet, 82, 293, 313; aroma, 299
Cabernet franc, 34, 216, 217
Cabernet Sauvignon, 34, 124, 125, 233, 216, 217, 293, 296, 298, 309, 316
California, 27, 46–49, 261–263, 273, 275–291, 293, 295, 299, 300–302, 313, 315, 316; Board of State Viticultural Commissioners, 279–280, 290; climate of, 46–49, 275–279; generic wines, 200–201; State Fair, 309; wine advertising, 284, 286, 291; Wine Association, 280–281; wineries in (numbers), 283, 287, 288, wines, 82–83, 275–291